# Tony Bennett
## Tracked Down

Copyright © 1996 by Mark Fox and C. A. Phasey

This book is copyrighted under the Berne Convention. No portion may be reproduced by any process without the copyright holder's written permission except for the purposes of reviewing or criticism, as permitted under the Copyright Act of 1956.

ISBN 0 7212 0950 5

Printed and bound in Great Britain by
Buckland Press Ltd., Dover, Kent.

# TONY BENNETT
## Tracked Down

*Compiled by Mark Fox and Chris Phasey*

Buckland Publications Ltd.
125 High Holborn, London WC1V 6QA

*Tony Bennett, 1993.*

ACKNOWLEDGMENTS

The Recordings and Covers of Columbia CBS, Sony, Philips, Fontana, Capitol, EMI, Horatio Nelson, DMG, and Roulette.

The many publishers of the songs.

The artistry of Tony Bennett.

All photographs used by kind permission of Mark Fox.

*Tony and Mark Fox.*
*Copthorne Hotel, Birmingham, 7th July, 1993.*

## THE
# TONY BENNETT
### APPRECIATION SOCIETY
Hon. President Anthony Dominick Benedetto

*A non-profit making organisation to honour the career and music of this unique song stylist. The aim is to circulate news, articles, interviews and album releases in their magazine, published four times a year.*

*Those wishing to join can contact Mark Fox by writing to TBAS, 13 Sunnyside, Heckmondwike, West Yorks, WF16 0LN, enclosing an SAE.*

*Harrogate, 1990.*
Photograph by Cynthia Guest.

*Tony in Harrogate, 1990, with Ralph Sharon.*

*Harrogate, 1990.*
Photograph by Cynthia Guest.

## TONY BENNETT

Anthony Dominick Benedetto was born 3 August 1926 in Astoria, New York to an Italian father and American mother. At the High School for Industrial Arts he studied music and art.

He used his tenor voice in the latter part of the Second World War when he served in the US Entertainment unit and afterwards, using the name Joe Bari, he worked in clubs. He joined a Pearl Bailey revue as singer and MC where he was seen by Bob Hope and joined his Paramount show. Bob Hope did not like the name but felt his real name was too long and shortened it to Tony Bennett.

A single was made in 1947 (using the name Joe Bari) but in 1950 he auditioned for Columbia Records producer Mitch Miller and "Boulevard of Broken Dreams" was released. It took another year to find the next hit but "Because of You" spent ten weeks at number one on billboard and over six months on the chart in 1951. "Cold, Cold Heart" was the follow-up, a Country & Western song by Hank Williams, it also reached number one in 1951. "Rags to Riches" was number one in 1953 after other hits including "Blue Velvet".

Shortly before the opening of "Kismet" in 1953, Tony Bennett recorded one of the songs, "Stranger in Paradise", and that became his first UK number one in 1955. The trend of the day was to record singles and albums were collections of singles. In 1953 Frank Sinatra had pioneered the concept album – a collection of songs to be listened to as a whole – and Tony Bennett was able to use this facility to express his own preferences for material to record with musicians of his choice. Consequently albums such as "A Treasure Chest of Hits" gave way to items such as "Cloud 7" and "Beat of my Heart" often allowing experimentation with jazz interpretations.

The 1958 album "Basie Swings-Bennett Sings" is an illustration of the jazz flavoured work and there were several outings with the Basie Band. His fifties albums had little UK reaction (an almost non-existent market)

and much of the material was heard on compilations later in the sixties. "Firefly" in 1958 was the last US single success until 1962 when "I Left my Heart in San Francisco" was released and went on to become a worldwide success – 3 Grammies and a UK hit in 1965. A 1962 Carnegie Hall Concert was recorded on two albums with close collaborator and pianist Ralph Sharon.

In the early and mid sixties a string of superb singles, "I Wanna be Around", "Who Can I Turn To?", "The Good Life", and "The Very Thought of You", were released from a similar stream of excellent albums which were now becoming the main product. However, chart life became unimportant against the long term sale of albums such as "I Left my Heart in San Francisco", "I Wanna Be Around", "This is all I Ask", "Who can I Turn To?", "The Many Moods of Tony", "When Lights are Low", "If I Ruled the World", "A Time For Love", "Tony Makes It Happen", and culminating in the first class quality of "The Movie Song Album" in 1966.

Tony has appeared in several roles on TV but his only film role was when he appeared in the Movie "The Oscar", the theme from it was a stand out track on the Movie Song album as was "The Shadow of your Smile". Appearing in a cameo role was Frank Sinatra and it was in the mid sixties that the publicity machine began to promote Bennett as "The Greatest Singer in the World – Frank Sinatra".

Although Tony had always recorded contemporary material, he had a preference for songs from the "Great American Songbook" and in the latter part of the sixties felt such new material was becoming more difficult to find and that producers were putting pressure on him to change his style to increase record sales by following current trends. Despite this, more excellent albums followed, "For Once In My Life", "Yesterday I Heard the Rain", "I've Gotta Be Me", "Something", "The Great Hits Of Today" but by the time of "Love Story" and "The Summer of '42" it was clear something was wrong as these albums contained recycled material. A 1970 retrospective had some tracks recorded using John Bunch and he began to feature on albums as pianist.

Tony had recorded a Christmas collection with Robert Farnon in the UK in 1968 and in 1971 returned to the UK for a live recording with Farnon conducting the London Philharmonic Orchestra – "Get Happy". A final magnificent album was made with Robert Farnon in London in 1972 for Columbia records – "With Love" was dedicated to Frank Sinatra and his Columbia contract ended.

Remaining with Robert Farnon in the UK he turned in "The Good Things in Life" with Philips and then Don Costa arranged and conducted "Listen Easy" also for Philips in 1973. Torrie Zito (who had arranged many Bennett tracks in the late sixties) had a hand in a few. These two albums and a few more tracks completed the Tony Bennett "Philips" spell as he seemed to leave the mainstream and concentrated on jazz associations.

A recording with jazz pianist Bill Evans was issued on Fantasy in 1975 and Tony Bennett set up his own label Improv which issued "Life is Beautiful", a typical excellent Bennett album arranged by Torrie Zito. These were followed by jazz orientated albums with the Ruby Braff/George Barnes Quartet, "10 Rodgers & Hart Songs", "More Great Rodgers & Hart", and with Bill Evans "Together Again" plus a guest appearance on an album with The MacPartlands & Friends. "The Special Magic" returned to an orchestra and Torrie Zito but the Improv business arrangements failed and most of the material now turns up in many different and confusing forms, most issued in the UK on the Horatio Nelson label with many tracks being duplicated and repeated.

Under the management of his son Danny, Tony Bennett returned to Columbia in 1986 and with "The Art of Excellence" re-established his popularity with his fans and earned many new ones. A tribute to Irving Berlin, "Bennett/Berlin" with Ralph Sharon, won a Grammy in 1987, "Jazz" collected some early tracks together as did "Forty Years – The Artistry of Tony Bennett", a 4cd 1991 set, "Astoria Portrait of an Artist" in 1990 continued his success and a further tribute to Sinatra in 1992, "Perfectly Frank", followed by an Astaire tribute, "Steppin' Out" in 1994, both won praise and awards and featured the Ralph Sharon Trio.

In 1994 he performed live with the trio, unplugged on MTV, to great acclaim and the live recording "MTV Unplugged" won the album of the year award and even more new fans. The 1995 "Here's to the Ladies" album kept the trio with orchestrations reminiscent of the sixties albums. That tenor voice has deepened over the years, Tony, who will be seventy on 3 August 1996, enjoys more popularity than ever and justifies that tag – "The Greatest Singer in The World".

Tony Bennett pursues a successful career as an artist who exhibits work that sells for five figure sums, using his family name Benedetto.

We look forward to this Discography becoming out of date with the release of future albums.

CHRIS PHASEY.

Recent press releases have this to say:–

## TONY BENNETT

"Tony Bennett is the best singer in the business, the best exponent of a song. He excites me whenever I watch him – he moves me."  – Frank Sinatra.
"Tony Bennett is the best singer I've ever heard."
– Bing Crosby.

With praise like that, many artists would feel they had reached a pinnacle in their career. For Tony Bennett however, it is just the start of a long list of accolades from artists across the musical spectrum and a new found audience which has made the five-time Grammy Award winner the most venerable "teen idol" (The Boston Globe) in musical history.

Bennett entered his fifth decade in popular music by releasing an album version of his highly-acclaimed appearance on 'MTV Unplugged' with k.d.lang and Elvis Costello (released as an album on 1st August 1994). **"Tony Bennett: MTV Unplugged" has now sold in excess of 600,000 copies worldwide and won the <u>1995 Grammy Award for Album Of The Year</u>**, bringing Tony's lifetime Grammy total to five!

It is a testament to his artistry that the consummate concert performer has been discovered by a new generation of music lovers and praised by musicians of all genres.

"Tony Bennett has not just bridged the generation gap, he has demolished it. He has solidly connected with a younger crowd weaned on rock. And there have been no compromises."  – New York Times.

Tony Bennett has never compromised and it is this which holds the key to the phenomenal success he has enjoyed recently around the world. He still sings the songs from the "Great American Songbook" he has always sung, he still sings in his own inimitable style and he still values artistry above all else.

"The thrill of performing hasn't changed in years, I learn something different every day. I've never gotten bored yet and I don't think I ever will." – Tony Bennett.

With a list of duets, opening slots, collaborations and appearances with k.d.lang, Elvis Costello, Evan Dando, J. Mascis, Teenage Fanclub, Belly Idol, Porno For Pyros, Smashing Pumpkins, U2, Wynton Marsalis and

even the first ever cameo appearance on The Simpsons, it seems unlikely that he could ever be bored! Even without doing all this, his recording schedule has been relentless.

Since his return to Columbia Records in 1986, Tony Bennett has been responsible for one of the most consistent, high-quality bodies of recorded work in American popular music: **The Art Of Excellence (May 1986)**, chosen by PULSE! magazine as one of the 200 best albums of the decade and the number one vocal record; the double-LP anthology **Tony Bennett Jazz** (April 1987); **Bennett/Berlin** (October 1988), a tribute to the composer in the year of his birthday; the Grammy-nominated **Astoria: Portrait Of The Artist** (February 1990); **Forty Years: The Artistry Of Tony Bennett** (July 1991), a four CD/Cassette box-set tribute with 87 songs and more than four hours of music, and his last two Columbia Records – **Perfectly Frank** (1992) and **Steppin' Out** (1993) – which each won a Grammy in the best Traditional Pop Vocal category.

### Tony Bennett: *'Here's To The Ladies'*

On **Monday 6 November 1995**, six time Grammy Award Winner **Tony Bennett** releases his new album – **'Here's To The Ladies'**.

Over the past five years Tony Bennett has sold in excess of three million records world-wide, has had two records certified gold and has received countless awards including the **Grammy** for **Best Selling Jazz Album** for 1994's **'Tony Bennett: MTV Unplugged'**.

With 'Here's To The Ladies' he pays homage to such great female artists as **Billie Holiday, Barbra Streisand, Doris Day, Ella Fitzgerald, Sarah Vaughan, Judy Garland, Liza Minnelli and Rosemary Clooney** with an album of 18 superb songs delivered in inimitable Tony Bennett style, accompanied by Trio, Big Band and Orchestra.

On the album's concept, Tony commented: **"I grew up listening to my mom and aunts sing and the freedom and emotion they had in their voices seemed to me uniquely feminine. I have tried to emulate that quality in my**

singing and since some of my all-time favourite singers are the ladies on the album, this concept really appealed to me."

In October 1995 a CBS TV Special called **'Tony Bennett: Here's To The Ladies – A Concert For Hope'** benefiting the Centre For Addiction and Drug Abuse will be recorded in Hollywood featuring guest appearances from Liza Minnelli, Patti LaBelle, Mary Chapin Carpenter, Roseanne Barr and Brandy which will be broadcast in the US on 1 December.

Having performed for six US Presidents and at four Royal Variety Performances, Tony is used to high profile audiences, but when his good friend, billionaire John Kluge, asked him whether he would perform at the **United Cerebral Palsey Benefit Gala** at which The Princess of Wales is to receive the organisation's **Humanitarian Award**, he gladly accepted.

The benefit concert, which is to be held at New York's Hilton Hotel on Monday 11 December 1995, is expected to raise thousands of dollars for the charity, with seats selling for up to £10,000!

General Colin Powell is also to be honoured at the event, with the **Outstanding Achievement Award**.

Tony, whose album **'Here's To The Ladies'** was released last month, said of the event:

> **"It's always a great honour to be invited to perform at such worthwhile events. When I was told that the Princess of Wales was coming I couldn't think of anything more suitable than singing songs from 'Here's To The Ladies' for *the* Lady. I know she does some great work for charity and it should be a wonderful evening."**

Tony Bennett is touring extensively throughout North America for the rest of the year and will tour Europe in Spring 1996.

\* \* \*

The son of a grocer and Italian-born immigrant, Anthony Dominick Benedetto was born in Astoria (New York City), in 1926. He grew up singing and drawing pictures and now enjoys a flourishing second career as an artist painting under his own name. He spent three years in the army and many more seasons singing wherever he could, including clubs in Long Island City with visiting stars like Al Cohn and Tyree Glenn.

"**My scuffling years began to end in 1949,**" recalls Tony, "**when I auditioned for a revue that Pearl Bailey was in at the old Greenwich Village Inn. Bob Hope heard me in the show and asked me to come up and sing at the Parament Theatre with him. He didn't like my stage name [Joe Bari] and asked me what my real name was . . . he thought for a moment and said, 'that's too long for the Marquee. We'll call you Tony Bennett'.**"

A year later he was auditioned by Columbia Records' Mitch Miller and sang '**Boulevard Of Broken Dreams**' which became his first hit and encouraged him to go on the road, working clubs in places like Philadelphia, Boston, Cleveland and Buffalo.

"**So I started this crazy adventure that has just lasted forty years. I had hits like 'Because Of You', 'Just In Time', 'Cold, Cold Heart', 'Stranger In Paradise' and 'Rags To Riches'. I became international in 1962 when I recorded 'I Left My Heart In San Francisco'.**"

'I Left My Heart In San Francisco' won him two Grammy Awards for Record Of The Year and Best Solo Vocal Performance (Male) and went on to become his signature tune, introducing him to audiences worldwide as the consummate concert performer.

\* \* \*

All those years later, there isn't much you could teach Tony Bennett about his profession, but the advice he received from Frank Sinatra in the 1950's when he was just starting out has stayed with him through all those years:

"**He gave me some very, very good pointers. He told me to just stay with good music. He said, 'Don't do any tricks or novelty songs just to get a hit. Don't compromise.' So I lived by those lessons. And many**

years later, just recently I said, 'Why do you think we've been around so long? I'm sailing 40 years now.' And he said, 'Well, we stayed with quality'."

It is this uncompromising belief in what he does that has ensured his continued success throughout the years and which has won him the respect and admiration of a whole new generation of artists and audiences. In a review of the MTV Unplugged programme, the New York Times asked:

"What accounts for the Bennett magic? Artistry certainly. The repertory is indeed classic . . . But perhaps more important is his ability to convey a sense of joy, of utter satisfaction, in what he is doing. When this session is over, an obviously delighted and energised performer assures his new fans, 'This has been one of the most wonderful nights of my career.' And you know he's not exaggerating."

The phenomenal success of Tony Bennett 'Unplugged' around the world has delighted and fascinated the media. As far as Tony Bennett is concerned however, there is no mystery. The quality performances, great songs and superb voice he has always delivered have simply been appreciated by a whole new audience.

"But make no mistake, this is not about kitsch but about a singer who's emotional and sincere, and that's the truest kind of style. He was modern to begin with, and the rest of us are just catching up." – Elvis Costello.

\* \* \*

## ABOUT THIS DISCOGRAPHY

Mark Fox is the founder of the Tony Bennett Appreciation Society and has been the recognised compiler of information on Tony Bennett releases and a lifetime collector of albums, singles and memorabilia. Mark has written many articles and has appeared on radio programmes – particularly about Frank Sinatra, and the easy listening group of vocalists (and of course Tony) and has a large collection of related albums and memorabilia. He has associations with the UK and USA antique trade and is married with two children and two grandchildren. His personal Discography has been available to society members and eventually was purchased by Chris Phasey who had been compiling his own on Computer for a few years and a correspondence began.

Chris Phasey began collecting Tony Bennett albums in 1965 when he could not make up his mind which album to buy – "I Left My Heart In San Francisco", "I Wanna Be Around" or "Who Can I Turn To?" – and compromised by buying all three and has collected most of the issues since then.

He is employed in the printing industry and late in 1995 persuaded his colleagues to allow him to publish his similar Sinatra catalogue as "Francis Albert Sinatra – Tracked Down". This has led to this publication which is a joint effort combining the work by Mark Fox and Chris Phasey.

The guide lists, in section one, the songs alphabetically (chronological order is not possible) and shows where possible the British album title, and single, plus composer, arranger and date where known, US Albums and Singles are shown when there is not a UK issue. Section two lists most of the albums issued by Tony Bennett followed by his appearance on Various Artists albums, EPs, Singles and his CDs.

Album titles refer mainly to the British release in the "song" section but we have tried to indicate the US equivalent in the album section (i.e. US Greatest Hits is referred to with UK title A String of Hits). In the

song section some album titles have been shortened to save room but will be obvious when checked to the album section. For international collectors a full US list is in section six. Only the main issues have been used as the list of compilations – reissues, etc. is phenomenal.

Tony Bennett recorded for Columbia until 1971. Early albums were not always released in the UK, but there were some releases on Philips. In the sixties the Columbia UK releases are on CBS.

We cannot guarantee that all our information is complete and accurate but have made every effort to make it as correct as possible. Comments are welcomed which may be included in future editions.

## CONTENTS

| Section 1 | The Songs of Tony Bennett. | 15 |
| --- | --- | --- |
| Section 2 | The Albums of Tony Bennett:– | |
| | Columbia Years 1950-71. | 103 |
| | Philips/Improv/Fantasy. | 121 |
| | Columbia from 1986. | 126 |
| | Appearances on Various Artist albums. | 132 |
| Section 3 | The EP's. | 139 |
| Section 4 | The Singles. | 143 |
| Section 5 | Worldwide CD releases. | 157 |
| Section 6 | US Album Discography. | 160 |
| Section 7 | Unreleased Concerts. | 163 |

# THE SONGS OF TONY BENNETT
compiled alphabetically January 1996

**A BEAUTIFUL FRIENDSHIP**     TONY MAKES IT HAPPEN     CBS     63055
D.Kahn/S.H.Styne     THE TROLLEY SONG     EMBASSY     31002
Columbia recorded 27/1/67
Marion Evans

**A BLOSSOM FELL**     ALL STAR POPS     COLUMBIA     CL728
Barnes/Cornelius
Columbia recorded 9/6/55
Sid Feller

**A CHILD IS BORN**     TOGETHER AGAIN     IMPROV     7117
T.Jones/A.Wilder     TOGETHER AGAIN     NELSON     CD1129
Improv recorded 27-30/9/76     UNFORGETTABLE     CASTLE     UNLP019
Bill Evans

**A COTTAGE FOR SALE**
W.Robinson/L.Conley
Columbia recorded 7/4/58
Frank De Vol
not released

✓ re-recorded Columbia 9/4/58     LONG AGO AND FAR AWAY     COLUMBIA     CL1186
Frank De Vol

**A FOGGY DAY**     ON THE GLORY ROAD+     COLUMBIA     CL1813
I.Gershwin/G.Gershwin
Columbia recorded 15/3/62
Ralph Sharon
+album unreleased

✓ re-recorded Columbia 1993     PERFECTLY FRANK     COLUMBIA     472222
with the Ralph Sharon Trio

live MTV recording 4/94     MTV UNPLUGGED     COLUMBIA     477170
with the Ralph Sharon Trio

**A FOOL OF FOOLS**     YESTERDAY I HEARD THE RAIN     CBS     63351
M.Curtis/J.Meyer     SINGLE     CBS     3370
Columbia recorded 21/12/67
Torrie Zito

**A LITTLE STREET WHERE OLD**
   **FRIENDS MEET**     ASTORIA:PORTRAIT OF THE
G.Kahn/H.Woods                        ARTIST     COLUMBIA     466005
Columbia recorded May 1989
Jorge Calandrelli

| | | | |
|---|---|---|---|
| **A LONELY PLACE**<br>P.Webster/J.Mandel<br>Columbia recorded 27/3/69<br>Torrie Zito | I'VE GOTTA BE ME | CBS | 63685 |
| **A NIGHTINGALE SANG IN<br>BERKELEY SQUARE**<br>E.Maschwitz/M.Sherwin<br>Columbia recorded 1993<br>with the Ralph Sharon Trio | PERFECTLY FRANK | COLUMBIA | 472222 |
| **A RAINY DAY**<br>Columbia recorded 1985<br>Jorge Calandrelli | THE ART OF EXCELLENCE<br>(CD only) | CBS | 40344 |
| **A SLEEPIN' BEE**<br>H.Arlen/T.Capote<br>Columbia recorded 29/10/59<br>Ralph Sharon | TONY SINGS FOR TWO<br>FORTY YEARS VOL 1 | COLUMBIA<br>COLUMBIA | CL1446<br>46843 |
| **A TASTE OF HONEY**<br>R.Marlow/B.Scott<br>Columbia recorded 11/9/63<br>Dick Hyman | THE MANY MOODS OF TONY<br>THE GOLDEN TOUCH<br>TONY BENNETT SINGS<br>FORTY YEARS VOL 2<br>GREATEST HITS<br>20 GREATEST HITS<br>LOVE STORY | CBS<br>COLUMBIA<br>R/DIGEST<br>COLUMBIA<br>CBS<br>WARWICK<br>CBS | 62245<br>P12789<br>8070<br>46843<br>62821<br>PA5021<br>64368 |
| **A TIME FOR LOVE**<br>P.Webster/J.Mandel<br>Columbia recorded 11/6/66<br>Johnny Mandel<br><br>live recording Columbia<br>H.Roberts (A&R) 11/8/67<br>not released | A TIME FOR LOVE<br>GREATEST HITS VOL 2<br>FORTY YEARS VOL 3<br>ALL-TIME GREATEST HITS | CBS<br>CBS<br>COLUMBIA<br>CBS | 62800<br>63612<br>46843<br>68200 |
| **A WEAVER OF DREAMS<br>/THERE WILL NEVER BE<br>ANOTHER YOU**<br>V.Young/J.Elliot,H.Warren/M.Gordon<br>Columbia recorded 1989<br>Jorge Calandrelli | ASTORIA:PORTRAIT OF THE<br>ARTIST | CBS | 466005 |
| **AFRAID OF THE DARK**<br>Columbia recorded 30/6/55<br>Percy Faith | SINGLE | PHILIPS | PB537 |
| **AFTER SUPPER**<br>Roulette recorded 1958 | BASIE/BENNETT* | ROULETTE | TOCS5378 |

*bonus track on Japan issue previously unreleased.

| | | | |
|---|---|---|---|
| ✓ **AFTER YOU'VE GONE**<br>H.Creamer/T.Layton<br>Columbia recorded 29/2/60<br>Frank De Vol | ALONE TOGETHER | COLUMBIA | CL 1471 |
| **AIN'T MISBEHAVIN'**<br>A.Razaf/T.Waller/H.Brooks<br>Columbia recorded 26/2/64<br>not released | | | |
| re-recorded Columbia<br>Ralph Sharon Trio 27/3/64 | WHEN LIGHTS ARE LOW | CBS | 62296 |
| live Columbia recorded 8/4/64<br>Louis Basil with Ralph Sharon Trio<br>not released | | | |
| **ALFIE**<br>B.Bacharach/H.David<br>Columbia recorded 25/2/69<br>Torrie Zito | TONY!<br>I'VE GOTTA BE ME<br>THE TROLLEY SONG | COLUMBIA<br>CBS<br>EMBASSY | KH32171<br>63685<br>31002 |
| **ALL MINE**<br>F.Hime/J.Livingston/R.Evans/R.Guerra<br>Improv recorded c1975<br>Torrie Zito | LIFE IS BEAUTIFUL | IMPROV | 7112 |
| **ALL MY LOVE**<br>Columbia recorded 14/7/50<br>Percy Faith<br>not released | | | |
| **ALL MY TOMORROWS**<br>J.Van Heusen/S.Cahn<br>Columbia recorded 19/2/66<br>Don Costa | SONGS FOR THE JET SET<br>IF I RULED THE WORLD | CBS<br>EMBASSY | 62544<br>31058 |
| **ALL OF MY LIFE**<br>I.Berlin<br>Columbia recorded 1987<br>Tony Bennett | BENNETT:BERLIN | CBS | 460450 |
| **ALL OF YOU**<br>C.Porter<br>Columbia recorded 28/10/59<br>Originally unissued | GREAT AMERICAN COMPOSERS<br>SERIES | COLUMBIA | |
| Re-recorded Columbia 1994<br>Tony Bennett & Ralph Sharon | STEPPIN' OUT | COLUMBIA | 474360 |
| ✓ live MTV recording 4/94<br>with the Ralph Sharon Trio | MTV UNPLUGGED | COLUMBIA | 477170 |

| | | | |
|---|---|---|---|
| **ALL THAT LOVE WENT TO WASTE**<br>Barrie/Cahn<br>Philips recorded c1973<br>with the George Barnes/<br>Ruby Braff Quartet<br>Torrie Zito | SPOTLIGHT ON . . . .<br>BRUT SINGLE<br>SINGLE | PHILIPS<br>BRUT<br>PHILIPS | 6641 297<br>BR813<br>6006372 |
| ✓ **ALL THE THINGS YOU ARE**<br>J.Kern/O.Hammerstein II<br>live Columbia recorded 9/6/62<br>Ralph Sharon | AT CARNEGIE HALL 1 | CBS | 62116 |
| **ALONE AT LAST**<br>Columbia recorded 4/2/58<br>Ralph Sharon | SINGLE | COLUMBIA | 41127 |
| ✓ **ALONE TOGETHER**<br>H.Deitz/A.Schwartz<br>Columbia released 1960<br>Frank De Vol | ALONE TOGETHER<br>LOVE SONGS<br>ALONE TOGETHER (EP) | COLUMBIA<br>CBS<br>PHILIPS | CL 1471<br>66297<br>BBE12461 |
| ✓ **ALWAYS**<br>I.Berlin<br>Columbia recorded 13/9/57<br>Ray Conniff | TONY<br>TONY BENNETT SHOWCASE<br>IRVING BERLIN | COLUMBIA<br>PHILIPS<br>COLUMBIA | CL 938<br>BBL7138<br>460999 |
| ✓ live Columbia recorded<br>Ralph Sharon 9/6/62 | AT CARNEGIE HALL 2 | CBS | 62117 |
| live Columbia recorded 8/4/64<br>Louis Basil with Ralph Sharon Trio<br>not released | | | |
| re-recorded Columbia 1994<br>Johnny Mandel | IT COULD HAPPEN TO YOU<br>(SOUNDTRACK) | COLUMBIA | CK66184 |
| **ALWAYS/REMEMBER**<br>I.Berlin<br>Columbia recorded Oct 1987<br>Ralph Sharon Trio<br>Recorded for "Bennett:Berlin" but not issued | | | |
| ✓ **ANGEL EYES**<br>E.Brett/M.Dennis<br>Columbia recorded 1993<br>with the Ralph Sharon Trio | PERFECTLY FRANK | COLUMBIA | 472222 |
| ✓ **ANTONIA**<br>R.Wells/J.Segal<br>Columbia recorded 18/5/89<br>Jorge Calandrelli | ASTORIA:PORTRAIT OF THE<br>ARTIST<br>FORTY YEARS VOL 4 | COLUMBIA<br>COLUMBIA | 466005<br>46843 |

| | | | |
|---|---|---|---|
| **ANYTHING GOES**<br>C.Porter<br>Roulette released 1961<br>Count Basie | STRIKE UP THE BAND<br>THE SINGER AND THE SONG<br>A ONE NIGHT STAND | ROULETTE<br>PREMIER<br>ALLEGRO | 25231<br>98859<br>799 |
| re-recorded Columbia 15/3/62<br>Ralph Sharon<br>not released | | | |
| ✓ live Columbia recording<br>Ralph Sharon 9/6/62 | AT CARNEGIE HALL 2 | CBS | 62117 |
| **ANYWHERE I WANDER**<br>F.Loesser<br>Columbia recorded 26/8/58<br>Percy Faith | A STRING OF HITS<br>TONY'S GREATEST HITS | CBS<br>COLUMBIA | 66010<br>CS8652 |
| **APPLAUSE**<br>Columbia recorded 30/1/70<br>Peter Matz<br>not released | | | |
| **APRIL IN PARIS**<br>Harburg/Duke<br>Columbia recorded 12/11/59<br>Frank De Vol | TO MY WONDERFUL ONE | COLUMBIA | CL 1429 |
| ✓ live recording 9/6/62<br>Ralph Sharon | AT CARNEGIE HALL 1<br>WHEN I FALL IN LOVE | CBS<br>HALLMARK | 62116<br>SHM 817 |
| ✓ live radio recording 1963<br>with Gene Krupa | MEETS GENE KRUPA | SANDY HOOK | SH 2067 |
| **ARE YOU HAVING ANY FUN?**<br>Fain/Yellen<br>Roulette released 1961<br>Count Basie | STRIKE UP THE BAND<br>ONE NIGHT STAND | ROULETTE<br>ALLEGRO | 25231<br>799 |
| **ARMY AIR CORPS SONG**<br>R.Crawford<br>Columbia recorded 21/10/57<br>Ralph Sharon | THE BEAT OF MY HEART | COLUMBIA | CL 1079 |
| ✓ **AS TIME GOES BY**<br>H.Hupfeld<br>Improv recorded c1975<br>Torrie Zito | LIFE IS BEAUTIFUL<br>STAGE AND SCREEN HITS<br>THE SPECIAL MAGIC OF . .<br>UNFORGETTABLE<br>HOLLYWOOD & BROADWAY<br>THE MAGIC OF TONY BENNETT | IMPROV<br>DBM<br>DRG<br>CASTLE<br>NELSON<br>NELSON | 7112<br>1001<br>801<br>ULP019<br>1145<br>CYU 106 |

| | | | |
|---|---|---|---|
| **ASK ANYONE IN LOVE** | A STRING OF HITS | CBS | 66010 |
| St Lynn/Shapiro | MORE TONY'S GREATEST HITS | COLUMBIA | 13301 |
| Columbia recorded 23/3/59 | SINGLE | PHILIPS | PB1079 |
| Ralph Burns | | | |
| | | | |
| **ASK ME (I KNOW)** | SINGLE | PHILIPS | PB1008 |
| Columbia recorded 13/1/60 | | | |
| Frank De Vol | | | |
| | | | |
| **AT LONG LAST LOVE** | LISTEN EASY | PHILIPS | 6308 157 |
| C.Porter | AT LONG LAST LOVE | PHILIPS | SON 014 |
| Philips recorded c1973 | SPOTLIGHT ON .... | PHILIPS | 6641 297 |
| Don Costa | | | |
| | | | |
| **AUTUMN IN ROME** | THIS IS ALL I ASK | CBS | 62205 |
| S.Cahn/P.Weston/A.Cicognini | | | |
| Columbia recorded 22/4/63 | | | |
| Ralph Burns | | | |
| | | | |
| **AUTUMN LEAVES** | TO MY WONDERFUL ONE | COLUMBIA | CL 1429 |
| J.Mercer/J.Kosma | | | |
| Columbia recorded 10/11/59 | | | |
| Frank De Vol | | | |
| | | | |
| re-recorded Columbia | WHO CAN I TURN TO | CBS | 62486 |
| George Siravo 14/10/64 | | | |
| | | | |
| **AUTUMN LEAVES/** | | | |
| **INDIAN SUMMER** | MTV UNPLUGGED | COLUMBIA | 477170 |
| J.Mercer/J.Kosma, A.Dubin/V.Herbert | | | |
| live MTV recorded 4/94 | | | |
| with the Ralph Sharon Trio | | | |
| | | | |
| **BABY DON'T YOU QUIT NOW** | | | |
| J.Rowles/J.Mercer | | | |
| Columbia recorded 16/10/67 | | | |
| Torrie Zito | | | |
| not released | | | |
| | | | |
| re-recorded Columbia | I'VE GOTTA BE ME | CBS | 63685 |
| Torrie Zito 25/11/68 | FORTY YEARS VOL 4 | COLUMBIA | 46843 |
| | | | |
| **BABY TALK TO ME** | MR BROADWAY | COLUMBIA | CL 1763 |
| L.Adams/C.Strouse | A STRING OF HITS | CBS | 66010 |
| Columbia recorded 6/5/60 | MORE TONY'S GREATEST HITS | COLUMBIA | 13301 |
| Frank De Vol | SINGLE | PHILIPS | PB1149 |
| | | | |
| **BABY, DREAM YOUR DREAM** | FOR ONCE IN MY LIFE | CBS | 63166 |
| C.Coleman/D.Fields | FORTY YEARS VOL 3 | COLUMBIA | 46843 |
| Columbia recorded 14/12/65 | LET'S FALL IN LOVE WITH .. | CBS | 88131 |
| David Rose | | | |

20

| | | | |
|---|---|---|---|
| **BE CAREFUL, IT'S MY HEART**<br>I.Berlin<br>Columbia recorded 9/4/58<br>Frank De Vol | LONG AGO AND FAR AWAY | COLUMBIA | CL 1186 |
| **BEAUTIFUL MADNESS**<br>Columbia recorded 17/1/51<br>Marty Manning | SINGLE<br>BECAUSE OF YOU | COLUMBIA<br>COLUMBIA | 39209<br>CL6221 |
| **BECAUSE OF YOU**<br>A.Hammerstein/D.Wilkinson<br>Columbia recorded 17/1/51<br>Percy Faith | BECAUSE OF YOU<br>POPULAR FAVORITES<br>ALL TIME HALL OF FAME HITS<br>BECAUSE OF YOU 56<br>A STRING OF HITS<br>MILLION DOLLAR MEMORIES<br>16 MOST REQUESTED SONGS<br>16 ORIGINAL HITS<br>ALL-TIME GREATEST HITS<br>COCA COLA PRESENTS<br>FORTY YEARS VOL 1<br>SINGLE | COLUMBIA<br>COLUMBIA<br>CBS<br>COLUMBIA<br>CBS<br>R/DIGEST<br>COLUMBIA<br>EVEREST<br>CBS<br>COLUMBIA<br>COLUMBIA<br>PHILIPS | CL6221<br>CL6205<br>64200<br>CL2550<br>66010<br>8061/9<br>57056<br>LP16-19<br>68200<br>26851<br>46843<br>DB2924 |
| live recording Columbia<br>Ralph Sharon 9/6/62 | AT CARNEGIE HALL 2 | CBS | 62117 |
| **BEFORE WE SAY GOODBYE**<br>A.Stillman/M.Lewis<br>Columbia record 7/10/69 | SINGLE | COLUMBIA | 45032 |
| **BEGIN THE BEGUINE**<br>C.Porter<br>Columbia recorded 21/10/57<br>Ralph Sharon<br>not released | THE BEAT OF MY HEART | | |
| re-recorded Columbia 14/1/60<br>Ralph Sharon | MR BROADWAY<br>FORTY YEARS VOL 2<br>SUNRISE, SUNSET | COLUMBIA<br>COLUMBIA<br>CBS | CL1763<br>46843<br>32239 |
| **BEING TRUE TO ONE ANOTHER**<br>Hilliard/Allen<br>Columbia recorded 2/11/58<br>Glenn Osser | SINGLE | PHILIPS | PB907 |
| **BETWEEN THE DEVIL AND<br>THE DEEP BLUE SEA**<br>T.Koehler/H.Arlen<br>Columbia recorded 4/9/64<br>George Siravo | WHO CAN I TURN TO | CBS | 62486 |

| | | | |
|---|---|---|---|
| **BEWITCHED** | TONY SINGS FOR TWO | COLUMBIA | CL1446 |
| L.Hart/R.Rodgers | LOVE SONGS | CBS | 66297 |
| Columbia recorded 28/10/59 | | | |
| Ralph Sharon | | | |
| | | | |
| **BLUE MOON** | LONG AGO AND FAR AWAY | COLUMBIA | CL1186 |
| L.Hart/R.Rodgers | | | |
| Columbia recorded 8/4/58 | | | |
| Ralph Sharon | | | |
| | | | |
| re-recorded Improv | 10 RODGERS & HART SONGS | IMPROV | 7113 |
| with the Ruby Braff/ | UNFORGETTABLE | CASTLE | ULP019 |
| George Barnes Quartet | RODGERS & HART SONGBOOK | NELSON | CD1129 |
| 28-30/9/73 | | | |
| | | | |
| **BLUE VELVET** | BLUE VELVET | COLUMBIA | CL1292 |
| B.Wayne/B.Morris | 16 ORIGINAL HITS | EVEREST | LP16-19 |
| Columbia recorded 17/7/51 | THE GOLDEN TOUCH | COLUMBIA | P12789 |
| Percy Faith | FORTY YEARS VOL 1 | COLUMBIA | 46843 |
| | THE LAST PICTURE SHOW | COLUMBIA | 70115 |
| | | | |
| live Columbia recording | AT CARNEGIE HALL 2 | CBS | 62117 |
| Ralph Sharon 9/6/62 | | | |
| | | | |
| **BLUES FOR BREAKFAST** | THE GOOD THINGS IN LIFE | PHILIPS | 6308 134 |
| Dennis/Gladstone | SPOTLIGHT ON . . . . | PHILIPS | 6641 297 |
| Philips recorded c1972 | | | |
| Robert Farnon | | | |
| | | | |
| **BLUES IN THE NIGHT** | THE BEAT OF MY HEART | COLUMBIA | CL1079 |
| J.Mercer/H.Arlen | JUST ONE OF THOSE THINGS | HALLMARK | 646 |
| Columbia recorded 21/10/57 | | | |
| Ralph Sharon | | | |
| | | | |
| **BODY AND SOUL** | ASTORIA: PORTRAIT OF THE | | |
| E.Heyman/R.Sour/F.Eyton/J.Green | ARTIST | COLUMBIA | 466005 |
| Columbia recorded 1989 | | | |
| Jorge Calandrelli | | | |
| | | | |
| live MTV recorded 4/94 | MTV UNPLUGGED | COLUMBIA | 477170 |
| with the Ralph Sharon Trio | | | |

**BOULEVARD OF BROKEN DREAMS**
A.Dubin/H.Warren
Demo disc recorded c1949
with Tony Tamburello (p) with his Orchestra
This Disc motivated Mitch Miller to sign Tony Bennett to Columbia Records
Several copies of the 78 rpm disc existed into the 1990's
(possibly in the late Tony Tamburello's effects).

| | | | |
|---|---|---|---|
| ✓ Columbia recorded 17/4/50 | BECAUSE OF YOU | COLUMBIA | CL6221 |
| Marty Manning | PHILIPS TV (EP) | PHILIPS | BBE1222 |
| | BECAUSE OF YOU 56 | COLUMBIA | CL2550 |
| | FORTY YEARS VOL 1 | COLUMBIA | 46843 |
| alternative take 17/4/50 | | | |
| not released | | | |
| | | | |
| re-recorded Columbia 13/9/56 | TONY | COLUMBIA | CL938 |
| ✓ Ray Conniff | A STRING OF HITS | CBS | 66010 |
| | ALL-TIME GREATEST HITS | CBS | 68200 |
| | 16 MOST REQUESTED SONGS | COLUMBIA | 57056 |
| | TONY BENNETT SHOWCASE | PHILIPS | BBL7138 |
| | | | |
| re-recorded Columbia 1989 | ASTORIA:PORTRAIT OF THE | | |
| Jorge Calandrelli | ARTIST | COLUMBIA | 466005 |
| | | | |
| **BRIDGES** | LIFE IS BEAUTIFUL | IMPROV | 7112 |
| G.Lees | | | |
| Improv recorded c1975 | | | |
| Torrie Zito | | | |
| | | | |
| **BROADWAY** | | | |
| T.McRae/H.Woode/B.Bird | | | |
| live recording Columbia | | | |
| H.Roberts (A&R) 11/8/67 | | | |
| not released | | | |
| | | | |
| **BROADWAY/CRAZY RYTHMN/** | | | |
| **LULLABY OF BROADWAY** | FOR ONCE IN MY LIFE | CBS | 63166 |
| T.McRae/H.Woode/B.Bird | | | |
| I.Caesar/R.Kahn/J.Meyer | | | |
| A.Dubin/H.Warren | | | |
| Columbia recorded 18/7/67 | | | |
| Torrie Zito | | | |
| | | | |
| **BUT BEAUTIFUL** | BENNETT/BILL EVANS ALBUM | FANTASY | FT527 |
| S.Burke/J.Van Heusen | FORTY YEARS VOL 4 | COLUMBIA | 46843 |
| ✓ Fantasy recorded 10-13/6/75 | | | |
| with Bill Evans | | | |
| | | | |
| **BY MYSELF** | HOMETOWN, MY TOWN | COLUMBIA | CL1301 |
| H.Dietz/A.Schwartz | | | |
| ✓ Columbia recorded 3/11/58 | | | |
| Ralph Burns | | | |

| | | | | |
|---|---|---|---|---|
| ✓✓ | re-recorded Columbia 1994<br>Tony Bennett & Ralph Sharon | STEPPIN' OUT | COLUMBIA | 474360 |
| ⌐<br>✓ | **CA, C'EST L'AMOUR**<br>C.Porter<br>Columbia recorded 19/9/57<br>Neal Hefti | A STRING OF HITS<br>16 ORIGINAL HITS<br>FORTY YEARS VOL 1<br>SINGLE | CBS<br>EVEREST<br>COLUMBIA<br>PHILIPS | 66010<br>LP16-19<br>46843<br>PB753 |
| ✓ | **CALL ME IRRESPONSIBLE**<br>S.Cahn/J.Van Heusen<br>Columbia recorded 1993<br>with the Ralph Sharon Trio | PERFECTLY FRANK | COLUMBIA | 472222 |

**CAN YOU FIND IT IN YOUR HEART?**
Columbia recorded 16/12/55
Percy Faith

| | | | |
|---|---|---|---|
| COCA COLA PRESENTS | COLUMBIA | 26851 |
| 16 ORIGINAL HITS | EVEREST | LP16-19 |
| THE GOLDEN TOUCH | COLUMBIA | P12789 |
| SINGLE | PHILIPS | PB501 |

**CANDY KISSES**
G.Morgan
Columbia recorded 6/9/61
Marty Manning

| | | | |
|---|---|---|---|
| I LEFT MY HEART IN<br>SAN FRANCISCO | CBS | 62201 |
| 20 GREATEST HITS | WARWICK | PA5021 |
| TONY BENNETT SINGS | R/DIGEST | 8070 |
| SINGLE | CBS | 201730 |
| SINGLE | CBS | AAG121 |

**CAN'T GET OUT OF
    THIS MOOD**
F.Loesser/J.McHugh
Columbia released 1967
Marion Evans

| | | |
|---|---|---|
| TONY MAKES IT HAPPEN | CBS | 63055 |

**CAPRI IN MAY**
Columbia recorded 16/12/55
Percy Faith

| | | |
|---|---|---|
| SINGLE | PHILIPS | PB563 |

**CARAVAN**
Mills/Tizol/D.Ellington
Columbia recorded 16/3/62
Ralph Sharon
+ album not issued

| | | |
|---|---|---|
| ON THE GLORY ROAD+ | COLUMBIA | CL1813 |
| THE MANY MOODS OF TONY | CBS | 62245 |

**CHANGE PARTNERS**
I.Berlin
Columbia recorded 10/86
Tony Bennett
with George Benson
not released recording from Bennett:Berlin sessions

| | | | |
|---|---|---|---|
| **CHEEK TO CHEEK**<br>I.Berlin<br>Columbia recorded 10/86<br>Tony Bennett<br>with George Benson | BENNETT:BERLIN | CBS | 460450 |
| **CHICAGO**<br>S.Cahn/J.Van Heusen<br>Roulette released 1961<br>Count Basie<br>R. SHARON 9/6/62 *(handwritten)*<br>live Columbia recorded 8/4/64<br>Louis Basil with Ralph Sharon Trio<br>not released | STRIKE UP THE BAND<br>ONE NIGHT STAND<br>COAST TO COAST<br>CARNEGIE HALL *(handwritten)* | ROULETTE<br>ALLEGRO<br>CAPITOL | 25231<br>799<br>80180 |
| **CHRISTMASLAND**<br>B.Farnon/D.Farnon<br>Columbia recorded 2/10/68<br>Robert Farnon | SNOWFALL, THE CHRISTMAS<br>ALBUM | COLUMBIA | 63782 |
| **CINNAMON SINNER**<br>Chase<br>Columbia recorded 13/5/56<br>Percy Faith | BECAUSE OF YOU 56<br>POPULAR FAVOURITES NO 1<br>SINGLE | COLUMBIA<br>PHILIPS<br>PHILIPS | CL2550<br>BBR8084<br>PB322 |
| **CITY OF THE ANGELS**<br>F.Astaire/T.Wolf<br>Columbia recorded 1985<br>Jorge Calandrelli | THE ART OF EXCELLENCE | CBS | 26990 |
| **CLIMB EVERY MOUNTAIN**<br>R.Rodgers/O.Hammerstein II<br>Columbia recorded 23/10/59<br>Ralph Sharon | MR BROADWAY<br>A STRING OF HITS<br>SUNRISE, SUNSET<br>GREAT SONGS FROM THE SHOWS<br>THE GOLDEN TOUCH<br>SINGLE | COLUMBIA<br>CBS<br>COLUMBIA<br>PICKWICK<br>COLUMBIA<br>PHILIPS | CL1763<br>66010<br>C32239<br>4171<br>P12790<br>PB1122 |
| live Columbia recording<br>with Ralph Sharon 9/6/62 | AT CARNEGIE HALL 1<br>TONY BENNETT SINGS | CBS<br>R/DIGEST | 62116<br>8070 |
| **CLOSE YOUR EYES**<br>B.Petkere<br>Columbia recorded 31/7/53<br>Gil Evans with The Pastels<br>not released | POSSIBLE RELEASE<br>(COLUMBIA PRICELESS EDITION) | COLUMBIA | PE6 |
| re-recorded Columbia 4/1/56<br>Percy Faith | THE VOICE OF YOUR CHOICE<br>BACK TO THE FIFTIES<br>BECAUSE OF YOU 56<br>SINGLE | PHILIPS<br>PICKWICK<br>COLUMBIA<br>PHILIPS | BBR 8051<br>4151<br>CL2550<br>PB445 |

| | | | | |
|---|---|---|---|---|
| ✓✓✓ | re-recorded Columbia<br>Ralph Burns 5/4/61 | MY HEART SINGS<br>FORTY YEARS VOL 2<br>JAZZ | COLUMBIA<br>COLUMBIA<br>COLUMBIA | CL1658<br>46843<br>450465 |
| ✓ | **CLOUDY MORNING**<br>J.McCarthy Jnr./M.Fisher<br>Columbia recorded 1995<br>Jorge Calandrelli & Bill Holman | HERE'S TO THE LADIES | COLUMBIA | 481266 |
| | **COCO**<br>A.J.Lerner/A.Previn<br>Columbia recorded 17/11/69<br>Peter Matz | SOMETHING | CBS | 64217 |
| | **COFFEE BREAK**<br>J.Moody<br>Columbia recorded 11/71<br>Torrie Zito | SUMMER OF '42 | CBS | 64648 |
| ✓ | **COLD, COLD HEART**<br>H.Williams<br>Columbia recorded 31/5/51<br>Percy Faith | BECAUSE OF YOU<br>FORTY YEARS VOL 1<br>THE GOLDEN TOUCH<br>16 ORIGINAL HITS<br>COCA COLA PRESENTS<br>A STRING OF HITS<br>THE LAST PICTURE SHOW<br>POPULAR FAVORITES<br>SINGLE | COLUMBIA<br>COLUMBIA<br>COLUMBIA<br>EVEREST<br>COLUMBIA<br>CBS<br>COLUMBIA<br>COLUMBIA<br>PHILIPS | CL6221<br>46843<br>P12789<br>LP16-19<br>26851<br>66010<br>70115<br>CL6205<br>DB2924 |
| | re-recorded Columbia<br>John Bunch 24/6/70 | ALL TIME HALL OF FAME HITS<br>16 MOST REQUESTED SONGS | CBS<br>COLUMBIA | 64200<br>57056 |
| ✓ | **COLE PORTER SELECTION**<br>**10 SONG MEDLEY**<br>C.Porter<br>Improv recorded c1975<br>Torrie Zito | THE SPECIAL MAGIC OF . . .<br>HOLLYWOOD & BROADWAY<br>THE MAGIC OF TONY BENNETT<br>STAGE & SCREEN HITS | DRG<br>NELSON<br>NELSON<br>DBM | 801<br>1145<br>CYU 106<br>1001 |

What is this thing called love
Love for sale
I'm in love again
You'd be so nice to come home to
Easy to love
It's alright by me
Night and Day
Dream dancing
I've got you under my skin
Get out of town

| | | | |
|---|---|---|---|
| **COME NEXT SPRING**<br>Adelson/Steiner<br>Columbia recorded 11/10/55<br>Percy Faith | POPULAR FAVOURITES 5<br>COCA COLA PRESENTS<br>SINGLE<br>COME NEXT SPRING (SOUNDTRACK) | PHILIPS<br>COLUMBIA<br>PHILIPS | BBR8084<br>26851<br>PB537 |
| **COME RAIN OR COME SHINE**<br>J.Mercer/H.Arlen<br>Columbia recorded 15/8/60<br>Glenn Osser | A STRING OF HAROLD ARLEN<br>LET'S FALL IN LOVE WITH.. | COLUMBIA<br>CBS | CL1559<br>88131 |
| **COME SATURDAY MORNING**<br>F.Karlin/D.Previn<br>Columbia recorded 1969<br>Peter Matz | SOMETHING | CBS | 64217 |
| re-recorded Columbia 30/1/70<br>Peter Matz<br>not released | | | |
| **COMES ONCE IN A LIFETIME**<br>B.Comden/A.Green<br>Columbia recorded 6/9/61 ✓ 9/6/62 | MR BROADWAY<br>*CARNEGIE HALL* | COLUMBIA | CL1763 |
| **CONGRATULATIONS TO SOMEONE**<br>Alfred/Frisch ✓<br>Columbia recorded 26/8/52<br>Percy Faith | BLUE VELVET<br>MUSIC FOR THE ENGAGED<br>POP HITS VOL 1 (EP) | COLUMBIA<br>COLUMBIA<br>COLUMBIA | CL1292<br>CL687<br>B1648 |
| **COUNTRY GIRL**<br>R.Farnon ✓<br>Columbia recorded 26/11/66<br>Marion Evans | TONY MAKES IT HAPPEN<br>FORTY YEARS VOL 3<br>LOVE STORY<br>WHEN I FALL IN LOVE<br>TONY BENNETT SINGS | CBS<br>COLUMBIA<br>CBS<br>HALLMARK<br>R/DIGEST | 63055<br>46843<br>64368<br>SHM817<br>8070 |
| live recording Columbia<br>H.Roberts (A&R) 11/8/67<br>not released | | | |
| live Columbia recording<br>Robert Farnon 31/1/71 ✓ | GET HAPPY | CBS | 64577 |
| **CRAZY RYTHMN**<br>Charig/Meyer ✓<br>Columbia recorded 27/6/57<br>Ralph Sharon | THE BEAT OF MY HEART<br>JUST ONE OF THOSE THINGS<br>JAZZ | COLUMBIA<br>HALLMARK<br>COLUMBIA | CL1079<br>SHM646<br>450465 |
| **CUTE**<br>N.Hefti/J.Styne ✓<br>Philips recorded c1972<br>Robert Farnon | THE GOOD THINGS IN LIFE<br>SPOTLIGHT ON ....<br>GREATEST HITS NO7 | PHILIPS<br>PHILIPS<br>VERVE | 6308134<br>6641497<br>SE4929 |

| | | | |
|---|---|---|---|
| **DANCING IN THE DARK** <br> H.Deitz/A.Schwartz <br> Columbia recorded 6/4/61 <br> Ralph Burns | MY HEART SINGS <br> FORTY YEARS VOL 2 <br> JAZZ | COLUMBIA <br> COLUMBIA <br> CBS | CL1658 <br> 46843 <br> 450465 |
| Re-recorded 1993 <br> Tony Bennett & Ralph Sharon | STEPPIN' OUT | COLUMBIA | 474360 |
| **DANNY BOY** <br> Trad <br> Columbia recorded 25/5/64 <br> Stan Getz <br> +album not released | JAZZ <br> TONY BENNETT, STAN GETZ <br>                  & FRIENDS+ | CBS <br><br> CBS | 450465 <br><br> 32276 |
| **DARN THAT DREAM** <br> De Lang/Van Heusen <br> Columbia recorded 11/8/54 <br> Chuck Wayne | CLOUD 7 | COLUMBIA | CL621 |
| **DAY IN, DAY OUT** <br> J.Mercer/R.Bloom <br> Columbia recorded 1993 <br> with the Ralph Sharon Trio | PERFECTLY FRANK | COLUMBIA | 472222 |
| **DAYBREAK** <br> H.Adamson/F.Grofe <br> Columbia recorded 1995 <br> Jorge Calandrelli & Bill Holman | HERE'S TO THE LADIES | COLUMBIA | 481266 |
| **DAYS OF LOVE** <br> D.Rose/P.F.Webster <br> Columbia recorded 20/4/67 <br> Marion Evans | FOR ONCE IN MY LIFE <br> FORTY YEARS VOL 4 | CBS <br> COLUMBIA | 63166 <br> 46843 |
| live recording Columbia <br> H.Roberts (A&R) 11/8/67 <br> not released | | | |
| **DE GLORY ROAD** <br> C.Wood/J.Wolfe <br> recorded Columbia 13/3/62 <br> Ralph Sharon <br> +this album unreleased | ON THE GLORY ROAD+ | COLUMBIA | CL1813 |
| Live Columbia recorded <br> Ralph Sharon 9/6/62 | AT CARNEGIE HALL 2 | CBS | 62117 |
| **DON'T CRY BABY** <br> Columbia recorded 1/10/50 <br> Marty Manning | SINGLE | COLUMBIA | 39060 |

| | | | |
|---|---|---|---|
| **DON'T GET AROUND MUCH ANYMORE**<br>S.Russell/E.Ellington<br>Columbia recorded 27/1/67<br>Marion Evans | TONY MAKES IT HAPPEN<br>JAZZ<br>THE VERY THOUGHT OF YOU<br>SUNRISE, SUNSET | CBS<br>CBS<br>HALLMARK<br>CBS | 63055<br>450465<br>SHM769<br>32239 |
| live recording Columbia<br>H.Roberts (A&R) 11/8/67<br>not released | | | |
| **DON'T TELL ME WHY**<br>Shanklin/Magenta<br>Columbia recorded 5/5/55<br>Percy Faith | SINGLE | PHILIPS | PB486 |
| **DON'T WAIT TOO LONG**<br>S.Skylar<br>Columbia recorded 11/9/63<br>Dick Hyman | THE MANY MOODS OF TONY<br>THE GOLDEN TOUCH<br>SINGLE | CBS<br>COLUMBIA<br>CBS | 62245<br>P12789<br>AAG176 |
| **DON'T WORRY 'BOUT ME**<br>T.Koehler/R.Bloom<br>Columbia recorded 4/4/61<br>Ralph Burns | MY HEART SINGS | COLUMBIA | CL1658 |
| re-recorded Columbia 1993<br>with the Ralph Sharon Trio | PERFECTLY FRANK | COLUMBIA | 472222 |
| **DOWN IN THE DEPTHS**<br>C.Porter<br>Columbia recorded 1995<br>Jorge Calandrelli & Bill Holman | HERE'S TO THE LADIES | COLUMBIA | 481266 |
| **DREAM**<br>J.Mercer<br>Columbia recorded 1/10/71<br>Robert Farnon | WITH LOVE | CBS | 64849 |
| **EAST OF THE SUN (WEST OF THE MOON)**<br>B.Bowman<br>Columbia recorded 1993<br>with the Ralph Sharon Trio | PERFECTLY FRANK | COLUMBIA | 472222 |
| **EASY COME, EASY GO**<br>J.Green/E.Heyman<br>Columbia recorded 1/10/71<br>Robert Farnon | WITH LOVE | CBS | 64849 |

**EASY STREET**
Columbia recorded 15/1/68
Torrie Zito with Dominic Germano
not released

| | | | |
|---|---|---|---|
| **ELEANOR RIGBY** | GREAT HITS OF TODAY | CBS | 63962 |
| J.Lennon/P.McCartney | SINGLE | CBS | S5255 |
| Columbia recorded 18/11/69 | | | |
| Peter Matz | | | |
| | | | |
| **EMILY** | THE MOVIE SONG ALBUM | CBS | 62677 |
| J.Mandel/J.Mercer | FORTY YEARS VOL 3 | COLUMBIA | 46843 |
| Columbia recorded 28/12/65 | | | |
| Johnny Mandel | | | |
| | | | |
| **END OF A LOVE AFFAIR** | THE GOOD THINGS IN LIFE | PHILIPS | 6308134 |
| Redding | SPOTLIGHT ON .... | PHILIPS | 6641297 |
| Philips recorded c1972 | AT LONG LAST LOVE | PHILIPS | SON 014 |
| Robert Farnon | | | |
| | | | |
| **EVERYBODY HAS THE BLUES** | THE ART OF EXCELLENCE | CBS | 26990 |
| J.Taylor | | | |
| Columbia recorded 1985 | | | |
| Jorge Calandrelli | | | |
| with Ray Charles | | | |
| | | | |
| **EVERYBODY'S TALKIN'** | SOMETHING | CBS | 64217 |
| F.Neil | | | |
| Columbia recorded 11/8/69 | | | |
| Peter Matz | | | |
| | | | |
| re-recorded Columbia | SINGLE | COLUMBIA | 4-45157 |
| Peter Matz 30/6/70 | | | |
| | | | |
| **EVERYTIME WE SAY** | | | |
| **GOODBYE** | LONG AGO AND FAR AWAY | COLUMBIA | CL1186 |
| C.Porter | | | |
| Columbia recorded 8/4/58 | | | |
| Frank De Vol | | | |
| | | | |
| **EXPERIMENT** | LIFE IS BEAUTIFUL | IMPROV | 7112 |
| C.Porter | HOLLYWOOD & BROADWAY | NELSON | 1145 |
| Improv recorded c1975 | THE MAGIC OF TONY BENNETT | NELSON | CYU106 |
| Torrie Zito | STAGE & SCREEN HITS | DBM | 1001 |

**FALLING IN LOVE WITH LOVE**
R.Rodgers/L.Hart
Columbia recorded 11/3/65
Ernie Altschuler
not released

30

**FASCINATIN' RHYTHM**        SINGLE                         LESLIE
G.Gershwin/I.Gershwin
Leslie recording c1947
recorded as Joe Bari

This is the first known recording by Tony Bennett using his first stage name,
Joe Bari. Both songs were issued on a 78 rpm by Leslie records, a company
owned by George Simon. The 1968 Billboard profile "20 years with Tony Bennett"
states that the only known copy of this record disintegrated sometime in the 60's.

| | | | |
|---|---|---|---|
| re-recorded Columbia | IN PERSON! | CBS | 62250 |
| Count Basie | 20 GREATEST HITS | WARWICK | PA 5021 |
| & Ralph Sharon 22/12/58 | THE TROLLEY SONG | EMBASSY | 31002 |
| 9/6/62 | CARNEGIE HALL | | |
| live radio recording 1963 | MEETS GENE KRUPA | SANDY HOOK | SH 2067 |
| with Gene Krupa | | | |
| | | | |
| **FIREFLY** | IN PERSON! | CBS | 62250 |
| C.Leigh/C.Coleman | ALL-TIME GREATEST HITS | CBS | 68200 |
| Columbia recorded 22/12/58 | FORTY YEARS VOL 1+ | COLUMBIA | 46843 |
| Count Basie | A STRING OF HITS+ | CBS | 66010 |
| & Ralph Sharon | PHILIPS TV (EP) | PHILIPS | BBE12223 |
| + no fake audience | 20 GREATEST HITS | WARWICK | PA 5021 |
| | 16 ORIGINAL HITS | EVEREST | LP16-19 |
| | LET'S FALL IN LOVE WITH .. + | CBS | 88131 |
| | SINGLE | PHILIPS | PB855 |
| | | | |
| live recording Columbia | AT CARNEGIE HALL 1 | CBS | 62116 |
| Ralph Sharon 9/6/62 | WHEN I FALL IN LOVE | HALLMARK | SHM817 |
| | | | |
| live Columbia recorded 8/4/64 | | | |
| Louis Basil with Ralph Sharon Trio | | | |
| not released | | | |
| | | | |
| live recording Columbia | | | |
| H.Roberts (A&R) 11/8/67 | | | |
| not released | | | |
| | | | |
| **FLY ME TO THE MOON** | SONGS FOR THE JET SET | CBS | 62544 |
| **(IN OTHER WORDS)** | THE GOLDEN TOUCH | COLUMBIA | P12790 |
| B.Howard | FORTY YEARS VOL 3 | COLUMBIA | 46843 |
| Columbia recorded 18/2/65 | GREATEST HITS VOL 2 | CBS | 63612 |
| Don Costa | TONY BENNETT SINGS | R/DIGEST | 8070 |
| | | | |
| live MTV recorded 4/94 | MTV UNPLUGGED | COLUMBIA | 477170 |
| with the Ralph Sharon Trio | | | |
| | | | |
| **FOLLOW ME** | MR BROADWAY | COLUMBIA | CL1763 |
| Lerner/Lowe | SINGLE | CBS | AAG208 |
| Columbia recorded 13/10/60 | | | |
| Glenn Osser | | | |

✓ **FOOLS RUSH IN**  LONG AGO AND FAR AWAY  COLUMBIA  CL1186
J.Mercer/J.Bloom
Columbia recorded 10/4/58
Frank De Vol

**FOR EVERY MAN THERE'S
A WOMAN**  A STRING OF HAROLD ARLEN  COLUMBIA  CL1559
H.Arlen
Columbia recorded 17/8/60
Glenn Osser

✓ **FOR HEAVEN'S SAKE**  ALONE TOGETHER  COLUMBIA  CL1471
D.Meyer/E.Bretton/S.Edwards
Columbia recorded 29/2/60
Frank De Vol

✓ **FOR ONCE IN MY LIFE**  FOR ONCE IN MY LIFE  CBS  63166
R.Miller/O.Murden  20 GREATEST HITS  WARWICK  PA5021
Columbia recorded 18/7/67  ALL TIME HALL OF FAME HITS  CBS  64200
Torrie Zito  16 MOST REQUESTED SONGS  CBS  57056
 THE GOLDEN TOUCH  COLUMBIA  P12789
 GREATEST HITS VOL 2  CBS  63612
 ALL-TIME GREATEST HITS  CBS  68200
 FORTY YEARS VOL 4  COLUMBIA  46843

live recording Columbia
H.Roberts (A&R) 11/8/67
not released

✓ live recording Columbia  GET HAPPY  CBS  64577
Robert Farnon 31/1/71

**FORGET HER**  SINGLE  PHILIPS  PB501
Columbia recorded 16/12/56
Marion Evans

**FORGET THE WOMAN**  THE ART OF EXCELLENCE  CBS  26990
E.Stratta/R.Whyte
Columbia recorded 1985
Jorge Calandrelli

**FRED**  GREAT AMERICAN COMPOSERS  COLUMBIA
S.Cahn/N.Hefti  SERIES*
Columbia recorded 25/1/71
Ralph Burns

re-recorded Columbia 21/5/71
Torrie Zito
* possibly either version has been issued on this US release

32

**FRIENDS BLUES**         2.38 AM RALPH SHARON &
R. Sharon                                      FRIENDS     ARGO               635
Argo released 1958
Scat only for the Ralph Sharon Trio

**FROM THE CANDY STORE ON**
   **THE CORNER (TO THE**     16 ORIGINAL HITS             EVEREST       LP16-19
   **CHAPEL ON THE HILL)**      SINGLE                             PHILIPS         PB628
Hilliard
Columbia recorded 6/6/56
Percy Faith
with Lois Winter

**FROM THIS MOMENT ON**
C.Porter
live Columbia recorded 8/4/64
Louis Basil with Ralph Sharon Trio
not released

**FUN TO BE FOOLED**           A STRING OF HAROLD ARLEN      COLUMBIA      CL1559
Gershwin/Harburg/Arlen        LET'S FALL IN LOVE WITH..         CBS               88131
Columbia recorded 18/8/60
Glenn Osser

✓ **FUNNY THING**                BLUE VELVET                      COLUMBIA      CL1292
Sigman/Williams                SINGLE                             PHILIPS         PB390
Columbia recorded 24/9/54
Percy Faith

**GEORGIA ROSE**                 A TIME FOR LOVE                CBS               62800
✓ Sullivan/Flynn/Rosenthal       GREATEST HITS VOL 2          CBS               63612
Columbia recorded 1/6/66
Ralph Burns

**GET HAPPY**                      YESTERDAY I HEARD THE RAIN    CBS               63351
T.Koehler/H.Arlen
Columbia recorded 22/5/68
Torrie Zito

✓ live recording Columbia         GET HAPPY                       CBS               64577
Robert Farnon 31/1/71

✓ **GIRL TALK**                       THE MOVIE SONG ALBUM       CBS               62677
B.Troup/N.Hefti                  THE TROLLEY SONG            EMBASSY       31002
Columbia recorded 14/12/65
Neal Hefti

live recording Columbia
H.Roberts (A&R) 11/8/67
not released

| | | | |
|---|---|---|---|
| **GIVE ME LOVE, GIVE ME PEACE**<br>Philips recorded c1972<br>Robert Farnon | GREATEST HITS NO7<br>SPOTLIGHT ON . . . .<br>SINGLE | VERVE<br>PHILIPS<br>PHILIPS | SE4929<br>6641297<br>6006326 |
| **GIVE ME THE SIMPLE LIFE**<br>Bloom/Ruby<br>Columbia recorded 6/8/54<br>Chuck Wayne<br>not released | | | |
| re-recorded Columbia 22/12/54<br>Chuck Wayne | CLOUD 7<br>JAZZ | COLUMBIA<br>CBS | CL621<br>450465 |
| **GOD BLESS THE CHILD**<br>A.Herzog/B.Holiday<br>Columbia recorded 28/10/59<br>Ralph Sharon<br>Unreleased | | | |
| re-recorded Columbia 1995<br>Jorge Callandrelli & Bill Holman | HERE'S TO THE LADIES | COLUMBIA | 481266 |
| **GOLDEN SLUMBERS**<br>Columbia recorded 3/4/70<br>Peter Matz<br>not released | | | |
| **GONE WITH THE WIND**<br>A.Wrubel/H.Magidson<br>Columbia recorded 29/2/60<br>Frank De Vol | ALONE TOGETHER | COLUMBIA | CL1471 |
| **GOODBYE JOHN**<br>Columbia recorded 14/7/50<br>Percy Faith<br>not released | | | |
| **GOT HER OFF MY HANDS (BUT CAN'T GET HER OFF MY MIND)**<br>Lewis/Young/Phillips<br>Columbia recorded 24/4/63<br>Ralph Burns | THIS IS ALL I ASK | CBS | 62205 |
| **GOT THE GATE ON THE GOLDEN GATE**<br>M.Torme<br>Columbia recorded 29/9/64<br>George Siravo | WHO CAN I TURN TO | CBS | 62486 |

re-recorded Columbia 14/10/64
George Siravo
not released

**GROWING PAINS**           STRIKE UP THE BAND          ROULETTE          25231
Stone                       ONE NIGHT STAND             ALLEGRO           799
Roulette released 1961
Count Basie

**HAPPINESS IS A THING
    CALLED JOE**            TONY SINGS FOR TWO          COLUMBIA          CL1446
E.Harburg/H.Arlen
Columbia recorded 28/10/59
Ralph Sharon

**HAPPINESS STREET
    (CORNER SUNSHINE SQ)**  TOP 12                      COLUMBIA          CL937
Woolfson/White              SINGLE                      PHILIPS           PB628
Columbia recorded 11/10/55
Percy Faith

**HARLEM BUTTERFLY**        WITH LOVE                   CBS               64849
J.Mercer
Columbia recorded 1/10/71
Robert Farnon

**HAVE A GOOD TIME**        BLUE VELVET                 COLUMBIA          CL1292
Bryant/Bryant
Columbia recorded 24/4/52
Percy Faith

**HAVE I TOLD YOU LATELY?** I LEFT MY HEART IN SAN
H.Rome                           FRANCISCO              CBS               62201
Columbia recorded 23/1/62
Marty Manning?
RALPH SHARON 9/6/62         CARNEGIE HA
live radio recording 1963   MEETS GENE KRUPA            SANDY HOOK        SH 2067
Gene Krupa

**HAVE YOU MET MISS JONES?** JAZZ                       CBS               450465
R.Rodgers/L.Hart            STAN GETZ & FRIENDS+        CBS               32276
Columbia recorded 15/10/64  GREAT SONGS FROM THE SHOWS  PICKWICK          4171
Stan Getz
+album unreleased

re-recorded Improv c1973    SINGS 10 RODGERS & HART
with Ruby Braff/                                SONGS  IMPROV            7113
George Barnes Quartet       RODGERS & HART SONGBOOK     NELSON            1129

**HAVE YOURSELF A MERRY
    LITTLE CHRISTMAS**      SNOWFALL, THE CHRISTMAS
H.Martin/R.Blare                                ALBUM  CBS               63782
Columbia recorded 1/10/68   NOEL                        TRAX              701
Robert Farnon

✓ **HE LOVES AND SHE LOVES**    STEPPIN' OUT    COLUMBIA    474360
G.Gershwin/I.Gershwin
Columbia recorded 1994
Tony Bennett & Ralph Sharon

**HEART**    ALL STAR POPS    COLUMBIA    CL728
Adler/Ross    POPULAR FAVOURITES NO7    PHILIPS    BBR8108
Columbia recorded 5/5/55    SINGLE    PHILIPS    PB672
Sid Feller

**HERE**    GREAT HITS OF TODAY    CBS    63962
G.Lees
Columbia recorded 7/10/69
Peter Matz

✓ **HERE COMES THAT HEARTACHE AGAIN**    BLUE VELVET    COLUMBIA    CL1292
Alfred/Frisch    SINGLE    PHILIPS    PB267
Columbia recorded 17/3/53
Percy Faith

**HERE IN MY HEART**    ALONE AT LAST    COLUMBIA    CL2507
Genaro/Levinson/Borelli    THE GOLDEN TOUCH    COLUMBIA    P12790
Columbia recorded 30/4/52
Percy Faith

**HERE, THERE & EVERYWHERE**    GREAT HITS OF TODAY    CBS    63962
J.Lennon/P.McCartney
Columbia recorded 17/11/69
Peter Matz

✓ **HERE'S THAT RAINY DAY**    WITH LOVE    CBS    64849
J.Burke/J.Van Heusen
Columbia recorded 1/10/71
Robert Farnon

✓ re-recorded Columbia 1993    PERFECTLY FRANK    COLUMBIA    472222
with the Ralph Sharon Trio

✓ **HI-HO**    YESTERDAY I HEARD THE RAIN    CBS    63351
G.Gershwin/I.Gershwin    FORTY YEARS VOL 4    COLUMBIA    46843
Columbia recorded 22/5/68
Torrie Zito

**HOME IS THE PLACE**    YESTERDAY I HEARD THE RAIN    CBS    63351
S.Sondheim/J.Styne
Columbia recorded 16/4/68
Torrie Zito

| | | | |
|---|---|---|---|
| **HONEYSUCKLE ROSE** ✓<br>T.Waller/H.Brooks/A.Razaf<br>Columbia recorded 1995<br>Jorge Calandrelli & Bill Holman | HERE'S TO THE LADIES | COLUMBIA | 481266 |
| **HOUSE OF FLOWERS**<br>T.Capote/H.Arlen<br>Columbia recorded 15/8/60<br>Glenn Osser | A STRING OF HAROLD ARLEN<br>LET'S FALL IN LOVE WITH . . | COLUMBIA<br>CBS | CL1559<br>88131 |
| **HOW ABOUT YOU** ✓<br>Freed/Lane<br>live Columbia recorded 9/6/62<br>Ralph Sharon | AT CARNEGIE HALL 1<br>WHEN I FALL IN LOVE | CBS<br>HALLMARK | 62116<br>SHM817 |
| **HOW BEAUTIFUL IS NIGHT<br>(WITH YOU)** ✓<br>M.Raskin/R.Farnon<br>Columbia recorded 11/8/71<br>Robert Farnon<br><br>re-recorded Columbia 1/10/71<br>Robert Farnon<br>not released | WITH LOVE | CBS | 64849 |
| **HOW CAN I REPLACE YOU?**<br>Gallup/Van Heusen<br>Columbia recorded 5/5/55<br>Percy Faith | THE VOICE OF YOUR CHOICE<br>SINGLE | PHILIPS<br>PHILIPS | BBR 8051<br>PB521 |
| **HOW DO YOU KEEP THE<br>MUSIC PLAYING?** ✓<br>Bergman/Bergman/LeGrand<br>Columbia recorded 1/86<br>Jorge Calandrelli | THE ART OF EXCELLENCE<br>FORTY YEARS VOL 4 | CBS<br>COLUMBIA | 26990<br>46843 |
| **HOW DO YOU SAY<br>AUF WIEDERSEHEN?**<br>J.Mercer/A.Scibetta<br>Columbia recorded 18/7/67<br>Torrie Zito | FOR ONCE IN MY LIFE | CBS | 63166 |
| **HOW INSENSITIVE**<br>A.C.Jobim/DeMoraes/Gimbel<br>Columbia recorded 18/2/65<br>Don Costa<br>*edited version | SONGS FOR THE JET SET<br>GREATEST HITS VOL 2* | CBS<br>CBS | 62544<br>63612 |

**HOW LITTLE WE KNOW**
**(HOW LITTLE IT MATTERS)**       LISTEN EASY                        PHILIPS       6308157
J.Mercer/H.Carmichael             SPOTLIGHT ON . . . .               PHILIPS       6641297
Philips recorded c1973            AT LONG LAST LOVE                  PHILIPS       SON 014
Don Costa

**HOW LONG HAS THIS BEEN**
 **GOING ON?**                  ALONE TOGETHER                  COLUMBIA      CL1471
G.Gershwin/I.Gershwin
Columbia recorded 29/2/60
Frank De Vol

re-recorded Columbia 26/2/64
not released

**HUSHABYE MOUNTAIN**             YESTERDAY I HEARD THE RAIN          CBS          63351
Sherman/Sherman
Columbia recorded 16/4/68
Torrie Zito

**I AM**                          A STRING OF HITS                    CBS          66010
Shuman/Edwards                    MORE TONY'S GREATEST HITS           COLUMBIA     13301
Columbia recorded 19/6/57         SINGLE                              PHILIPS      PB724
Ray Ellis

**I CAN'T BELIEVE YOU'RE**
 **IN LOVE WITH ME**          CLOUD 7                            COLUMBIA      CL621
McHugh/Gaskill                    JAZZ                                CBS          450465
Columbia recorded 22/12/54
Chuck Wayne

**I CAN'T GET STARTED**           ONCE MORE WITH FEELING              AMHERST      AMH 94405
V.Duke/I.Gershwin
recorded c1992/3
Doc Severinsen

**I CAN'T GIVE YOU**
 **ANYTHING BUT LOVE**        BECAUSE OF YOU 56                   COLUMBIA     CL2550
Columbia recorded 17/4/56
Marty Manning

re-recorded Columbia              TONY                                COLUMBIA     CL938
Ray Conniff 13/9/56               TONY BENNETT SHOWCASE               PHILIPS      BBL7138

**I CONCENTRATE ON YOU**          LISTEN EASY                         PHILIPS      6308157
C.Porter                          SPOTLIGHT ON . . .                  PHILIPS      6641297
Philips recorded c1973            AT LONG LAST LOVE                   PHILIPS      SON 014
Don Costa

re-recorded Columbia 1994         STEPPIN' OUT                        COLUMBIA     474360
with the Ralph Sharon Trio

| | | | |
|---|---|---|---|
| I COULD WRITE A BOOK<br>R.Rodgers/L.Hart<br>Improv recorded c1973<br>with the Ruby Braff/<br>George Barnes Quartet | 10 RODGERS & HART SONGS<br>UNFORGETTABLE<br>RODGERS & HART SONGBOOK | IMPROV<br>CASTLE<br>NELSON | 7113<br>UNLP019<br>CD1129 |
| I COVER THE WATERFRONT<br>E.Heyman/J.Green<br>Columbia recorded 4/11/58<br>Ralph Burns' | HOMETOWN, MY TOWN<br>LOVE SONGS | COLUMBIA<br>CBS | CL1301<br>66297 |
| I DIDN'T KNOW WHAT<br>  TIME IT WAS<br>R.Rodgers/L.Hart<br>Columbia recorded 28/10/59<br>Ralph Sharon | TONY SINGS FOR TWO | COLUMBIA | CL1446 |
| I DO NOT KNOW A DAY<br>  I DID NOT LOVE YOU<br>R.Rodgers/M.Charnin<br>Columbia recorded 28/9/70<br>Torrie Zito | LOVE STORY<br>FORTY YEARS VOL 4 | CBS<br>COLUMBIA | 64368<br>46843 |
| I DON'T KNOW WHY<br>  (I JUST DO)<br>R.Turk/F.Ahlert<br>Columbia recorded 12/1/67<br>Marion Evans<br><br>re-recorded Columbia 18/1/67<br>Marion Evans<br>not released | TONY MAKES IT HAPPEN | CBS | 63055 |
| I FALL IN LOVE TOO EASILY<br>S.Cahn/J.Styne<br>Columbia recorded 6/8/54<br>Chuck Wayne | CLOUD 7<br>PHILIPS TV (EP) | COLUMBIA<br>PHILIPS | CL621<br>BBE12223 |
| re-recorded Columbia 1993<br>with the Ralph Sharon Trio | PERFECTLY FRANK | COLUMBIA | 472222 |
| I GET A KICK OUT OF YOU<br>C.Porter<br>Columbia recorded 14/10/57<br>Ralph Sharon | FORTY YEARS VOL 1<br>THE BEAT OF MY HEART | COLUMBIA | 46843 |
| I GOT LOST IN HER ARMS<br>I.Berlin<br>Columbia recorded 10/1/86<br>Jorge Calandrelli | THE ART OF EXCELLENCE<br>FORTY YEARS VOL 4 | CBS<br>COLUMBIA | 26990<br>46843 |

| | | | |
|---|---|---|---|
| ✓ I GOT RHYTHM<br>I.Gershwin/G.Gershwin<br>Columbia recorded 1995<br>Jorge Calandrelli & Bill Holman | HERE'S TO THE LADIES | COLUMBIA | 481266 |
| I GUESS I'LL HAVE TO<br>CHANGE MY PLAN<br>Dietz/Schwartz<br>Roulette released 1961<br>Count Basie | STRIKE UP THE BAND<br>ONE NIGHT STAND | ROULETTE<br>ALLEGRO | 25231<br>799 |
| ✓ re-recorded Columbia 1994<br>Tony Bennett & Ralph Sharon | STEPPIN' OUT | COLUMBIA | 474360 |
| (I LEFT MY HEART) IN<br>SAN FRANCISCO<br>✓ D.Cross/G.Cory<br>Columbia recorded 23/1/62<br>✓ Marty Manning | I LEFT MY HEART IN<br>SAN FRANCISCO<br>ALL-TIME GREATEST HITS<br>16 MOST REQUESTED SONGS<br>16 ORIGINAL HITS<br>ALL TIME HALL OF FAME HITS<br>FORTY YEARS VOL 2<br>20 GREATEST HITS<br>THE GOLDEN TOUCH<br>MILLION DOLLAR MEMORIES<br>GREATEST HITS<br>SINGLE<br>SINGLE | CBS<br>CBS<br>CBS<br>EVEREST<br>CBS<br>COLUMBIA<br>WARWICK<br>COLUMBIA<br>R/DIGEST<br>CBS<br>CBS<br>CBS | 62201<br>68200<br>57056<br>LP16-19<br>64200<br>46843<br>PA5021<br>P12789<br>8061/9<br>62821<br>201730<br>AAG121 |
| ✓ live Columbia recording<br>Ralph Sharon 9/6/62 | AT CARNEGIE HALL 1 | CBS | 62116 |
| ✓ live radio recording 1963<br>with Gene Krupa | MEETS GENE KRUPA | SANDY HOOK | SH 2067 |
| live Columbia recorded 8/4/64<br>Louis Basil with Ralph Sharon Trio<br>not released | | | |
| live recording Columbia<br>H.Roberts (A&R) 11/8/67<br>not released | | | |
| ✓ live Columbia recording<br>with Robert Farnon 31/1/71 | GET HAPPY | CBS | 64577 |
| live Palladium recording<br>intro Max Bygraves 1972 | 25 YEARS OF ROYAL VARIETY | CGD | RVP252S |
| live Sullivan recording<br>from Ed Sullivan Show | 20 COMMAND PERFORMANCES | RONCO | 2005 |

| | | | |
|---|---|---|---|
| live Improv recording<br>with the MacPartlands 5/77 | MACPARTLANDS & FRIENDS<br>MAKE BEAUTIFUL MUSIC | IMPROV | 7123 |
| live MTV recorded 4/94<br>with the Ralph Sharon Trio | MTV UNPLUGGED | COLUMBIA | 477170 |

✓ **I LET A SONG GO OUT
   OF MY HEART**
E.Ellington/I.Mills/
H.Nemo/J.Redmond
Columbia recorded 27/1/67
Marion Evans

| | | |
|---|---|---|
| TONY MAKES IT HAPPEN<br>JAZZ | CBS<br>COLUMBIA | 63055<br>450465 |

**I LOVE A PIANO**
I.Berlin
Columbia recorded 10/86
Ralph Sharon Trio
unreleased track fron "Bennett:Berlin" session

| | | | |
|---|---|---|---|
| live MTV recorded 4/94<br>with the Ralph Sharon Trio | MTV UNPLUGGED | COLUMBIA | 477170 |

✓ **I LOVE THE WINTER WEATHER/
   I'VE GOT MY LOVE TO
   KEEP ME WARM**
T.Freeman/E.Brown, I.Berlin
Columbia released 1967
Robert Farnon

| | | |
|---|---|---|
| SNOWFALL, THE CHRISTMAS<br>ALBUM | CBS | 63782 |

**I LOVE YOU**
Grieg/Wright/Forrest
Columbia recorded 23/1/62
Marty Manning
+album unreleased

| | | |
|---|---|---|
| ON THE GLORY ROAD+ | COLUMBIA | CL1813 |

**I NEVER FELT MORE LIKE
   FALLING IN LOVE**
R.Freed/R.Allen
Columbia recorded 19/6/57
Ralph Sharon

| | | |
|---|---|---|
| SINGLE | PHILIPS | PB786 |

✓ **I ONLY HAVE EYES FOR YOU**
✓ A.Dubin/H.Warren
Columbia recorded 12/11/57
Percy Faith
not released

*THE BEAT OF MY HEART*

| | | |
|---|---|---|
| re-recorded Columbia 1968<br>Torrie Zito | YESTERDAY I HEARD THE RAIN<br>LOVE SONGS | CBS<br>CBS | 63351<br>66297 |

| | | | |
|---|---|---|---|
| **I SEE YOUR FACE BEFORE ME**<br>H.Dietz/A.Schwartz<br>Columbia recorded 1993<br>with the Ralph Sharon Trio ✓ | PERFECTLY FRANK | COLUMBIA | 472222 |
| **I THOUGHT ABOUT YOU**<br>J.Mercer/J.Van Heusen<br>Columbia recorded 1993<br>with the Ralph Sharon Trio ✓ | PERFECTLY FRANK | COLUMBIA | 472222 |
| **I USED TO BE COLOUR BLIND**<br>I.Berlin<br>Improv recorded c1975<br>Torrie Zito | LIFE IS BEAUTIFUL<br>HOLLYWOOD & BROADWAY<br>STAGE & SCREEN HITS<br>THE MAGIC OF TONY BENNETT | IMPROV<br>NELSON<br>DBM<br>NELSON | 7112<br>1145<br>1001<br>CYU 106 |
| **I WALK A LITTLE FASTER**<br>C.Leigh/C/Coleman<br>Columbia recorded 29/9/64 ✓<br>George Siravo | WHO CAN I TURN TO<br>LET'S FALL IN LOVE WITH..<br>FORTY YEARS VOL 3 | CBS<br>CBS<br>COLUMBIA | 62486<br>88131<br>46843 |

**I WANNA BE AROUND**
S.Vimmerstedt/J.Mercer
Columbia recorded 12/10/62
Marty Manning
Not released

| | | | |
|---|---|---|---|
| ✓ re-recorded Columbia<br>Marty Manning 19/10/62 | I WANNA BE AROUND<br>ALL-TIME GREATEST HITS<br>20 GREATEST HITS<br>16 MOST REQUESTED SONGS<br>THE GOLDEN TOUCH<br>16 ORIGINAL HITS<br>ALL TIME HALL OF FAME HITS<br>GREATEST HITS<br>FORTY YEARS VOL 2<br>SINGLE | CBS<br>CBS<br>WARWICK<br>CBS<br>COLUMBIA<br>EVEREST<br>CBS<br>CBS<br>COLUMBIA<br>CBS | 62149<br>68200<br>PA5021<br>57056<br>P12790<br>LP16-19<br>64200<br>62821<br>46843<br>AAG137 |

live Columbia recorded 8/4/64
Louis Basil with Ralph Sharon Trio
not released

✓ **I WANNA BE IN LOVE AGAIN**
see entry for "I Wish I Were In Love Again"

**I WANNA BE LOVED**
Columbia recorded 17/4/50
Marty Manning
not released

| | | | |
|---|---|---|---|
| re-recorded Colymbia<br>Marty Manning 20/4/52 | BECAUSE OF YOU | COLUMBIA | CL6221 |

42

| | | | |
|---|---|---|---|
| **I WANT TO BE HAPPY**<br>I.Caesar/V.Youmans<br>Columbia recorded 25/1/71<br>Ralph Burns | LOVE STORY | CBS | 64368 |
| ✓ live Columbia recording<br>Robert Farnon 31/1/71 | GET HAPPY | CBS | 64577 |
| **I WAS LOST I WAS DRIFTING**<br>B.Kaper/K.Gannon<br>Columbia recorded 1989<br>Jorge Calandrelli | ASTORIA: PORTRAIT OF THE<br>ARTIST | CBS | 466005 |
| **I WILL LIVE MY LIFE**<br>**FOR YOU**<br>Salvadore/Stellman<br>Columbia recorded 19/10/62<br>Marty Manning | I WANNA BE AROUND<br>SINGLE | CBS<br>CBS | 62149<br>AAG137 |
| **I WISH I WERE IN LOVE**<br>**AGAIN**<br>R.Rodgers/L.Hart<br>✓ Improv recorded c1973<br>with the Ruby Braff/<br>George Barnes Quartet | MORE GREAT RODGERS & HART<br>HOLLYWOOD & BROADWAY<br>STAGE & SCREEN HITS<br>RODGERS & HART SONGBOOK<br>SINGLE | IMPROV<br>NELSON<br>DBM<br>NELSON<br>IMPROV | 7120<br>1145<br>1001<br>CD1129<br>713106 |
| ✓ Columbia recorded 1993<br>with the Ralph Sharon Trio<br>(the album sleeve notes show title incorrect) | PERFECTLY FRANK | COLUMBIA | 472222 |
| ✓ **I WISHED ON THE MOON**<br>D.Parker/R.Rainger<br>Columbia recorded 1993<br>with the Ralph Sharon Trio | PERFECTLY FRANK | COLUMBIA | 472222 |
| **I WON'T CRY ANYMORE**<br>Wise/Frisch<br>✓ Columbia recorded 4/4/51<br>Percy Faith | BECAUSE OF YOU<br>16 ORIGINAL HITS<br>BLUE VELVET | COLUMBIA<br>EVEREST<br>COLUMBIA | CL6221<br>LP16-19<br>CL1292 |
| **I, YES ME! THAT'S WHO**<br>Columbia recorded 30/1/70<br>Peter Matz | GREAT AMERICAN COMPOSERS<br>SERIES | COLUMBIA | |
| Re-recorded 2/4/70<br>Peter Matz | HOUSE MUSIC COLLECTION | COLUMBIA | |
| **IF I COULD GO BACK**<br>B.Bacharach/H.David<br>Philips recorded c1973<br>Don Costa | LISTEN EASY<br>SPOTLIGHT ON . . . .<br>AT LONG LAST LOVE | PHILIPS<br>PHILIPS<br>PHILIPS | 6308157<br>6641297<br>SON 014 |

IF I LOVE AGAIN
B.Oakland/J.Murray
Columbia recorded 12/10/62
Marty Manning
not released

✓ re-recorded Columbia | I WANNA BE AROUND | CBS | 62149
Marty Manning | FORTY YEARS VOL 2 | COLUMBIA | 46843
19/10/62 | THE VERY THOUGHT OF YOU | HALLMARK | SHM769

IF I RULED THE WORLD | SONGS FOR THE JET SET | CBS | 62544
L.Bricuse/C.Ornadel | THE BEST OF TONY BENNETT | CBS | 6151
✓ Columbia recorded 4/1/65 | GREATEST HITS | CBS | 62821
Don Costa | TONY BENNETT SINGS | R/DIGEST | 8070
 | FORTY YEARS VOL 3 | COLUMBIA | 46843
 | GREAT SONGS FROM THE SHOWS | PICKWICK | 4171
 | 20 GREATEST HITS | WARWICK | PA502
 | THE GOLDEN TOUCH | COLUMBIA | P12789
 | SINGLE | CBS | 201735

live recording Columbia
H.Roberts (A&R) 11/8/67
not released

✓ live recording Columbia | GET HAPPY | CBS | 64577
Robert Farnon 31/1/71

IF YOU WERE MINE | I WANNA BE AROUND | CBS | 62149
J.Mercer/Malneck
Columbia recorded 19/12/62
Marty Manning

IMAGINATION
J.Burke/J.Van Heusen
Columbia recorded 28/10/59
Ralph Sharon
not released

IN A MELLOW TONE | THE MACPARTLANDS & FRIENDS
live Improv recorded 5/77 | MAKE BEAUTIFUL MUSIC | IMPROV | 7123
with the MacPartlands

IN SANDY'S EYES
✓ Columbia recorded 27/6/57     THE BEAT OF MY HEART
Ralph Sharon
not released

IN THE MIDDLE OF AN ISLAND | A STRING OF HITS | CBS | 66010
Varnick/Acquaviva | 16 ORIGINAL HITS | EVEREST | LP16-19
Columbia recorded 19/6/57 | COCA COLA PRESENTS | COLUMBIA | 26851
 | THE GOLDEN TOUCH | COLUMBIA | P12789
 | SINGLE | PHILIPS | PB724

| | | | |
|---|---|---|---|
| ✓ IN THE WEE SMALL HOURS<br>OF THE MORNING<br>B.Hilliard/D.Mann<br>Columbia recording 1966<br>Ralph Sharon | A TIME FOR LOVE | CBS | 62800 |
| INDIAN SIGN<br>Columbia recorded 1/8/58<br>Ray Ellis<br>not released | | | |
| INDIAN SUMMER<br>A.Dubin/V.Herbert<br>Columbia recorded 16/3/62<br>Ralph Sharon<br>not released | | | |
| ✓ re-recorded Columbia 1993<br>with the Ralph Sharon Trio | PERFECTLY FRANK | CBS | 472222 |
| AUTUMN LEAVES/<br>INDIAN SUMMER<br>J.Mercer/J.Kosma, A.Dubin/V.Herbert<br>live MTV recorded 4/94<br>with the Ralph Sharon Trio | MTV UNPLUGGED | COLUMBIA | 477170 |
| INDIVIDUAL THING<br>B.Merrill/J.Styne<br>Columbia recorded 25/1/71<br>Ralph Burns | LOVE STORY | CBS | 64368 |
| INVITATION<br>✓ B.Kaper/P.Webster<br>Philips recorded c1972<br>Robert Farnon | THE GOOD THINGS IN LIFE<br>SPOTLIGHT ON . . . . | PHILIPS<br>PHILIPS | 6308134<br>6641297 |
| IRENA<br>R.Farnon<br>Columbia recorded 15/11/71<br>Robert Farnon | SUMMER OF '42 | CBS | 64648 |
| IS THAT ALL THERE IS?<br>J.Leiber/M.Stoller<br>Columbia recorded 7/10/69<br>Peter Matz | GREAT HITS OF TODAY | CBS | 63962 |
| ISN'T IT ROMANTIC?<br>✓ R.Rodgers/L.Hart<br>Improv recorded c1973<br>with the Ruby Braff/<br>George Barnes Quartet | SINGS 10 RODGERS & HART<br>SONGS<br>RODGERS & HART SONGBOOK | IMPROV<br>NELSON | 711<br>CD1129 |

**ISN'T THIS A LOVELY DAY?**     BENNETT:BERLIN     CBS     460450
I.Berlin
Columbia recorded 1987
Tony Bennett

**IT AMAZES ME**     LONG AGO AND FAR AWAY     COLUMBIA     CL1186
C.Leigh/C.Coleman     FORTY YEARS VOL 1     COLUMBIA     46843
Columbia recorded 9/4/58     LET'S FALL IN LOVE WITH ..     CBS     88131
Frank De Vol

live Columbia recording     AT CARNEGIE HALL 1     CBS     62116
Ralph Sharon 9/6/62

live Columbia recorded 8/4/64
Louis Basil with Ralph Sharon Trio
not released

live MTV recorded 4/94     MTV UNPLUGGED     COLUMBIA     477170
with the Ralph Sharon Trio

**IT COULD HAPPEN TO YOU**     LONG AGO AND FAR AWAY     COLUMBIA     CL1186
J.Burke/J.Van Heusen
Columbia recorded 7/4/58
Frank De Vol

re-recorded Columbia 1964     WHEN LIGHTS ARE LOW     CBS     62296
Ralph Sharon

**IT DON'T MEAN A THING IF**
   **IT AIN'T GOT THAT SWING**
I.Mills/D.Ellington
Columbia recorded 15/1/68
Torrie Zito with Dominic Germano
not released

live MTV recorded 4/94     MTV UNPLUGGED     COLUMBIA     477170
with the Ralph Sharon Trio

live recording Improv     MACPARTLANDS & FRIENDS     IMPROV     7123
MacPartlands 13-14/5/77     MAKE BEAUTIFUL MUSIC

**IT HAD TO BE YOU**     TONY     COLUMBIA     CL938
G.Kahn/I.Jones     PHILIPS TV (EP)     PHILIPS     BBE12223
Columbia recorded 11/9/56     TONY BENNETT SHOWCASE     PHILIPS     BBL7138
Ray Conniff

re-recorded Columbia     WHEN LIGHTS ARE LOW     CBS     62296
Ralph Sharon 27/3/64     LOVE SONGS     CBS     66297
    FORTY YEARS VOL 3     COLUMBIA     46843

live recording MTV 4/94     MTV UNPLUGGED     COLUMBIA     477170
with the Ralph Sharon Trio

**ONE FOR MY BABY/**
**IT HAD TO BE YOU**     ALL TIME HALL OF FAME HITS     CBS     64200
J.Mercer/H.Arlen, G.Kahn/I.Jones
Columbia recorded 1971
John Bunch

**IT NEVER WAS YOU**     MY HEART SINGS     COLUMBIA     CL1658
K.Weill/M.Anderson
Columbia recorded 5/4/61
Ralph Burns

**IT ONLY HAPPENS WHEN**
**I DANCE WITH YOU**     STEPPIN' OUT     COLUMBIA     474360
I.Berlin
Columbia recorded 1994
Tony Bennett & Ralph Sharon

**IT WAS ME**     I WANNA BE AROUND     CBS     62149
G.Becaud/N.Gimbel     FORTY YEARS VOL 2     COLUMBIA     46843
Columbia recorded 19/12/62     SUMMER OF '42     CBS     64648
Marty Manning

**IT WAS WRITTEN IN**
**THE STARS**     A STRING OF HAROLD ARLEN     COLUMBIA     CL1559
H.Arlen/L.Robin     LET'S FALL IN LOVE WITH . .     CBS     88131
Columbia recorded 17/8/60
Glenn Osser

**IT WAS YOU**     THE GOOD THINGS IN LIFE     PHILIPS     6308134
Coleman/Lipton     AT LONG LAST LOVE     PHILIPS     SON 014
Philips recorded 15/11/71     SPOTLIGHT ON . . . .     PHILIPS     6641297
Robert Farnon

**IT'S A SIN TO TELL A LIE**
B.Mayhew
Columbia recorded 26/2/64
not released

re-recorded Columbia     WHEN LIGHTS ARE LOW     CBS     62296
Ralph Sharon 26/3/64

live recording Columbia     SINGLE     COLUMBIA     4-43073
Ralph Sharon Trio 8/4/64
Sahara Hotel, Las Vegas
Louis Basil – this was the only track released from this recorded concert

**IT'S LIKE REACHING FOR**     ASTORIA: PORTRAIT OF THE
**THE MOON**     ARTIST     CBS     466005
Sherman/Lewis/Marqusee
Columbia recorded 1989
Jorge Calandrelli

| | | | |
|---|---|---|---|
| IT'S MAGIC<br>S.Cahn/J.Styne<br>Columbia recorded 1/3/60<br>Frank De Vol | ALONE TOGETHER<br>THE VERY THOUGHT OF YOU | COLUMBIA<br>HALLMARK | CL1471<br>SHM769 |
| IT'S SO PEACEFUL IN<br>  THE COUNTRY<br>Wilder<br>Columbia recorded 27/1/57<br>Percy Faith | BLUE VELVET<br>SINGLE<br><br>*THE BEAT OF MY HEART* | COLUMBIA<br>PHILIPS | CL1292<br>PB907 |
| IT'S TOO SOON TO KNOW<br>Chessler<br>Columbia recorded 4/1/55<br>Percy Faith | SINGLE | PHILIPS | PB445 |
| I'LL BE AROUND<br>A.Wilder<br>Columbia recorded 6/11/63<br>Dick Hyman | THE MANY MOODS OF TONY<br>THE VERY THOUGHT OF YOU<br>FORTY YEARS VOL 2 | CBS<br>HALLMARK<br>COLUMBIA | 62245<br>SHM769<br>46843 |
| I'LL BE HOME FOR<br>  CHRISTMAS<br>B.Ram/W.Kent/K.Gannon<br>live recording 1994<br>from The Jon Stewart TV Show<br>with the Ralph Sharon Trio | SNOWFALL (CD only) | COLUMBIA | 477597 |
| I'LL BE SEEING YOU<br>I.Kahal<br>Columbia recorded 12/9/57<br>Ray Conniff | TONY<br>TONY BENNETT SHOWCASE | COLUMBIA<br>PHILIPS | CL938<br>BBL7138 |
| re-recorded Columbia 1993<br>with the Ralph Sharon Trio | PERFECTLY FRANK | COLUMBIA | 472222 |
| I'LL BEGIN AGAIN<br>L.Bricusse<br>Columbia recorded 25/1/71<br>Torrie Zito | LOVE STORY | CBS | 64368 |
| live Columbia recording<br>Robert Farnon 31/1/71 | GET HAPPY | CBS | 64577 |
| I'LL BRING YOU A RAINBOW<br>D.V.Silvers<br>Columbia recorded 13/1/60<br>Frank De Vol | A STRING OF HITS<br>SINGLE | CBS<br>PHILIPS | 66010<br>PB1008 |

**I'LL GO**
Columbia recorded 17/3/53

SINGLE                    COLUMBIA        40004

**I'LL ONLY MISS HER WHEN
I THINK OF HER**
S.Cahn/J.Van Heusen
Columbia recorded 26/9/65
Johnny Mandel

A TIME FOR LOVE           CBS             62800
FORTY YEARS VOL 3         COLUMBIA        46843
GREAT SONGS FROM THE
                 SHOWS    PICKWICK        4171

**I'M A FOOL TO WANT YOU**
Wolf/Heron/Sinatra
Columbia recorded 12/11/59
Frank De Vol

TO MY WONDERFUL ONE       COLUMBIA        CL1429

**I'M ALWAYS CHASING
RAINBOWS**
McCarthy/Carrol
Columbia recorded 28/2/60
Frank De Vol

ALONE TOGETHER            COLUMBIA        CL1471
I LEFT MY HEART IN        CBS             62201
    SAN FRANCISCO

**I'M CONFESSIN'
(THAT I LOVE YOU)**
Neiburg/Daugherty/Reynolds
Columbia recorded 15/1/68
Torrie Zito with Dominic Germano
not released

**I'M COMING VIRGINIA**
D.Heywood/W.Cook
Columbia recorded 4/4/61
Ralph Burns

MY HEART SINGS            COLUMBIA        CL1658

**I'M GLAD THERE IS YOU**
P.Medeira/J.Dorsey
Columbia recorded 1993
with the Ralph Sharon Trio

PERFECTLY FRANK           COLUMBIA        472222

**I'M GONNA SIT RIGHT DOWN
AND WRITE MYSELF A LETTER**
F.Ahlert/J.Young
Columbia recorded 15/1/68
Torrie Zito with Dominic Germano
not released

**I'M IN LOVE AGAIN**
C.Coleman/P.Lee/B.Schluger
Columbia recorded 25/11/68
Torrie Zito
not released

re-recorded Columbia 1995     HERE'S TO THE LADIES     COLUMBIA    481266
Jorge Calandrelli & Bill Holman

| | | | |
|---|---|---|---|
| **I'M JUST A LUCKY SO AND SO**<br>David/Ellington<br>Columbia recorded 11/9/57<br>Ray Conniff | TONY | COLUMBIA | CL938 |
| live Columbia recording<br>Ralph Sharon 9/6/62 | AT CARNEGIE HALL 1 | CBS | 62117 |
| re-recorded Concord c1977<br>Scott Hamilton Quartet | TRIBUTE TO DUKE | CONCORD | CJ50 |
| **I'M LOSING MY MIND**<br>S.Sondheim<br>Columbia recorded 21/5/72<br>Torrie Zito | SUMMER OF '42 | CBS | 64648 |
| **I'M LOST AGAIN**<br>Dee/Lipman<br>Columbia recorded 1950<br>Percy Faith | SINGLE | COLUMBIA | 39745 |
| **I'M THE KING OF BROKEN HEARTS**<br>F.Tobias/J.Tobias<br>Columbia recorded 4/9/52<br>Percy Faith | SINGLE | COLUMBIA | 39964 |
| **I'M THRU' WITH LOVE**<br>Malneck/Kahn/Livingston<br>Columbia recorded 28/10/59<br>Ralph Sharon | TONY SINGS FOR TWO<br>JAZZ<br>LOVE SONGS | COLUMBIA<br>CBS<br>CBS | CL1446<br>450465<br>66297 |
| **I'M WAY AHEAD OF THE GAME**<br>Columbia recorded 26/2/64<br>not released | | | |
| live Columbia recorded 8/4/64<br>Louis Basil with Ralph Sharon Trio<br>not released | | | |
| **I'VE COME HOME AGAIN**<br>C.DeForest<br>Columbia recorded 1989<br>Jorge Calandrelli | ASTORIA: PORTRAIT OF THE<br>ARTIST | CBS | 466005 |
| **I'VE GOT FIVE DOLLARS**<br>R.Rodgers/L.Hart<br>Improv recorded c1973<br>with the Ruby Braff/<br>George Barnes Quartet | MORE RODGERS & HART SONGS<br>HOLLYWOOD & BROADWAY<br>RODGERS & HART SONGBOOK<br>STAGE & SCREEN HITS | IMPROV<br>NELSON<br>NELSON<br>DBM | 7120<br>1145<br>CD1129<br>1001 |

**I'VE GOT JUST ABOUT**
**EVERYTHING**
R.Dorough
Columbia recorded 26/2/64
not released

re-recorded Columbia          WHEN LIGHTS ARE LOW        CBS           62296
Ralph Sharon 26/3/64          FORTY YEARS VOL 3          COLUMBIA      46843

**I'VE GOT THE WORLD ON**
**A STRING**                  A STRING OF HAROLD ARLEN   COLUMBIA      CL1559
T.Koehler/H.Arlen             LET'S FALL IN LOVE WITH..  CBS           88131
Columbia recorded 17/8/60
Glenn Osser
*[handwritten: Ralph Sharon 9/6/62 Carnegie Hall]*
re-recorded Columbia 1993     PERFECTLY FRANK            COLUMBIA      472222
with the Ralph Sharon Trio

**I'VE GOT YOUR NUMBER**      LET'S FALL IN LOVE WITH..  CBS           88131
C.Coleman/C.Leigh
Columbia recorded 19/10/62

**I'VE GOTTA BE ME**          I'VE GOTTA BE ME           CBS           63685
W.Marks                       THE TROLLEY SONG           EMBASSY       31002
Columbia recorded 27/3/69
Torrie Zito

**I'VE GROWN ACCUSTOMED**
**TO HER FACE**               STRIKE UP THE BAND         ROULETTE      25231
Lerner/Lowe                   ONE NIGHT STAND            ALLEGRO       799
Roulette released 1961
Count Basie

**I'VE NEVER SEEN**           WHO CAN I TURN TO          CBS           62486
D.Cochran/D.Marcotte
Columbia recorded 4/9/64
George Siravo

**I'VE WAITED FOR A WALTZ**
Columbia recorded 14/8/64
George Siravo
not released

**JEEPERS CREEPERS**          STRIKE UP THE BAND         ROULETTE      25231
Warren/Mercer                 ONE NIGHT STAND            ALLEGRO       799
Roulette released 1961
Count Basie

**JUDY**                      WHEN LIGHTS ARE LOW        CBS           62296
H.Carmichael                  JAZZ                       CBS           450465
Columbia recorded 26-27/3/64
Ralph Sharon

51

**JUST A GIGOLO**
Columbia recorded 15/1/68
Torrie Zito with Dominic Germano
not released

| | | | |
|---|---|---|---|
| **JUST FRIENDS**<br>Lewis/Kleiner<br>Columbia recorded 28/10/59<br>Ralph Sharon | TONY SINGS FOR TWO | COLUMBIA | CL1446 |
| ✓ re-recorded Columbia<br>with Stan Getz 15/10/64<br>+album unreleased | JAZZ<br>STAN GETZ & FRIENDS+ | CBS<br>CBS | 450465<br>32276 |
| **JUST IN TIME**<br>J.Styne/B.Comden/A.Green<br>Columbia recorded 19/9/56<br>Percy Faith | MR BROADWAY<br>20 GREATEST HITS<br>A STRING OF HITS<br>16 MOST REQUESTED SONGS<br>ALL-TIME GREATEST HITS<br>THE VERY THOUGHT OF YOU<br>THE GOLDEN TOUCH<br>SINGLE | COLUMBIA<br>WARWICK<br>CBS<br>CBS<br>CBS<br>HALLMARK<br>COLUMBIA<br>PHILIPS | CL1763<br>PA5021<br>66010<br>57056<br>68200<br>SHM769<br>P12789<br>PB753 |
| ✓ edited version of original<br>no strings | FORTY YEARS VOL 1 | COLUMBIA | 46843 |
| re-recorded Columbia 1958<br>Ralph Sharon | IN PERSON! | CBS | 62250 |
| ✓ live recording Columbia<br>Ralph Sharon 9/6/62 | AT CARNEGIE HALL 1 | CBS | 62116 |
| ✓ live radio recording 1963<br>with Gene Krupa | MEETS GENE KRUPA | SANDY HOOK | 2067 |
| ✓ **JUST ONE OF THOSE THINGS**<br>C.Porter<br>Columbia recorded 14/10/57<br>Ralph Sharon | THE BEAT OF MY HEART<br>JAZZ<br>JUST ONE OF THOSE THINGS | COLUMBIA<br>COLUMBIA<br>HALLMARK | CL1079<br>450465<br>SHM646 |
| **JUST SAY I LOVE HER**<br>**(DICITENCELLO VIVIE)**<br>M.Kamanoff/S.Ward/<br>J.Val/J.Dale/R.Flavo<br>Columbia recorded 20/7/50<br>Marty Manning | SINGLE<br>JUST SAY I LOVE HER (EP) | COLUMBIA<br>COLUMBIA | 38926<br>B2620 |
| **KEEP SMILING AT TROUBLE**<br>**(TROUBLE'S A BUBBLE)**<br>A.Jolson/B.DeSylva/L.Gensier<br>Columbia recorded 22/4/63<br>Ralph Burns | THIS IS ALL I ASK | CBS | 62205 |

live Columbia recorded 8/4/64
Louis Basil with Ralph Sharon Trio
not released

live recording Columbia
H.Roberts (A&R) 11/8/67
not released

| re-recorded Columbia | FOR ONCE IN MY LIFE | CBS | 63166 |
| Ralph Burns 20/4/67 | FORTY YEARS VOL 4 | COLUMBIA | 46843 |

**KISS YOU**      SINGLE      COLUMBIA      38989
Columbia recorded 23/8/50
Marty Manning

**KISSES I'LL NEVER FORGET**      SINGLE      PHILIPS      PB477
Columbia recorded 11/5/54
Percy Faith

re-recorded Columbia 24/9/54
Percy Faith
not released

**LAST NIGHT WHEN WE
    WERE YOUNG**      TO MY WONDERFUL ONE      COLUMBIA      CL1429
H.Arlen/E.V.Harburg
Columbia recorded 12/11/59
Frank De Vol

re-recorded Columbia 1993      PERFECTLY FRANK      COLUMBIA      472222
with the Ralph Sharon Trio

| **LAURA** | TO MY WONDERFUL ONE | COLUMBIA | CL1429 |
| J.Mercer/Raskin | THE VERY THOUGHT OF YOU | HALLMARK | SHM769 |
| Columbia recorded 10/11/59 | LOVE SONGS | CBS | 66297 |
| Frank De Vol | | | |

| **LAZY AFTERNOON** | THE BEAT OF MY HEART | COLUMBIA | CL1079 |
| Latouche/Moross | JUST ONE OF THOSE THINGS | HALLMARK | SHM646 |
| Columbia recorded 27/6/57 | SONGS FOR THE JET SET | CBS | 62544 |
| Ralph Sharon | MR BROADWAY | COLUMBIA | CL1763 |
| | FORTY YEARS VOL 1 | COLUMBIA | 46843 |

live Columbia recording      AT CARNEGIE HALL 2      CBS      62117
Ralph Sharon 9/6/62

**LAZY DAY IN LOVE**      WITH LOVE      CBS      64849
M.Raskin/R.Farnon
Columbia recorded 11/8/71
Robert Farnon

| | | | |
|---|---|---|---|
| **LET THERE BE LOVE**<br>Grant/Rand<br>Columbia recorded 21/10/57<br>Ralph Sharon | THE BEAT OF MY HEART<br>JUST ONE OF THOSE THINGS | COLUMBIA<br>HALLMARK | CL1079<br>SHM646 |
| Live Columbia recording<br>Robert Farnon 31/1/71 | GET HAPPY | CBS | 64577 |
| **LET YOURSELF GO**<br>I.Berlin<br>Columbia recorded 1987<br>Tony Bennett | BENNETT:BERLIN | CBS | 460450 |
| **LET'S FALL IN LOVE**<br>T.Koekler/H.Arlen<br>Columbia recorded 15/8/60<br>Glenn Osser | A STRING OF HAROLD ARLEN<br>LET'S FALL IN LOVE WITH . . | COLUMBIA<br>CBS | CL1559<br>88131 |
| **LET'S BEGIN**<br>J.Kern<br>Columbia recorded 14/10/57<br>Ralph Sharon | THE BEAT OF MY HEART<br>JUST ONE OF THOSE THINGS | COLUMBIA<br>HALLMARK | CL1079<br>SHM646 |
| **LET'S DO IT**<br>**(LET'S FALL IN LOVE)**<br>C.Porter<br>Philips recorded c1972/3<br>Torrie Zito | GREATEST HITS NO 7 | VERVE | SE4929 |
| **LET'S FACE THE MUSIC<br>AND DANCE**<br>I.Berlin<br>Columbia recorded 21/10/57<br>Ralph Sharon | THE BEAT OF MY HEART<br>JUST ONE OF THOSE THINGS<br>IRVING BERLIN<br>JAZZ<br>I WANNA BE AROUND | COLUMBIA<br>HALLMARK<br>COLUMBIA<br>COLUMBIA<br>CBS | CL1079<br>SHM646<br>460999<br>450465<br>62149 |
| re-recorded Columbia 1987<br>Tony Bennett | BENNETT:BERLIN | COLUMBIA | 460450 |
| **LET'S MAKE LOVE**<br>Columbia recorded 20/4/50<br>Marty Manning | SINGLE | COLUMBIA | 38856 |
| **LIFE IN A LOOKING GLASS**<br>H.Mancini/L.Briausse<br>Recorded for the film "That's Life"<br>Starring Jack Lemmon and Julie Andrews<br>Released 1986 | THAT'S LIFE (SOUNDTRACK) | COLUMBIA | |
| **LIFE IS A SONG**<br>Ahlert/Young<br>Roulette released 1961<br>Count Basie | STRIKE UP THE BAND<br>ONE NIGHT STAND | ROULETTE<br>ALLEGRO | 25231<br>799 |

| | | | |
|---|---|---|---|
| **LIFE IS BEAUTIFUL**<br>F.Astaire/T.Wolf<br>Improv recorded c1974/5<br>Torrie Zito | LIFE IS BEAUTIFUL<br>UNFORGETTABLE<br>SINGLE | IMPROV<br>CASTLE<br>IMPROV | 7112<br>UNLP019<br>711105 |
| **LIMEHOUSE BLUES**<br>D.Furber/P.Braham<br>Columbia recorded 11/9/63<br>Dick Hyman | THE MANY MOODS OF TONY<br>SINGLE | CBS<br>CBS | 62245<br>AAG176 |
| ✓ **LISTEN LITTLE GIRL**<br>F.Landesman/T.Wolf<br>Columbia recorded 14/10/64<br>George Siravo | WHO CAN I TURN TO | CBS | 62486 |
| **LITTLE GREEN APPLES**<br>B.Russell<br>Columbia recorded 7/10/69<br>Dee Barton | GREAT HITS OF TODAY | CBS | 63962 |
| **LIVE FOR LIFE**<br>N.Gimbel/F.Lai<br>Columbia recorded 7/10/69<br>Peter Matz | GREAT HITS OF TODAY | CBS | 63962 |
| **LIVING TOGETHER,**<br>**GROWING TOGETHER**<br>B.Bacharach/H.David<br>Philips recorded c1972/3<br>Don Costa | AT LONG LAST LOVE<br>SINGLE | PHILIPS<br>PHILIPS | SON 014<br>6006260 |
| ✓ **LONDON BY NIGHT**<br>E.Coates<br>Philips recorded c1972<br>Robert Farnon | THE GOOD THINGS IN LIFE<br>SPOTLIGHT ON .... | PHILIPS<br>PHILIPS | 6308134<br>6641297 |
| ✓ **LONELY GIRL**<br>Hefti/Livingston/Evans<br>Improv recorded c1976<br>Bill Evans | TOGETHER AGAIN<br>UNFORGETTABLE<br>HOLLYWOOD & BROADWAY<br>STAGE & SCREEN HITS | IMPROV<br>CASTLE<br>NELSON<br>DBM | 7117<br>UNLP019<br>1145<br>1001 |
| **LONG ABOUT NOW**<br>F.Hellerman/F.Minkoff<br>Columbia recorded 26/4/63<br>Ralph Burns | THIS IS ALL I ASK | CBS | 62205 |
| ✓ **LONG AGO (AND FAR AWAY)**<br>I.Gershwin/J.Kern<br>Columbia recorded 1958<br>Frank De Vol | LONG AGO AND FAR AWAY | COLUMBIA | CL1186 |

55

| | | | |
|---|---|---|---|
| ✓ LOST IN THE STARS<br>K.Weill/M.Anderson<br>Columbia recorded 6/6/57<br>Percy Faith | TONY<br>TONY BENNETT SHOWCASE | COLUMBIA<br>PHILIPS | CL938<br>BBL7138 |
| ✓ re-recorded Columbia 22/12/58<br>Ralph Sharon<br>with Count Basie | IN PERSON!<br>FORTY YEARS VOL 1 | CBS<br>COLUMBIA | 62250<br>46843 |
| ✓ Live Columbia recording<br>Ralph Sharon 9/6/62 | AT CARNEGIE HALL 2 | CBS | 62117 |
| re-recorded Improv c1975<br>Torrie Zito | LIFE IS BEAUTIFUL<br>HOLLYWOOD & BROADWAY<br>STAGE & SCREEN HITS<br>THE MAGIC OF TONY BENNETT | IMPROV<br>NELSON<br>DBM<br>NELSON | 7112<br>1145<br>1001<br>CYU 106 |
| ✓ LOVE<br>H.Martin/R.Blane<br>Columbia recorded 1/10/71<br>Robert Farnon | WITH LOVE | CBS | 64849 |
| ✓ LOVE FOR SALE<br>C.Porter<br>Columbia recorded 21/10/57<br>Ralph Sharon | THE BEAT OF MY HEART<br>JUST ONE OF THOSE THINGS<br>I LEFT MY HEART IN SAN F'CO<br>GREAT SONGS FROM THE SHOWS<br>LOVE SONGS | COLUMBIA<br>HALLMARK<br>CBS<br>PICKWICK<br>CBS | CL1079<br>SHM646<br>62201<br>4171<br>66297 |
| LOVE IS HERE TO STAY<br>I.Gershwin/G.Gershwin<br>Columbia recorded 4/11/58<br>Ralph Burns | HOMETOWN, MY TOWN | COLUMBIA | CL1301 |
| Live Columbia recording<br>Ralph Sharon 9/6/62 | AT CARNEGIE HALL 1 | CBS | 62116 |
| re-recorded Columbia<br>Torrie Zito 16/4/68 | YESTERDAY I HEARD THE RAIN | CBS | 63351 |
| LOVE IS THE THING<br>Washington/Young<br>Philips recorded c1973<br>Don Costa | LISTEN EASY<br>SPOTLIGHT ON ....<br>SINGLE | PHILIPS<br>PHILIPS<br>PHILIPS | 6308157<br>6641297<br>6006309 |
| ✓ LOVE LETTERS<br>Young/Heyman<br>Columbia recorded 11/8/54<br>Chuck Wayne | CLOUD 7 | COLUMBIA | CL621 |

| | | | |
|---|---|---|---|
| LOVE LOOK AWAY<br>R.Rodgers/O.Hammerstein II<br>Columbia recorded 2/11/58<br>Glenn Osser<br><br>✓ Live Columbia recording<br>Ralph Sharon 9/6/62 | MR BROADWAY<br>I WANNA BE AROUND<br>ALL-TIME GREATEST HITS<br>A STRING OF HITS<br>SINGLE<br>AT CARNEGIE HALL 2 | COLUMBIA<br>CBS<br>CBS<br>CBS<br>PHILIPS<br>CBS | CL1763<br>62149<br>68200<br>66010<br>PB996<br>62117 |
| LOVE ME, LOVE ME, LOVE ME<br>Columbia recording | SINGLE | PHILIPS | PB786 |
| LOVE ME TENDER<br>E.Presley/V.Matson<br>Live TV Special 1994<br>Ralph Sharon | ELVIS – IT'S NOW OR NEVER | MERCURY | 524072 |
| ✓ LOVE SCENE<br>✓ D.Ellington<br>✓ Columbia recorded 19/2/65<br>Don Costa | SONGS FOR THE JET SET<br>JAZZ<br>FORTY YEARS VOL 3 | CBS<br>CBS<br>COLUMBIA | 62544<br>450465<br>46843 |
| LOVE SONG FROM BEAUTY<br>   AND THE BEAST<br>David/Livingston<br>Columbia recorded 12/11/57<br>Percy Faith | SINGLE | COLUMBIA | 41086 |
| LOVE STORY<br>   (WHERE DO I BEGIN)<br>C.Sigman/F.Lai<br>Columbia recorded 3/12/70<br>Peter Matz | LOVE STORY<br>SUNRISE, SUNSET<br>16 MOST REQUESTED SONGS | CBS<br>CBS<br>COLUMBIA | 64368<br>32239<br>57056 |
| ✓ Live recording Columbia<br>✓ Robert Farnon 31/1/71 | GET HAPPY<br>ALL-TIME GREATEST HITS | CBS<br>CBS | 64577<br>68200 |
| ✓ LOVE WALKED IN<br>G.Gershwin/I.Gershwin<br>Columbia recorded 12/9/56<br>Ray Conniff | TONY<br>TONY BENNETT SHOWCASE | COLUMBIA<br>PHILIPS | CL938<br>BBL7138 |
| LOVER<br>R.Rodgers/L.Hart<br>✓ Improv recorded c1973<br>with the Ruby Braff/<br>George Barnes Quartet | 10 RODGERS & HART SONGS<br>UNFORGETTABLE<br>RODGERS & HART SONGBOOK | IMPROV<br>CASTLE<br>NELSON | 7113<br>UNLP019<br>1129 |
| LOVER MAN<br>   (OH! WHERE CAN YOU BE)<br>J.Davis/R.Ramirez/J.Sherman<br>Columbia recorded 4/4/61<br>Ralph Burns | MY HEART SINGS | COLUMBIA | CL1658 |

✓ **LUCKY TO BE ME**  TOGETHER AGAIN  IMPROV  7117
L.Bernstein/B.Comden/A.Green  STAGE & SCREEN HITS  DBM  1001
Improv recorded c1977  TOGETHER AGAIN  NELSON  1122
Bill Evans

✓ **LULLABY OF BROADWAY**  THE BEAT OF MY HEART  COLUMBIA  CL1079
Dubin/Warren  JUST ONE OF THOSE THINGS  HALLMARK  SHM646
Columbia recorded 21/10/57
Ralph Sharon

✓✓ re-recorded Columbia  IN PERSON!  CBS  62250
Ralph Sharon  FORTY YEARS VOL 1  COLUMBIA  46843
with Count Basie 22/12/58  JAZZ  CBS  450465

Live reording Columbia  AT CARNEGIE HALL 1  CBS  62116
Ralph Sharon 9/6/62

live Columbia recorded 8/4/64
Louis Basil with Ralph Sharon Trio
not released

**MADONNA MADONNA**  SINGLE  PHILIPS  PB357
Columbia recorded 11/5/54
Percy Faith

**MAKE IT EASY ON YOURSELF**
B.Bacharach/H.David
Columbia recorded 30/7/70
Peter Matz
not released

re-recorded Columbia 11/8/70  SOMETHING  CBS  64217
Peter Matz

✓ **MAKE SOMEONE HAPPY**  TOGETHER AGAIN  IMPROV  7117
J.Styne/A.Green/B.Comden  TOGETHER AGAIN  NELSON  CD1122
Improv recorded c1977  UNFORGETTABLE  CASTLE  UNLP019
Bill Evans  STAGE & SCREEN HITS  DBM  1001
  HOLLYWOOD & BROADWAY  NELSON  1145

**MAM'SELLE**  TONY SINGS FOR TWO  COLUMBIA  CL1446
Gordon/Goulding
Columbia recorded 28/10/59
Ralph Sharon

live Columbia recorded 8/4/64
Louis Basil with Ralph Sharon Trio
not released

58

| | | | |
|---|---|---|---|
| ✓ MANHATTAN<br>R.Rodgers/L.Hart<br>Improv recorded c1973<br>with the Ruby Braff/<br>George Barnes Quartet | 10 RODGERS & HART SONGS<br>THE RODGERS & HART<br>    SONGBOOK<br>UNFORGETTABLE<br>STAGE & SCREEN HITS<br>HOLLYWOOD & BROADWAY | IMPROV<br><br>NELSON<br>CASTLE<br>DBM<br>NELSON | 7113<br><br>CD1129<br>UNLP019<br>1001<br>1145 |
| MARRIAGE-GO-ROUND<br>L.Spence/M.Keith/A.Bergman<br>Columbia recorded 13/10/60<br>Glenn Osser | SINGLE<br>TONY BENNETT SINGS | PHILIPS<br>PHILIPS | PB1089<br>BBE12424 |
| MARRY YOUNG<br>C.Leigh/C.Coleman<br>Columbia recorded 10/7/60<br>Marty Manning | I LEFT MY HEART IN<br>    SAN FRANCISCO<br>SINGLE | CBS<br>CBS | 62201<br>AAG126 |
| ✓ MAY I NEVER LOVE AGAIN<br>✓ S.Marco/J.Erickson<br>✓ Columbia recorded 5/5/55<br>Percy Faith | BLUE VELVET<br>BECAUSE OF YOU 56<br>FORTY YEARS VOL 1<br>SINGLE | COLUMBIA<br>COLUMBIA<br>COLUMBIA<br>PHILIPS | CL1292<br>CL2550<br>46843<br>PB486 |
| SONG FROM "THE OSCAR"<br>✓   MAYBE SEPTEMBER<br>P.Faith/J.Livingston/R.Evans<br>Columbia recorded 27/12/65<br>Larry Wilcox & Johnny Mandel | THE MOVIE SONG ALBUM<br>FORTY YEARS VOL 3<br>THE OSCAR – SOUNDTRACK | CBS<br>COLUMBIA<br>CBS | 62677<br>46843<br>62684 |
| re-recorded Improv c1977<br>Bill Evans | TOGETHER AGAIN<br>TOGETHER AGAIN<br>UNFORGETTABLE | IMPROV<br>NELSON<br>CASTLE | 7117<br>CD1122<br>UNLP019 |
| ✓ MAYBE THIS TIME<br>J.Kander/F.Ebb<br>live Columbia recording<br>Robert Farnon 1/10/71 | ALL-TIME GREATEST HITS<br>GREAT SONGS FROM THE SHOWS<br>FORTY YEARS VOL 4<br>WITH LOVE (US only)<br>SINGLE | CBS<br>PICKWICK<br>COLUMBIA<br>COLUMBIA<br>CBS | 68200<br>4171<br>46843<br>31460<br>S8095 |
| ✓ re-recorded Columbia 1995<br>Jorge Calandrelli & Bill Holman | HERE'S TO THE LADIES | COLUMBIA | 481266 |
| MacARTHUR PARK<br>J.Webb<br>Columbia recorded 7/10/69<br>Peter Matz | GREAT HITS OF TODAY<br>TONY!<br>SINGLE | CBS<br>COLUMBIA<br>CBS | 63962<br>KH32171<br>S5255 |

✓ **MEDLEY/CAROLS**  SNOWFALL, THE CHRISTMAS   CBS        63782
Various                ALBUM
Columbia recorded Nov 1968
Robert Farnon

We Wish you a Merry Christmas
Silent Night
O Come all ye Faithfull
Jingle Bells
Where is love?

**MICHELLE**
P.McCartney/J.Lennon
Columbia recorded 7/10/69
Peter Matz
not released

✓ **MIMI**                    THE GOOD THINGS IN LIFE   PHILIPS    6308134
R.Rodgers/L.Hart         SPOTLIGHT ON . . . .      PHILIPS    6641297
Philips recorded c1972
Robert Farnon

**MOMENTS LIKE THIS**         THE ART OF EXCELLENCE     CBS        26990
F.Loesser/B.Lane
Columbia recorded 1985
Jorge Calandrelli

**MOONGLOW**                  MTV UNPLUGGED             COLUMBIA   477170
Hudson/DeLange/Mills
live MTV recorded 4/94
with the Ralph Sharon Trio
duet with kd lang

✓ **MOONLIGHT IN VERMONT**    HERE'S TO THE LADIES      COLUMBIA   481266
J.Blackburn/K.Suessdorf
Columbia recorded 1995
Jorge Calandrelli & Bill Holman

**MORE AND MORE**             SUMMER OF '42             CBS        64648
S.Distel/R.Allen              SINGLE                    CBS        S8095
Columbia recorded Nov 71
Torrie Zito

**MORE THAN YOU KNOW**        MY HEART SINGS            COLUMBIA   CL1658
B.Rose/E.Eliscu/V.Youmans
Columbia recorded 4/4/61
Ralph Burns

| | | | |
|---|---|---|---|
| MOUNTAIN GREENERY ✓ R.Rodgers/L.Hart Improv recorded c1973 with the Ruby Braff/ George Barnes Quartet | MORE RODGERS & HART SONGS STAGE & SCREEN HITS RODGERS & HART SONGBOOK | IMPROV DBM NELSON | 7120 1001 1129 |
| MR MAGIC MacDonald/Slater Improv recorded c1975 Torrie Zito | THE MAGIC OF TONY BENNETT STAGE & SCREEN HITS HOLLYWOOD & BROADWAY SINGLE | NELSON DBM NELSON IMPROV | CYU 106 1001 1145 715 107 |
| MY BABY JUST CARES FOR ME Kahn/Donaldson ✓ Columbia recorded 22/12/54 Chuck Wayne | CLOUD 7 | COLUMBIA | CL621 |
| MY CHERIE AMOUR S.Wonder Columbia recorded 7/10/69 Peter Matz | GREAT HITS OF TODAY | CBS | 63962 |
| MY FAVOURITE THINGS ✓ R.Rodgers/O.Hammerstein II Columbia recorded 1/10/68 Robert Farnon | SNOWFALL, THE CHRISTMAS ALBUM HITS GREATEST HITS VOL 2 TONY BENNETT SINGS 20 GREATEST HITS | CBS CBS R/DIGEST WARWICK | 63782 63612 8070 PA5021 |
| MY FOOLISH HEART V.Young/N.Washington ✓ Columbia recorded 7/4/58 Ralph Sharon | LONG AGO AND FAR AWAY | COLUMBIA | CL1186 |
| re-recorded Fantasy ✓ Bill Evans 10-13/6/75 | BENNETT/BILL EVANS ALBUM FORTY YEARS VOL 4 | FANTASY COLUMBIA | F9489 46843 |
| MY FUNNY VALENTINE R.Rodgers/L.Hart Columbia recorded 28/10/59 Ralph Sharon | TONY SINGS FOR TWO GREAT SONGS FROM THE SHOWS LOVE SONGS THE GOLDEN TOUCH | COLUMBIA PICWICK CBS COLUMBIA | CL1446 4171 66297 P12790 |
| re-recorded Columbia 1966 ✓ Ralph Sharon | A TIME FOR LOVE | CBS | 62800 |
| re-recorded Philips c1973 Don Costa | LISTEN EASY SPOTLIGHT ON.... | PHILIPS PHILIPS | 6308157 6641297 |
| (ALL OF A SUDDEN) MY HEART SINGS Jambian/Herpin/Rome Columbia recorded 4/4/61 Ralph Burns | MY HEART SINGS | COLUMBIA | CL1658 |

| | | | | |
|---|---|---|---|---|
| ✓ | MY HEART STOOD STILL<br>R.Rodgers/L.Hart<br>Improv recorded c1973<br>with the Ruby Braff/<br>George Barnes Quartet | MORE RODGERS & HART SONGS<br>RODGERS & HART SONGBOOK | IMPROV<br>NELSON | 7120<br>1129 |
| ✓ | MY HEART TELLS ME<br>M.Gordon/H.Warren<br>Columbia recorded 22/12/54<br>Chuck Wayne | CLOUD 7 | COLUMBIA | CL621 |
| ✓ | live recording Columbia<br>Ralph Sharon 9/6/62 | AT CARNEGIE HALL 2 | CBS | 62117 |
| ✓ | MY HEART WON'T SAY<br>   GOODBYE<br>Robin/Romberg<br>Columbia recorded 27/12/53<br>Percy Faith | BLUE VELVET | COLUMBIA | CL1292 |
| ✓ | MY IDEAL<br>B.Whiting/N.Chase/I.Robin<br>Columbia recorded 1995<br>Jorge Calandrelli & Bill Holman | HERE'S TO THE LADIES | COLUMBIA | 481266 |
| | MY INAMORATA<br>J.Williams/J.Mercer<br>Columbia recorded 15/11/71<br>Marion Evans | SUMMER OF '42 | CBS | 64648 |
| | MY KIND OF TOWN<br>S.Cahn/J.Van Heusen<br>live recording 1977<br>with Frank Sinatra<br>from TV Show "Sinatra & Friends" | THE FRANK SINATRA DUETS | PJI | 001 |
| | MY LOVE<br>P.McCartney<br>Philips recorded c1973<br>Torrie Zito | SPOTLIGHT ON . . . .<br>AT LONG LAST LOVE<br>SINGLE | PHILIPS<br>PHILIPS<br>PHILIPS | 6641297<br>SON 014<br>6006326 |
| ✓ | MY LOVE WENT TO LONDON<br>J.Wallowitch/T.Scibetta<br>Columbia recorded 1995<br>Jorge Calandrelli & Bill Holman | HERE'S TO THE LADIES | COLUMBIA | 481266 |
| | MY REVERIE<br>Clinton<br>Columbia recorded 11/8/54<br>Chuck Wayne<br>not released | | | |

✓ re-recorded Columbia 22/12/54    CLOUD 7                      COLUMBIA    CL621
  Chuck Wayne

  **MY ROMANCE**                   MORE RODGERS & HART SONGS    IMPROV      7120
  R.Rodgers/L.Hart                 STAGE & SCREEN HITS          DBM         1001
✓ Improv recorded c1973            RODGERS & HART SONGBOOK      NELSON      1129
  with the Ruby Braff/
  George Barnes Quartet

  **MY SHIP**                      MY HEART SINGS               COLUMBIA    CL1658
  G.Gershwin/K.Weill               SONGS FOR THE JET SET        CBS         62544
  Columbia recorded 6/4/61
  Ralph Burns
  R. Shannon 9/6/62
  **NANCY**                                                     COLUMBIA    472222
                                   CARNEGIE HALL
                                   PERFECTLY FRANK
  P.Silvers/J.Van Heusen
  Columbia recorded 1993
  with the Ralph Sharon Trio

  **(IT'S) NEVER TOO LATE**        THE MOVIE SONG ALBUM         CBS         62677
  J.Livingston/R.Evans/R.Rose
✓ Columbia recorded 14/12/65
  David Rose

  live recording Columbia
  H.Roberts (A&R) 11/8/67
  not released

  **NEW YORK, NEW YORK**           DUETS                        CAPITOL     28067
  F.Ebb/J.Kander
  Capitol released 1993
  Patrick Williams, Tony recorded 1993
  with Frank Sinatra (pre-recorded c1980)

  **NICE WORK IF YOU CAN
  GET IT**                         STEPPIN' OUT                 COLUMBIA    474360
✓ G.Gershwin/I.Gershwin
  Columbia recorded 1994
  Tony Bennett & Ralph Sharon

  **NIGHT AND DAY**                PERFECTLY FRANK              COLUMBIA    472222
✓ C.Porter
  Columbia recorded 1993
  with the Ralph Sharon Trio

  **NO HARD FEELINGS**             SINGLE                       PHILIPS     PB710
  Columbia recorded 19/1/57
  Percy Faith

| | | | |
|---|---|---|---|
| **NO ONE WILL EVER KNOW**<br>Force/Rose<br>Columbia recorded 4/9/52<br>Percy Faith | SINGLE | PHILIPS | PB216 |
| ✓ **NOBODY ELSE BUT ME**<br>J.Kern/O.Hammerstein II<br>Columbia recorded 26/3/64<br>Ralph Sharon | WHEN LIGHTS ARE LOW<br>FORTY YEARS VOL 3 | CBS<br>COLUMBIA | 62296<br>46843 |
| **NOBODY'S HEART BELONGS TO ME**<br>Columbia recorded 1959<br>Ralph Sharon | TONY SINGS FOR TWO | COLUMBIA | CL1446 |
| **NOT AS A STRANGER**<br>J.Van Heusen/B.Kaye<br>Columbia recorded 11/5/54<br>Percy Faith | SINGLE | PHILIPS | PB357 |
| **NOW I LAY ME DOWN TO SLEEP**<br>Columbia recorded 8/4/58<br>Frank De Vol | SINGLE | PHILIPS | PB831 |
| **NOW IT CAN BE TOLD**<br>I.Berlin<br>Columbia recorded 1987<br>Tony Bennett | BENNETT:BERLIN | COLUMBIA | 460450 |
| ✓ **O SOLE MIO**<br>Trad/Zito<br>Philips recorded c1972<br>Torrie Zito | THE GOOD THINGS IN LIFE<br>SPOTLIGHT ON . . . .<br>AT LONG LAST LOVE | PHILIPS<br>PHILIPS<br>PHILIPS | 6308134<br>6641297<br>SON 014 |
| ✓ **OH! LADY BE GOOD**<br>G.Gershwin/I.Gershwin<br>Philips recorded c1972<br>Robert Farnon | THE GOOD THINGS IN LIFE<br>SPOTLIGHT ON . . . . | PHILIPS<br>PHILIPS | 6308134<br>6641297 |
| **OH! YOU CRAZY MOON**<br>J.Burke/J.Van Heusen<br>Columbia recorded 26/2/64<br>not released | | | |
| re-recorded Columbia<br>Ralph Sharon 27/3/64 | WHEN LIGHTS ARE LOW | CBS | 62296 |
| ✓ **OLD DEVIL MOON**<br>E.Harburg/B.Lane<br>Columbia recorded 5/8/54<br>Chuck Wayne | CLOUD 7 | COLUMBIA | CL621 |

| | | | |
|---|---|---|---|
| re-recorded Columbia<br>Marion Evans 18/1/67 | TONY MAKES IT HAPPEN<br>THE TROLLEY SONG | CBS<br>EMBASSY | 63055<br>31002 |
| live recording Columbia<br>H.Roberts (A&R) 11/8/67<br>not released | | | |
| ✓ live Columbia recording<br>✓ Marion Evans & Robert Farnon<br>31/1/71 | GET HAPPY<br>GREAT SONGS FROM THE SHOWS<br>FORTY YEARS VOL 4 | CBS<br>PICKWICK<br>COLUMBIA | 64577<br>4171<br>46843 |
| live MTV recorded 4/94<br>with the Ralph Sharon Trio | MTV UNPLUGGED | COLUMBIA | 477170 |

**OLD FOLKS**
Columbia recorded 15/1/68
Torrie Zito with Dominic Germano
not released

**OL' MAN RIVER**
J.Kern/O.Hammerstein II
Columbia recorded 22/12/58
Count Basie
not released

| | | | |
|---|---|---|---|
| re-recorded 30/12/58<br>Ralph Sharon & Count Basie | IN PERSON!<br>GREAT SONGS FROM THE SHOWS | CBS<br>PICKWICK | 62250<br>4171 |
| ✓ live Columbia recording<br>✓ Ralph Sharon 9/6/62 | AT CARNEGIE HALL 1<br>WHEN I FALL IN LOVE | CBS<br>HALLMARK | 62116<br>SHM 817 |

**ON A CLEAR DAY**
   **(YOU CAN SEE FOREVER)**
A.Lerner/B.Lane
Columbia recorded 24/6/70
John Bunch
not released

re-recorded columbia 30/6/70
Peter Matz
not released

| | | | |
|---|---|---|---|
| re-recorded Columbia 11/8/70<br>Peter Matz | SOMETHING<br>GREAT SONGS FROM THE SHOWS | CBS<br>PICKWICK | 64217<br>4171 |
| **ON GREEN DOLPHIN STREET**<br>✓ Kaper/Washington<br>Columbia recorded 27/3/64<br>Ralph Sharon | WHEN LIGHTS ARE LOW<br>JAZZ | CBS<br>CBS | 62296<br>450465 |

**ON THE OTHER SIDE OF**
**THE TRACKS**  THIS IS ALL I ASK  CBS  62205
C.Leigh/C.Coleman  LET'S FALL IN LOVE WITH . .  CBS  88131
Columbia recorded 22/4/63
Ralph Burns

**ON THE SUNNY SIDE OF**
**THE STREET**  TONY MAKES IT HAPPEN  CBS  63055
D.Fields/J.McHugh
Columbia recorded 27/1/67
Marion Evans

live recording Columbia
H.Roberts (A&R) 11/8/67
not released

✓ live Columbia recording  GET HAPPY  CBS  64577
Robert Farnon 31/1/71

re-recorded Philips c1973  LISTEN EASY  PHILIPS  6308157
Don Costa  SPOTLIGHT ON . . . .  PHILIPS  6641297

**ON TREASURE ISLAND**
Columbia recorded 3/12/70
Peter Matz
not released

**ONCE THERE LIVED A FOOL**  BECAUSE OF YOU  COLUMBIA  CL6221
Columbia recorded 10/10/50
Percy Faith

**ONCE UPON A SUMMERTIME**  I WANNA BE AROUND  CBS  62149
Mercer/Marnay/LeGrand/Barclay
Columbia recorded 19/12/62
Marty Manning

**ONCE UPON A TIME**  I LEFT MY HEART IN SAN
P.Webster/Fain  FRANCISCO  CBS  62201
✓ Columbia recorded 23/1/62  GREATEST HITS  CBS  62821
Marty Manning  FORTY YEARS VOL 2  COLUMBIA  46843

live Columbia recorded 8/4/64
Louis Basil with Ralph Sharon Trio
not released

**ONE**
M.Hamlisch
Columbia recorded 30/7/70
Peter Matz
not released

| | | | |
|---|---|---|---|
| re-recorded Improv c1975<br>Torrie Zito | THE MAGIC OF TONY BENNETT<br>STAGE & SCREEN HITS<br>HOLLYWOOD & BROADWAY<br>SINGLE | NELSON<br>DBM<br>NELSON<br>IMPROV | CYU 106<br>1001<br>1145<br>715 107 |
| **ONE FOR MY BABY**<br>J.Mercer/H.Arlen<br>fake "live" recording<br>Columbia 13/9/56<br>Ray Conniff | SINGLE | PHILIPS | PB710 |
| ✓ live recording Columbia<br>Ralph Sharon 9/6/62 | AT CARNEGIE HALL 2<br>THE GOLDEN TOUCH | CBS<br>COLUMBIA | 62117<br>P12789 |
| live Columbia recorded 8/4/64<br>Louis Basil with Ralph Sharon Trio<br>not released | | | |
| ✓ re-recorded Columbia 1993<br>with the Ralph Sharon Trio | PERFECTLY FRANK | COLUMBIA | 472222 |
| **ONE FOR MY BABY/<br>IT HAD TO BE YOU**<br>J.Mercer/H.Arlen, G.Kahn/I.Jones<br>Columbia recorded 1971<br>John Bunch | ALL TIME HALL OF FAME HITS | CBS | 64200 |
| **ONE KISS AWAY FROM<br>HEAVEN**<br>Columbia recorded 19/9/56<br>Percy Faith | SINGLE | PHILIPS | PB689 |
| **ONE LIE LEADS TO ANOTHER**<br>Columbia recorded 1/10/50<br>Marty Manning | SINGLE | COLUMBIA | 39060 |
| **ONLY THE YOUNG**<br>R.Ahlert/M.Fisher<br>Columbia recorded 16/10/67<br>Torrie Zito | YESTERDAY I HEARD THE RAIN | CBS | 63351 |
| **OUR LADY OF FATIMA**<br>Columbia recorded 14/7/50<br>Percy Faith | SINGLE | COLUMBIA | 38926 |
| **OUR LOVE IS HERE TO STAY**<br>Columbia recorded 6/11/58<br>Ralph Burns<br>not released | | | |

✓ 9/6/62

CARNEGIE HALL

| | | | |
|---|---|---|---|
| ✓ OUT OF THIS WORLD<br>J.Mercer/H.Arlen<br>Columbia recorded 1/3/60<br>Frank De Vol | ALONE TOGETHER | COLUMBIA | CL1471 |
| ✓ Columbia recorded 16/10/64<br>Stan Getz<br>+Unissued album | STAN GETZ & FRIENDS+<br>JAZZ | COLUMBIA<br>CBS | 32276<br>450465 |
| re-recorded Columbia 1967<br>Marion Evans | FOR ONCE IN MY LIFE | CBS | 63166 |
| (SOMEWHERE)<br>OVER THE RAINBOW<br>E.Harburg/H.Arlen<br>Columbia record 15/8/60<br>Glenn Osser | A STRING OF HAROLD ARLEN<br>LET'S FALL IN LOVE WITH . . | COLUMBIA<br>CBS | CL1559<br>88131 |
| re-recorded Columbia 1995<br>Jorge Calandrelli & Bill Holman | HERE'S TO THE LADIES | COLUMBIA | 481266 |
| OVER THE SUN<br>J.Moran/A.Castro<br>Columbia recorded 17/1/69<br>Torrie Zito | I'VE GOTTA BE ME | CBS | 63685 |
| PAPER FLOWERS, COLOURED LIGHTS<br>Columbia recorded 4/2/58<br>Ralph Sharon<br>not released | | | |
| ✓ PASSING STRANGERS<br>Mitchell/Mann<br>Philips recorded c1972<br>Robert Farnon | THE GOOD THINGS IN LIFE<br>SPOTLIGHT ON . . . .<br>AT LONG LAST LOVE | PHILIPS<br>PHILIPS<br>PHILIPS | 6308134<br>6641297<br>SON 014 |
| PENNIES FROM HEAVEN<br>J.Burke/A.Johnston<br>Columbia recorded 30/12/58<br>Ralph Sharon & Count Basie<br>✓ R. SHARON 9/6/62 | IN PERSON!<br>WHEN I FALL IN LOVE<br>MAGIC MOMENTS<br>CARNEGIE HALL | CBS<br>HALLMARK<br>CBS | 62250<br>SHM 817<br>54680 |
| ✓ PENTHOUSE SERENADE<br>(WHEN WE'RE ALONE)<br>W.Jason/V.Burton<br>Columbia recorded 6/11/58<br>Ralph Burns | HOMETOWN, MY TOWN<br>FORTY YEARS VOL 1<br>LOVE SONGS | COLUMBIA<br>COLUMBIA<br>CBS | CL1301<br>46843<br>66297 |
| PEOPLE<br>J.Styne/B.Merrill<br>Columbia recorded 25/11/68<br>Torrie Zito | GREATEST HITS VOL 2<br>20 GREATEST HITS<br>SINGLE | CBS<br>WARWICK<br>COLUMBIA | 63612<br>PA5021<br>44755 |

| | | | |
|---|---|---|---|
| ✓ re-recorded Columbia 1995<br>Jorge Calandrelli & Bill Holman | HERE'S TO THE LADIES | COLUMBIA | 481266 |
| **WHY DO PEOPLE FALL IN LOVE?/PEOPLE**<br>Lambert/Potter,Styne/Merrill<br>Columbia recorded 11/1/86<br>Jorge Calandrelli | THE ART OF EXCELLENCE<br>FORTY YEARS VOL 4 | CBS<br>COLUMBIA | 26990<br>46843 |
| **PLAY IT AGAIN, SAM**<br>H.Hackady/L.Grossman<br>Columbia recorded 27/3/69<br>Torrie Zito | I'VE GOTTA BE ME<br>WHEN I FALL IN LOVE | CBS<br>HALLMARK | 63685<br>SHM817 |
| **PLEASE DRIVER (ONCE AROUND THE PARK AGAIN)**<br>C.Price<br>Columbia recorded 4/12/53<br>Percy Faith | ALONE AT LAST<br>SINGLE | COLUMBIA<br>PHILIPS | CL2507<br>PB390 |
| **PLEASE, MY LOVE**<br>Columbia recorded 4/52 | SINGLE | COLUMBIA | 39764 |
| **POOR BUTTERFLY**<br>J.Golden/R.Hubbell<br>✓ Columbia recorded 29/2/60<br>Frank De Vol | ALONE TOGETHER | COLUMBIA | CL1471 |
| ✓ re-recorded Columbia 1995<br>Jorge Calandrelli & Bill Holman | HERE'S TO THE LADIES | COLUMBIA | 481266 |
| **POOR LITTLE RICH GIRL**<br>N.Coward<br>Roulette released 1961<br>Count Basie | STRIKE UP THE BAND<br>ONE NIGHT STAND | ROULETTE<br>ALLEGRO | 25231<br>799 |
| **PUNCH AND JUDY LOVE**<br>B.Meril<br>Columbia recorded 24/9/54<br>Percy Faith | STRANGER IN PARADISE<br>SINGLE | PHILIPS<br>PHILIPS | BBE12009<br>PB477 |
| **PUT ON A HAPPY FACE**<br>C.Strouse/L.Adams<br>✓ Columbia recorded 6/5/60<br>Frank De Vol | MR BROADWAY<br>SUNRISE, SUNSET<br>20 GREATEST HITS<br>TONY BENNETT SINGS<br>ALL-TIME GREATEST HITS<br>A STRING OF HITS<br>FORTY YEARS VOL 2<br>SINGLE | COLUMBIA<br>COLUMBIA<br>WARWICK<br>R/DIGEST<br>CBS<br>CBS<br>COLUMBIA<br>PHILIPS | CL1763<br>C32239<br>PA5021<br>8070<br>68200<br>66010<br>46843<br>PB1140 |

live Columbia recorded 8/4/64
Louis Basil with Ralph Sharon Trio
not released

| | | | |
|---|---|---|---|
| **QUIET NIGHTS OF QUIET STARS (CORCOVADO)**<br>A.C.Jobim/G.Lees<br>Columbia recorded 19/12/62<br>Marty Manning | I WANNA BE AROUND<br>GREATEST HITS<br>SINGLE | CBS<br>CBS<br>CBS | 62149<br>62821<br>AAG225 |
| live Columbia recorded 8/4/64<br>Louis Basil with Ralph Sharon Trio<br>not released | | | |
| **RAGS TO RICHES**<br>R.Adler/J.Ross<br>Columbia recorded 17/3/53<br>Percy Faith | MUSIC FOR BABYSITTERS<br>POPULAR FAVORITES 3<br>COCA COLA PRESENTS<br>ALL TIME HALL OF FAME HITS<br>16 MOST REQUESTED SONGS<br>A STRING OF HITS<br>16 ORIGINAL HITS<br>HALL OF FAME VARIOUS<br>ALL-TIME GREATEST HITS<br>TONY BENNETT SPOTLITE<br>THE GOLDEN TOUCH<br>FORTY YEARS VOL 1<br>MILLION DOLLAR MEMORIES<br>SINGLE | COLUMBIA<br>COLUMBIA<br>COLUMBIA<br>CBS<br>CBS<br>CBS<br>EVEREST<br>COLUMBIA<br>CBS<br>COLUMBIA<br>COLUMBIA<br>COLUMBIA<br>R/DIGEST<br>PHILIPS | CL688<br>CL6284<br>26851<br>64200<br>57056<br>66010<br>LP16-19<br>CL2600<br>68200<br>B1842<br>P12789<br>46843<br>8061/9<br>PB216 |
| live Columbia recording<br>Ralph Sharon 9/6/62 | AT CARNEGIE HALL 2 | CBS | 62117 |
| live Columbia recorded 8/4/64<br>Louis Basil with Ralph Sharon Trio<br>not released | | | |
| live MTV recording 4/94<br>Ralph Sharon | MTV UNPLUGGED | COLUMBIA | 477170 |
| **RAIN, RAIN, (DON'T GO AWAY)**<br>Barer/Wilder<br>Philips recorded c1973<br>Don Costa | LISTEN EASY<br>SPOTLIGHT ON . . . . | PHILIPS<br>PHILIPS | 6308157<br>6641297 |
| **RAMONA**<br>Wolfe/Gilbert/Wayne<br>Columbia recorded 13/10/60<br>Glenn Osser | SINGLE | PHILIPS | PB1122 |
| **REFLECTIONS**<br>D.Ellington/M.Raskin/M.Raskin<br>Improv recorded c1975<br>Torrie Zito | LIFE IS BEAUTIFUL | IMPROV | 7112 |

**REMEMBER/ALWAYS**
I.Berlin
Columbia recorded 10/86
Tony Bennett
un-released recording from Bennett:Berlin sessions

| | | | |
|---|---|---|---|
| **REMIND ME** <br> D.Fields/J.Kern <br> Columbia recorded 1/10/71 <br> Robert Farnon | WITH LOVE <br> FORTY YEARS VOL 4 | CBS <br> COLUMBIA | 64849 <br> 46843 |
| **REVOLVIN' JONES** <br> unreleased <br> Columbia recorded 16/3/62 <br> Ralph Sharon <br> +unissued album | ON THE GLORY ROAD+ | COLUMBIA | CL1813 |
| **RIGHT AS THE RAIN** <br> Y.Harburg/H.Arlen <br> Columbia recorded 17/8/60 <br> Glenn Osser | A STRING OF HAROLD ARLEN <br> LET'S FALL IN LOVE WITH.. | COLUMBIA <br> CBS | CL1559 <br> 88131 |
| **ROSES OF YESTERDAY** <br> Columbia recorded 30/4/52 <br> Percy Faith | SINGLE | COLUMBIA | 39815 |
| **RUSSIAN LULLABY** <br> I.Berlin <br> Columbia recorded 1987 <br> Tony Bennett | BENNETT:BERLIN | CBS | 460450 |
| **SAMBA DE ORFEU** <br> L.Bonfa <br> Columbia recorded 28/12/65 <br> Johnny Mandel <br> with Luiz Bonfa | THE MOVIE SONG ALBUM | CBS | 62677 |
| **SANDY'S SMILE** <br> T.Burrell/T.Murray <br> Columbia recorded 26/4/63 <br> Ralph Burns | THIS IS ALL I ASK | CBS | 62205 |
| **SANTA CLAUS IS COMING TO TOWN** <br> M.Gillespie/J.Coots <br> Columbia released 1967 | GREAT SONGS OF CHRISTMAS <br> GREAT SONGS OF CHRISTMAS 7 | CBS <br> COLUMBIA | CSP859 <br> CSS547 |

**SENTIMENTAL**
Columbia recorded 6/6/56
Percy Faith
not released

| | | | |
|---|---|---|---|
| ✓ SENTIMENTAL JOURNEY<br>B.Green/L.Brown/H.Homer<br>Columbia recorded 1995<br>Jorge Calandrelli & Bill Holman | HERE'S TO THE LADIES | COLUMBIA | 481266 |
| ✓ SEPTEMBER SONG<br>K.Weill/M.Anderson<br>Columbia recorded 11/11/59<br>Frank de Vol | TO MY WONDERFUL ONE<br>LOVE SONGS<br>FORTY YEARS VOL 1<br>GREAT SONGS FROM THE SHOWS | COLUMBIA<br>CBS<br>COLUMBIA<br>PICKWICK | CL1429<br>66297<br>46843<br>4171 |
| ✓ SHAKIN' THE BLUES AWAY<br>I.Berlin<br>Columbia recorded 29/5/87<br>Tony Bennett | BENNETT:BERLIN<br>FORTY YEARS VOL 4 | CBS<br>COLUMBIA | 460450<br>46843 |
| ✓ SHALL WE DANCE<br>G.Gershwin/I.Gershwin<br>Columbia recorded 1994<br>Tony Bennett & Ralph Sharon | STEPPIN' OUT | COLUMBIA | 474360 |
| (I GOT A WOMAN CRAZY FOR ME)<br>SHE'S FUNNY THAT WAY<br>R.Whiting/C.Daniels<br>Columbia recorded 18/1/67<br>Marion Evans | TONY MAKES IT HAPPEN<br>THE TROLLEY SONG<br>SUNRISE, SUNSET | CBS<br>EMBASSY<br>COLUMBIA | 63055<br>31002<br>C32239 |
| live recording Columbia<br>H.Roberts (A&R) 11/8/67<br>not released | | | |
| ✓ SHINE ON YOUR SHOES<br>H.Dietz/A.Schwartz<br>Columbia recorded 1994<br>Tony Bennett & Ralph Sharon | STEPPIN' OUT | COLUMBIA | 474360 |
| SHOO-GAH (MY PRETTY<br>SUGAR)<br>Columbia recorded 24/9/54<br>Percy Faith | SINGLE | COLUMBIA | 40376 |
| SILLY DREAMER<br>Columbia recorded 17/10/51<br>Percy Faith | SINGLE | COLUMBIA | 39635 |
| SINCE MY LOVE HAS GONE<br>Wasserman/Aaron<br>Columbia recorded 31/5/51<br>Percy Faith | ALONE AT LAST | COLUMBIA | CL2507 |

| | | | |
|---|---|---|---|
| SING YOU SINNERS | ALONE AT LAST | COLUMBIA | CL2507 |
| S.Coslow/W.Harling | FORTY YEARS VOL 1 | COLUMBIA | 46843 |
| Columbia recorded 16/12/55 | ALL-TIME GREATEST HITS | CBS | 68200 |
| Percy Faith | A STRING OF HITS | CBS | 66010 |
| | SINGLE | PHILIPS | PB563 |
| | | | |
| live recording Columbia | AT CARNEGIE HALL 2 | CBS | 62117 |
| Ralph Sharon 9/6/62 | | | |
| | | | |
| live Columbia recorded 8/4/64 | | | |
| Louis Basil with Ralph Sharon Trio | | | |
| not released | | | |
| | | | |
| SKYLARK | FORTY YEARS VOL 1 | COLUMBIA | 46843 |
| H.Carmichael/J.Mercer | | | |
| Columbia recorded 28/10/59 | | | |
| Ralph Sharon | | | |
| | | | |
| outake Columbia 28/10/59 | TONY SINGS FOR TWO (CD only) | SONY | A8242 |
| | | | |
| SLEEPLESS | SINGLE | COLUMBIA | 39695 |
| Columbia recorded 17/10/51 | | | |
| Percy Faith | | | |
| | | | |
| SLEEPY TIME GAL | A TIME FOR LOVE | CBS | 62800 |
| R.Alden/R.Egan/ | SINGLE | CBS | 202021 |
| A.Lorenzo/R.Whiting | | | |
| Columbia recorded 1/66 | | | |
| Johnny Keating | | | |
| with Bobby Hackett | | | |
| | | | |
| SMALL WORLD IS'NT IT? | MEETS GENE KRUPA | SANDY HOOK | 2067 |
| live radio recorded 1963 | | | |
| Gene Krupa Guard Sessions | | | |
| | | | |
| SMILE | I LEFT MY HEART IN SAN | | |
| C.Chaplin/J.Turner/G.Parsons | FRANCISCO | CBS | 62201 |
| Columbia recorded c1959 | A STRING OF HITS | CBS | 66010 |
| Marty Manning | THE GOLDEN TOUCH | COLUMBIA | P12789 |
| | MILLION DOLLAR MEMORIES | R/DIGEST | 8061/9 |
| | SINGLE | PHILIPS | PB961 |
| *R. SHARON 9/6/62* | *CARNEGIE HALL* | | |
| re-recorded Columbia | THE MOVIE SONG ALBUM | CBS | 62677 |
| Al Cohn & Johnny Mandel | FORTY YEARS VOL 3 | COLUMBIA | 46843 |
| 27/12/65 | ALL-TIME GREATEST HITS | CBS | 68200 |
| | 16 MOST REQUESTED SONGS | CBS | 57056 |
| | TONY! | COLUMBIA | KH32171 |
| | | | |
| SMILE/WHEN YOUR SMILING | | | |
| live Columbia recorded 8/4/64 | | | |
| Louis Basil with Ralph Sharon Trio | | | |
| not released | | | |

| | | | |
|---|---|---|---|
| ✓ SNOWFALL<br>C.Thornhill<br>Columbia recorded 1/10/68<br>Robert Farnon | SNOWFALL, THE CHRISTMAS<br>ALBUM | CBS | 63782 |
| ✓ SO BEATS MY HEART<br>FOR YOU<br>P.Ballard/C.Hendeson/Waring<br>Columbia recorded 21/10/57<br>Ralph Sharon | THE BEAT OF MY HEART | COLUMBIA | CL1079 |
| ✓ SO FAR<br>R.Rodgers/O.Hammerstein II<br>Columbia recorded 8/4/58<br>Frank De Vol | LONG AGO AND FAR AWAY | COLUMBIA | CL1186 |
| SO LONG, BIG TIME<br>D.Langdon/H.Arlen<br>Columbia recorded 17/9/63<br>with the Ralph Sharon Trio<br>Marty Manning & Harold Arlen | THE MANY MOODS OF TONY | CBS | 62245 |
| SO MANY STARS<br>Mendes/Bergman/Bergman<br>Columbia recorded 1985<br>Jorge Calandrelli | THE ART OF EXCELLENCE<br>(CD only) | CBS | 26990 |
| SOLD TO THE MAN WITH<br>THE BROKEN HEART<br>Columbia recorded 19/1/567<br>Percy Faith | SINGLE | PHILIPS | PB689 |
| edited version released 1995<br>without string accompaniement | GREAT US COMPOSERS<br>SERIES | COLUMBIA | |
| ✓ SOLITAIRE<br>Borek/Nutter/Guion<br>Columbia recorded 17/7/51<br>Percy Faith | BLUE VELVET<br>LAST PICTURE SHOW (S'TRACK)<br>THE GOLDEN TOUCH | COLUMBIA<br>COLUMBIA<br>COLUMBIA | CL1292<br>70115<br>P12790 |
| ✓ SOLITUDE<br>Ellington/DeLange/Mills<br>Columbia recorded 22/12/58<br>Ralph Sharon & Count Basie | IN PERSON!<br>JAZZ | CBS<br>CBS | 62250<br>450465 |
| ✓ live recording Columbia<br>Ralph Sharon 9/6/62 | AT CARNEGIE HALL 1<br>WHEN I FALL IN LOVE | CBS<br>HALLMARK | 62116<br>SHM817 |
| SOME OF THESE DAYS<br>Philips recorded c1972<br>Don Costa | SPOTLIGHT ON . . . .<br>BRUT SINGLE<br>SINGLE | PHILIPS<br>BRUT<br>PHILIPS | 6641297<br>BR813<br>6006372 |

**SOME OTHER TIME**     BENNETT/BILL EVANS ALBUM     FANTASY     F9489
L.Bernstein/B.Comden/A.Green     FORTY YEARS VOL 4     COLUMBIA     4684
Fantasy recorded 10-13/6/75
Bill Evans

**SOMEBODY**     TONY BENNETT SINGS     PHILIPS     BBE12424
H.Warren/J.Brooks     SINGLE     PHILIPS     PB1089
Columbia recorded 13/10/60
Glenn Osser

**SOMEONE TO LIGHT UP**
**MY LIFE**     THE GOOD THINGS IN LIFE     PHILIPS     6308134
Jobim/Lees/Moraes     AT LONG LAST LOVE     PHILIPS     SON 014
Philips recorded c1972     SPOTLIGHT ON . . . .     PHILIPS     6641297
Robert Farnon

**SOMEONE TO LOVE**
B.Warren
Columbia recorded 12/10/62
Marty Manning
not released

re-recorded Columbia 19/12/62     I WANNA BE AROUND     CBS     62149
Marty Manning

**SOMEONE TO WATCH OVER ME**
G.Gershwin/I.Gershwin
Columbia recorded 17/1/69
Torrie Zito
not released

**SOMEONE TURNED THE MOON**
**UPSIDE DOWN**     SINGLE     COLUMBIA     40004
Columbia recorded 17/3/53
Percy Faith

**SOMETHING**     SOMETHING     CBS     64217
G.Harrison     GREAT HITS OF TODAY     CBS     63962
Columbia recorded 17/11/69     TONY!     COLUMBIA     32171
Peter Matz     20 GREATEST HITS     WARWICK     PA5021
    ALL-TIME GREATEST HITS     CBS     68200
    FORTY YEARS VOL 4     COLUMBIA     46843

**SOMETHING IN YOUR SMILE**     FOR ONCE IN MY LIFE     CBS     63166
L.Bricusse
Columbia recorded 20/4/67
Marion Evans

**SOMETHING TO LIVE FOR**
Columbia recorded 3/12/70
Peter Matz
not released

re-recorded Columbia 11/8/71
John Bunch
not released

**SOMETHING'S GOTTA GIVE**    ALL STAR POPS    COLUMBIA    CL728
J.Mercer    THE VOICE OF YOUR CHOICE    PHILIPS    BBR8051
Columbia recorded 9/6/55
Sid Feller

**SOMETIME AGO**
Columbia recorded 26/2/64
not released

**SOMETIMES I'M HAPPY**    ON THE GLORY ROAD+    COLUMBIA    CL1813
C.Grey/I.Caesar/V.Youmans
Columbia recorded 15/3/62
+album unreleased

✓ live recording Columbia    AT CARNEGIE HALL 2    CBS    62117
Ralph Sharon 9/6/62

✓ live radio recording 1963    MEETS GENE KRUPA    SANDY HOOK    2067
Gene Krupa Guard Sessions

re-recorded Columbia    FOR ONCE IN MY LIFE    CBS    63166
Marion Evans 1/9/67

**SOMEWHERE ALONG
THE LINE**    SUMMER OF '42    CBS    64648
D.Washington/M.Merrick
Columbia recorded 15/11/71
Torrie Zito

**SOMEWHERE ALONG
THE WAY**    ALONE AT LAST    COLUMBIA    CL2507
K.Adams/S.Gallop
Columbia recorded 17/10/51
Percy Faith

**(SOMEWHERE) OVER
THE RAINBOW**    SINGS A STRING OF HAROLD    COLUMBIA    CL1559
H.Arlen/Y.Harburg    ARLEN
Columbia recorded 30/7/60    LET'S FALL IN LOVE WITH...    CBS    88131
Glenn Osser

✓ re-recording Columbia 1995    HERE'S TO THE LADIES    COLUMBIA    481266
Jorge Calandrelli & Bill Holman

| | | | |
|---|---|---|---|
| **SONG OF THE JET** (SAMBA DO AVIAO) A.C.Jobim/G.Lees Columbia recorded 19/2/65 Don Costa | SONGS FOR THE JET SET | CBS | 62544 |
| **SOON IT'S GONNA RAIN** T.Jones/H.Schmidt Columbia recorded 16/3/62 Ralph Sharon +album unreleased | ON THE GLORY ROAD+ THE MANY MOODS OF TONY LOVE STORY SINGLE | COLUMBIA CBS CBS CBS | CL1813 62245 64368 AAG208 |
| **SOPHISTICATED LADY** I.Mills/M.Parish/D.Ellington Columbia recorded 28/2/60 Frank De Vol | ALONE TOGETHER | COLUMBIA | CL1471 |
| re-recorded Verve c1973 Bernie Leighton | GREATEST HITS NO7 | VERVE | SE4929 |
| **SPEAK LOW** O.Nash/K.Weill Columbia recorded 10/11/59 Frank De Vol | TO MY WONDERFUL ONE | COLUMBIA | CL1429 |
| re-recorded Columbia 13/3/62 +album unreleased | ON THE GLORY ROAD+ | COLUMBIA | CL1813 |
| re-recorded Columbia 27/3/64 Ralph Sharon | WHEN LIGHTS ARE LOW | CBS | 62296 |
| live Columbia recorded 8/4/64 Louis Basil with Ralph Sharon Trio not released | | | |
| re-recorded Columbia 1989 Jorge Calandrelli | ASTORIA:PORTRAIT OF THE ARTIST | CBS | 466005 |
| live MTV recorded 4/94 Ralph Sharon | MTV UNPLUGGED | COLUMBIA | 477170 |
| **SPRING IN MANHATTAN** A.Reach/A.Scribetta Columbia recorded 8/4/63 Don Costa | THE MANY MOODS OF TONY THE GOLDEN TOUCH FORTY YEARS VOL 2 SINGLE | CBS COLUMBIA COLUMBIA CBS | 62245 P12790 46843 AAG153 |
| live Columbia recorded 8/4/64 Louis Basil with Ralph Sharon Trio not released | | | |

| | | | |
|---|---|---|---|
| **SPRING IS HERE**<br>R.Rodgers/L.Hart<br>Improv recorded c1973<br>with the Ruby Braff/<br>George Barnes Quartet | 10 RODGERS & HART SONGS<br>RODGERS & HART SONGBOOK<br>UNFORGETTABLE | IMPROV<br>NELSON<br>CASTLE | 7113<br>CD1129<br>UNLP019 |
| **STAY WHERE YOU ARE**<br>Columbia recorded 26/8/52<br>Percy Faith | SINGLE | COLUMBIA | 39866 |
| **STELLA BY STARLIGHT**<br>V.Young/N.Washington<br>Columbia recorded 6/4/61<br>Ralph Burns | MY HEART SINGS<br>JAZZ<br>LOVE SONGS<br>FORTY YEARS VOL 2<br>THE VERY THOUGHT OF YOU | COLUMBIA<br>CBS<br>CBS<br>COLUMBIA<br>HALLMARK | CL1658<br>450465<br>66297<br>46843<br>SHM769 |
| **STEPPIN' OUT WITH MY BABY**<br>I.Berlin<br>Columbia recorded 1994<br>Tony Bennett & Ralph Sharon | STEPPIN' OUT | COLUMBIA | 474360 |
| live MTV recorded 4/94<br>with the Ralph Sharon Trio | MTV UNPLUGGED | COLUMBIA | 477170 |
| **STRAIGHTEN UP AND FLY RIGHT**<br>I.Mills<br>Columbia recorded 25/2/69<br>not released | | | |
| **STRANGER IN PARADISE**<br>Borodin/Wright/Forrest<br>Columbia recorded 13/10/53<br>Percy Faith | STRANGER IN PARADISE<br>ALL-TIME GREATEST HITS<br>16 MOST REQUESTED SONGS<br>FORTY YEARS VOL 1<br>THE 50'S REVISTED<br>MILLION DOLLAR MEMORIES<br>POPULAR FAVORITES 3<br>A STRING OF HITS<br>16 ORIGINAL HITS<br>MR BROADWAY<br>GREAT SONGS FROM THE SHOWS<br>20 GREATEST HITS<br>ALONE AT LAST<br>TONY BENNETT SPOTLITE<br>THE VOICE OF YOUR CHOICE<br>FABULOUS FIFTIES<br>THE VERY THOUGHT OF YOU<br>THE GOLDEN TOUCH<br>SINGLE | PHILIPS<br>CBS<br>CBS<br>COLUMBIA<br>PICKWICK<br>R/DIGEST<br>COLUMBIA<br>CBS<br>EVEREST<br>COLUMBIA<br>PICKWICK<br>WARWICK<br>COLUMBIA<br>COLUMBIA<br>PHILIPS<br>DITTO<br>HALLMARK<br>COLUMBIA<br>PHILIPS | BBE12009<br>68200<br>57056<br>46843<br>4152<br>8061/9<br>CL6284<br>66010<br>LP16-19<br>CL1763<br>4171<br>PA502<br>CL2507<br>B1842<br>BBR 8051<br>10252<br>SHM769<br>P12790<br>PB420 |
| live recording Columbia<br>Ralph Sharon 9/6/62 | AT CARNEGIE HALL 1 | CBS | 62116 |

| | | | |
|---|---|---|---|
| **STREET OF DREAMS**<br>Lewis/Young<br>Columbia recorded 28/10/59<br>Ralph Sharon | TONY SINGS FOR TWO<br>LOVE SONGS<br>JAZZ | COLUMBIA<br>CBS<br>CBS | CL1446<br>66297<br>450465 |
| re-recorded Columbia<br>Robert Farnon 1/10/71 | WITH LOVE | CBS | 64849 |
| **STRIKE UP THE BAND**<br>G.Gershwin/I.Gershwin<br>Roulette released 1961<br>Count Basie | STRIKE UP THE BAND<br>ONE NIGHT STAND | ROULETTE<br>ALLEGRO | 25231<br>799 |
| **SUDDENLY**<br>Cochran/Heuberger<br>Columbia recorded 12/11/59<br>Frank De Vol | TO MY WONDERFUL ONE | COLUMBIA | CL1429 |
| **SUNDAY**<br>Miller/Krueger/Conn/Styne<br>live radio recorded 1963<br>Gene Krupa Guard Sessions | MEETS GENE KRUPA | SANDY HOOK | 2067 |
| live Columbia recorded 8/4/64<br>Louis Basil with Ralph Sharon Trio<br>not released | | | |
| **SUNRISE, SUNSET**<br>S.Harnick/J.Bock<br>Columbia recorded 17/11/69<br>Peter Matz | GREAT HITS OF TODAY<br>SUNRISE, SUNSET | CBS<br>CBS | 63962<br>32239 |
| **SWEET GEORGIE FAME**<br>B.Dearie/S.Harris<br>Columbia recorded 26/2/68<br>Torrie Zito | YESTERDAY I HEARD THE RAIN | CBS | 63351 |
| **SWEET LORRAINE**<br>M.Parish/C.Burwell<br>Columbia recorded 11/3/65<br>Don Costa | SONGS FOR THE JET SET<br>TONY BENNETT SINGS<br>FORTY YEARS VOL 3<br>JAZZ | CBS<br>R/DIGEST<br>COLUMBIA<br>CBS | 62544<br>8070<br>46843<br>450465 |
| **S' WONDERFUL**<br>G.Gershwin/I.Gershwin<br>live Improv recording 13-14/5/77<br>with the MacPartlands | THE MACPARTLANDS & FRIENDS<br>MAKE BEAUTIFUL MUSIC | IMPROV | 7123 |
| **TAKE ME**<br>R.Bloome/M.David<br>Columbia recorded 4/9/52<br>Percy Faith | SINGLE | COLUMBIA | 39910 |

| | | | |
|---|---|---|---|
| **TAKE ME BACK AGAIN**<br>Evans/Kahn/Berman<br>Columbia recorded 27/12/53<br>Percy Faith | STRANGER IN PARADISE<br>THE VOICE OF YOUR CHOICE<br>SINGLE | PHILIPS<br>PHILIPS<br>PHILIPS | BBE12009<br>BBR 8051<br>PB420 |
| **TAKE THE MOMENT**<br>S.Sondheim/R.Rodgers<br>Columbia recorded 4/1/65<br>Don Costa | IF I RULED THE WORLD<br>SONGS FOR THE JET SET (US) | EMBASSY<br>COLUMBIA | 31058<br>CL1559 |
| **TAKING A CHANCE ON LOVE**<br>Latouche/Fetter/Duke<br>Columbia recorded 1957<br>Ray Conniff | TONY<br>TONY BENNETT SHOWCASE | COLUMBIA<br>PHILIPS | CL938<br>BBL7138 |
| live Columbia recording 1956<br>New York House Party<br>with Mitch Miller intro. | COLUMBIA HOUSE PARTY | COLUMBIA | XLP36210 |
| re-recorded Columbia 1959<br>Ralph Sharon & Count Basie<br>*no fake audience<br><br>R SHARON 9/6/6L | IN PERSON!<br>20 GREATEST HITS*<br>GREAT SONGS FROM THE SHOWS*<br>WHEN I FALL IN LOVE*<br>I LEFT MY HEART IN SAN<br>CARNEGIE FRANCISCO*<br>HALL | CBS<br>WARWICK<br>PICKWICK<br>HALLMARK<br>CBS | 62250<br>PA5021<br>4171<br>SHM817<br>62201 |
| **TANGERINE**<br>J.Mercer/V.Schertzinger<br>Columbia recorded 1995<br>Jorge Calandrelli & Bill Holman | HERE'S TO THE LADIES | COLUMBIA | 481266 |
| **TEA FOR TWO**<br>I.Caesar/V.Youmans<br>Columbia recorded 25/1/71<br>Ralph Burns | LOVE STORY | CBS | 64368 |
| live Columbia recording<br>Robert Farnon &<br>Ralph Burns 31/1/71 | GET HAPPY | CBS | 64577 |
| **TELL HER THAT IT'S<br>SNOWING**<br>Heiman/Mallows/Marnay<br>Philips recorded c1973<br>Don Costa | LISTEN EASY<br>SPOTLIGHT ON . . . . | PHILIPS<br>PHILIPS | 6308157<br>6641297 |
| edited short version | GREATEST HITS NO7 | VERVE | SE4929 |

**(COME BACK AND) TELL ME**
**THAT YOU LOVE ME**          THE VOICE OF YOUR CHOICE          PHILIPS          BBR8051
Chase                         SINGLE                            PHILIPS          PB521
Columbia recorded 30/6/55
Percy Faith

**TENDER IS THE NIGHT**       I LEFT MY HEART IN SAN
Webster/Fain                                 FRANCISCO          CBS              62201
Columbia recorded 6/9/61      LOVE SONGS                        CBS              66297
Marty Manning                 16 MOST REQUESTED SONGS           CBS              57056
                              FORTY YEARS VOL 2                 COLUMBIA         46843
                              SINGLE                            PHILIPS          PB1218

**TENDERLY**                  TO MY WONDERFUL ONE               COLUMBIA         CL1429
J.Lawrence                    LOVE SONGS                        CBS              66297
Columbia recorded 10/11/59
Frank De Vol

re-recorded Columbia 1995     HERE'S TO THE LADIES              COLUMBIA         481266
Jorge Calandrelli & Bill Holman

**THAT NIGHT**                I'VE GOTTA BE ME                  CBS              63685
N.Gimbel/L.Schifrin
Columbia recorded 25/2/69
Torrie Zito

**THAT OLD BLACK MAGIC**      ON THE GLORY ROAD+                COLUMBIA         CL1813
J.Mercer/H.Arlen
Columbia recorded 13/3/62
Ralph Sharon
+album unreleased
R SHARON 9/6/62              CARNEGIE HALL
live recording Columbia 1962  MUSIC FROM THE LATE SHOW          CBS              86356
Dave Brubeck                  SUMMIT SESSIONS                   CBS              30522

**THAT'S ENTERTAINMENT**      STEPPIN' OUT                      COLUMBIA         474360
A.Schwartz/H.Dietz
Columbia recorded 1994
Tony Bennett & Ralph Sharon

**THE AUTUMN WALTZ**          16 ORIGINAL HITS                  EVEREST          LP16-19
Hilliard/Coleman              SINGLE                            COLUMBIA         40770
Columbia recorded 19/9/56
Percy Faith

**THE BAD AND THE BEAUTIFUL** TOGETHER AGAIN                    IMPROV           7117
D.Raskin/D.Langdon
Improv recorded c1977
Bill Evans solo
Tony Bennett does not feature on this track

81

| | | | |
|---|---|---|---|
| ✓ **THE BEAT OF MY HEART**<br>Burke/Spina<br>Columbia recorded 27/6/57<br>Ralph Sharon | THE BEAT OF MY HEART<br>JUST ONE OF THOSE THINGS | COLUMBIA<br>HALLMARK | CL1079<br>SHM646 |
| ✓ **THE BEST IS YET TO COME**<br>C.Leigh/C.Coleman<br>Columbia recorded 30/7/60<br>Cy Coleman | I LEFT MY HEART IN SAN<br>    FRANCISCO<br>GREATEST HITS<br>LET'S FALL IN LOVE WITH..<br>FORTY YEARS VOL 2<br>SINGLE | CBS<br>CBS<br>CBS<br>COLUMBIA<br>PHILIPS | 62201<br>62821<br>88131<br>46843<br>PB1218 |
| ✓ R SHARON 9/6/62<br>✓ **THE BEST THING TO BE<br>   IS A PERSON**<br>B.Haymes/A.Brandt<br>Columbia recorded 4/9/64<br>George Siravo | CARNEGIE HALL<br><br>WHO CAN I TURN TO | CBS | 62486 |
| ✓ **THE BRIGHTEST SMILE<br>   IN TOWN**<br>B.De Vorzon/B.Sherman/R.Charles<br>Columbia recorded 14/8/64<br>George Siravo | WHO CAN I TURN TO | CBS | 62486 |
| **THE CHRISTMAS SONG**<br>M.Torme/R.Wells<br>Columbia released 1967 | GREAT SONGS OF CHRISTMAS 7<br>MANHATTAN TRANSFER<br>   CHRISTMAS ALBUM | COLUMBIA<br>COLUMBIA | CSS547<br>CK52968 |
| ✓ re-recorded Columbia 1968<br>Robert Farnon | SNOWFALL, THE CHRISTMAS<br>   ALBUM | CBS | 63782 |
| **THE COOL SCHOOL**<br>Wayne/Frisch<br>Columbia recorded 23/3/59<br>Ralph Sharon | SINGLE | PHILIPS | PB996 |
| **(ON) THE DAY YOU LEAVE ME**<br>C.Coleman/C.Gore<br>Columbia recorded 1985<br>Jorge Calandrelli | THE ART OF EXCELLENCE | CBS | 26990 |
| **THE DAYS OF WINE<br>   AND ROSES**<br>J.Mercer/H.Mancini<br>✓ Columbia recorded 29/12/65<br>Johnny Mandel & Larry Wilcox | THE MOVIE SONG ALBUM<br>SUNRISE, SUNSET<br>LOVE SONGS<br>THE TROLLEY SONG | CBS<br>CBS<br>CBS<br>EMBASSY | 62677<br>32239<br>66297<br>31002 |
| ✓ re-recorded Fantasy<br>Bill Evans 10-13/6/75 | BENNETT/ BILL EVANS ALBUM | FANTASY | FT527 |

| | | | |
|---|---|---|---|
| THE FOLKS WHO LIVE ON THE HILL<br>J.Kern/O.Hammerstein II<br>Columbia recorded 1989<br>Jorge Calandrelli | ASTORIA: PORTRAIT OF THE ARTIST | CBS | 466005 |
| THE GARDEN (ONCE IN A GARDEN)<br>DeSeca/Lees<br>Philips recorded c1973<br>Don Costa | LISTEN EASY<br>SPOTLIGHT ON .... | PHILIPS<br>PHILIPS | 6308157<br>6641297 |
| THE GENTLE RAIN<br>M.Dubey/L.Bonfa<br>Columbia recorded 28/12/65<br>Johnny Mandel<br>with Luiz Bonfa | THE MOVIE SONG ALBUM<br>GREATEST HITS VOL 2<br>LOVE STORY<br>WHEN I FALL IN LOVE | CBS<br>CBS<br>CBS<br>HALLMARK | 62677<br>63612<br>64368<br>SHM817 |
| THE GIRL I LOVE<br>(The Man I Love)<br>G.Gershwin/I.Gershwin<br>Columbia recorded 1989<br>Jorge Calandrelli | ASTORIA: PORTRAIT OF THE ARTIST | CBS | 466005 |
| live MTV recorded 4/94<br>with the Ralph Sharon Trio | MTV UNPLUGGED | COLUMBIA | 477170 |
| THE GLORY OF LOVE<br>B.Hill<br>Columbia recorded 1/68<br>Torrie Zito<br>duet with Dominic Germano | SINGLE<br>SINGLE | COLUMBIA<br>CBS | 44443<br>3370 |
| THE GOOD LIFE<br>S.Distel/Reardon<br>Columbia recorded 19/12/62<br>Marty Manning | I WANNA BE AROUND<br>GREATEST HITS<br>FORTY YEARS VOL 2<br>16 ORIGINAL HITS<br>25 YEARS OF ROCK N ROLL 63<br>THE GOLDEN TOUCH<br>20 GREATEST HITS<br>SINGLE | CBS<br>CBS<br>COLUMBIA<br>EVEREST<br>CONNOISSEUR<br>COLUMBIA<br>WARWICK<br>CBS | 62149<br>62821<br>46843<br>LP16-19<br>63<br>P12790<br>PA5021<br>AAG153 |
| re-recorded Columbia 24/6/70<br>John Bunch | ALL TIME HALL OF FAME HITS<br>16 MOST REQUESTED SONGS | CBS<br>CBS | 64200<br>57056 |
| THE GOOD LIFE/<br>I WANNA BE AROUND<br>S.Distel/Reardon,J.Mercer/Vimmerstedt<br>live MTV recorded 4/94<br>with the Ralph Sharon Trio | MTV UNPLUGGED | COLUMBIA | 477170 |

| | | | | |
|---|---|---|---|---|
| ✓ | THE GOOD THINGS IN LIFE<br>L.Bricusse/T.Newley<br>Philips recorded c1972<br>Robert Farnon | THE GOOD THINGS IN LIFE<br>SPOTLIGHT ON . . . .<br>SINGLE<br>SINGLE | PHILIPS<br>PHILIPS<br>PHILIPS<br>PHILIPS | 6308134<br>6641297<br>6006260<br>6006309 |
| ✓ | closing version | THE GOOD THINGS IN LIFE | PHILIPS | 6308134 |
| | THE HANDS OF TIME<br>(THEME FROM BRIAN'S SONG)<br>A.Bergman/M.LeGrand<br>Philips recorded c1973<br>Don Costa | LISTEN EASY<br>SPOTLIGHT ON . . . . | PHILIPS<br>PHILIPS | 6308157<br>6641297 |
| | THE KID'S A DREAMER<br>H.Hendler/D.Arthur<br>Columbia recorded 6/11/63<br>Ralph Sharon featuring Bobby Hackett | THE MANY MOODS OF TONY<br>SINGLE | CBS<br>CBS | 62245<br>AAG191 |
| ✓ | THE LADY IS A TRAMP<br>R.Rodgers/L.Hart<br>Improv recorded c1973<br>with the Ruby Braff/<br>George Barnes Quartet | 10 RODGERS & HART SONGS<br>RODGERS & HART SONGBOOK<br>STAGE & SCREEN HITS<br>UNFORGETTABLE<br>HOLLYWOOD & BROADWAY | IMPROV<br>NELSON<br>DBM<br>CASTLE<br>NELSON | 7113<br>CD1129<br>1001<br>UNLP019<br>1145 |
| ✓ | re-recorded Columbia 1993<br>with the Ralph Sharon Trio | PERFECTLY FRANK | COLUMBIA | 472222 |
| | THE LADY SINGS THE BLUES<br>A.Wilder<br>released 1977 | THE SONGS OF ALEC WILDER | JAZZ ARC | 19795 |
| | THE LADY'S IN LOVE<br>  WITH YOU<br>F.Loesser/B.Lane<br>Columbia recorded 12/1/67<br>Marion Evans | TONY MAKES IT HAPPEN | CBS | 63055 |
| | live recording Columbia<br>H.Roberts (A&R) 11/8/67<br>not released | | | |
| | THE LAMP IS LOW<br>Columbia recorded 15/3/62<br>Ralph Sharon<br>+album unreleased | ON THE GLORY ROAD+ | COLUMBIA | CL1813 |
| | THE LITTLE BOY<br>A.Stillman/C.Wood<br>Columbia recorded 6/11/63<br>Dick Hyman | THE MANY MOODS OF TONY<br>SINGLE | CBS<br>CBS | 62245<br>AAG184 |

| | | | |
|---|---|---|---|
| **THE LONG AND WINDING ROAD**<br>J.Lennon/P.McCartney<br>Columbia recorded 13/8/70<br>Peter Matz | SOMETHING | CBS | 64217 |
| **THE LOOK OF LOVE**<br>B.Bacharach/H.David<br>Columbia recorded 17/11/69<br>Peter Matz | GREAT HITS OF TODAY<br>TONY! | CBS<br>CBS | 63962<br>32171 |
| **THE LOVELIEST GIRL I KNOW**<br>Columbia recorded 14/7/50<br>Percy Faith<br>not released | | | |
| **THE MAN THAT GOT AWAY**<br>H.Arlen/I.Gershwin<br>Columbia recorded 28/10/59<br>Ralph Sharon | TONY SINGS FOR TWO | COLUMBIA | CL1446 |
| ✓ alternative take of above | FORTY YEARS VOL 1 | COLUMBIA | 46843 |
| **THE MIDNIGHT SUN**<br>Hampton/Burke/Mercer<br>Philips recorded c1972<br>Robert Farnon | THE GOOD THINGS IN LIFE<br>SPOTLIGHT ON . . . .<br>AT LONG LAST LOVE | PHILIPS<br>PHILIPS<br>PHILIPS | 6308134<br>6641297<br>SON 014 |
| **THE MOMENT OF TRUTH**<br>T.Satterwhite/F.Scott<br>Columbia recorded 24/4/63<br>Ralph Burns | THIS IS ALL I ASK<br>FORTY YEARS VOL 2<br>GREATEST HITS<br>SINGLE | CBS<br>COLUMBIA<br>CBS<br>CBS | 62205<br>46843<br>62821<br>AAG184 |
| live Columbia recorded 8/4/64<br>Louis Basil with Ralph Sharon Trio<br>not released | | | |
| live recording Columbia<br>H.Roberts (A&R) 11/8/67<br>not released | | | |
| **THE MOST BEAUTIFUL GIRL IN THE WORLD**<br>R.Rodgers/L.Hart<br>Improv recorded c1973<br>with the Ruby Braff/<br>George Barnes Quartet | MORE RODGERS & HART SONGS<br>RODGERS & HART SONGBOOK<br>STAGE & SCREEN HITS<br>HOLLYWOOD & BROADWAY | IMPR<br>NELSON<br>DBM<br>NELSON | OV7120<br>CD1129<br>1001<br>1145 |

**THE NIGHT THAT
HEAVEN FELL**
B.Bacharach/H.David
Columbia recorded 1/8/58
Ray Ellis

A STRING OF HITS
SINGLE

CBS
PHILIPS

66010
PB855

**THE PARTY'S OVER**
Styne/Comden/Green
Columbia recorded 4/11/58
Ralph Burns
*edited version

HOMETOWN, MY TOWN
MR BROADWAY*
SUNRISE, SUNSET*

COLUMBIA
COLUMBIA
CBS

CL1301
CL1763
32239

✓ **THE PAWNBROKER**
J.Lawrence/Q.Jones
Columbia recorded 14/12/65
Quincy Jones

THE MOVIE SONG ALBUM

CBS

62677

**THE RIGHT TO LOVE**
L.Schifrin/G.Lees
Columbia recorded 18/2/65
Don Costa

SONGS FOR THE JET SET

CBS

62544

✓ **THE RIVIERA**
C.Coleman/J.McCarthy
Columbia recorded 1/10/71
Robert Farnon

WITH LOVE
LET'S FALL IN LOVE WITH ..

CBS
CBS

64849
88131

**THE RULES OF THE ROAD**
C.Leigh/C.Coleman
Columbia released 1962
Ralph Burns
re-recorded Columbia 26/2/64
not released

✓ R. SHARON 9/6/62
re-recorded Columbia
Ralph Sharon 27/3/64

live Columbia recorded 8/4/64
Louis Basil with Ralph Sharon Trio
not released

I LEFT MY HEART IN SAN
FRANCISCO

CARNEGIE HALL
WHEN LIGHTS ARE LOW
LET'S FALL IN LOVE WITH ..

CBS

CBS
CBS

62201

62296
88131

✓ **THE SECOND TIME AROUND**
S.Cahn/J.Van Heusen
Columbia recorded 27/12/65
Johnny Mandel & Al Cohn

THE MOVIE SONG ALBUM
TONY!
THE VERY THOUGHT OF YOU
LOVE SONGS

CBS
CBS
HALLMARK
CBS

62677
32171
SHM769
66297

**THE SHADOW OF YOUR SMILE**  THE MOVIE SONG ALBUM        CBS        62677
P.Webster/J.Mandel                FORTY YEARS VOL 3            COLUMBIA   46843
Columbia recorded 26/9/65         THE GOLDEN TOUCH             COLUMBIA   P12790
Johnny Mandel                     GREATEST HITS 2              CBS        63612
                                  20 GREATEST HITS             WARWICK    PA5021
                                  ALL-TIME GREATEST HITS       CBS        68200
                                  16 MOST REQUESTED SONGS      CBS        57056
                                  TRUE LOVE                    TELSTAR    TCD2692
                                  ALL TIME HALL OF FAME HITS   CBS        64200

live recording Columbia
H.Roberts (A&R) 11/8/67
not released

**THE SHINING SEA**               A TIME FOR LOVE              CBS        62800
J.Mandel/P.Lee                    SUMMER OF '42                CBS        64648
Columbia recorded 11/6/66
Johnny Mandel

**THE SHOW MUST GO ON**
Columbia recorded 26/2/64
not released

live Columbia recorded 8/4/64
Louis Basil with Ralph Sharon Trio
not released

**THE SKYSCRAPER BLUES**
Adair/Jenkins
Columbia recorded 6/11/58
Ralph Burns
not released

re-recorded Columbia 1959         HOMETOWN, MY TOWN            COLUMBIA   CL1301
Ralph Burns

**THE SONG IS ENDED**             BENNETT:BERLIN               CBS        460450
I.Berlin
Columbia recorded 1987
Tony Bennett

**THE TOUCH OF YOUR LIPS**        BENNETT/BILL EVANS ALBUM     FANTASY    FT527
R.Noble
Fantasy recorded 10-13/6/75
Bill Evans

**THE TROLLEY SONG**              THE MOVIE SONG ALBUM         CBS        62677
H.Martin/R.Blane                  THE TROLLEY SONG             EMBASSY    31002
Columbia recorded 29/12/65        TONY BENNETT SINGS           R/DIGEST   8070
Johnny Mandel & Al Cohn

live recording Columbia
H.Roberts (A&R) 11/8/67
not released

✓ live Columbia recording  GET HAPPY              CBS        64577
  Robert Farnon 31/1/71

**THE TWO LONELY PEOPLE**   TOGETHER AGAIN        IMPROV     7117
B.Evans/C.Hall              TOGETHER AGAIN        NELSON     CD1122
Improv recorded c1977
Bill Evans

**THE VALENTINO TANGO**     BECAUSE OF YOU        COLUMBIA   CL6221
Columbia recorded 17/1/51   SINGLE                COLUMBIA   39209
Percy Faith

**THE VERY THOUGHT OF YOU** A TIME FOR LOVE       CBS        62800
R.Noble                     THE BEST OF TONY BENNETT CBS     6151
✓ Columbia recorded 1/66    THE VERY THOUGHT OF YOU HALLMARK SHM769
Johnny Keating              LOVE SONGS            CBS        66297
featuring Bobby Hackett     FORTY YEARS VOL 3     COLUMBIA   46843
                            SINGLE                CBS        202021

**THE WAY THAT I FEEL**     THIS IS ALL I ASK     CBS        62205
F.Brooks
Columbia recorded 26/4/63
Ralph Burns

**THE WAY YOU LOOK
  TONIGHT**                 LONG AGO AND FAR AWAY COLUMBIA   CL1186
✓ Columbia recorded 7/4/58
Frank De Vol

**THEME FROM THE SUMMER OF '42
(THE SUMMER KNOWS)**        SUMMER OF '42         CBS        64648
A.Bergman/M.Bergman/M.LeGrand
Columbia recorded 15/11/71
Torrie Zito

**THEME FROM
" VALLEY OF THE DOLLS"**    I'VE GOTTA BE ME      CBS        63685
D.Previn/A.Previn
Columbia recorded 17/1/69
Torrie Zito

**THEN WAS THEN AND
  NOW IS NOW**              SONGS FOR THE JET SET CBS        62544
P.Lee/C.Coleman             LET'S FALL IN LOVE WITH.. CBS    88131
Columbia recorded 18/2/65
Don Costa

88

| | | | |
|---|---|---|---|
| **THERE WILL NEVER BE ANOTHER YOU**<br>M.Gordon/H.Warren<br>Columbia recorded 22/12/58<br>Ralph Sharon & Count Basie | IN PERSON!<br>THE TROLLEY SONG | CBS<br>EMBASSY | 62250<br>31002 |
| re-recorded Columbia<br>Torrie Zito 22/5/68 | YESTERDAY I HEARD THE RAIN | CBS | 63351 |
| ✓ live Columbia recording<br>Robert Farnon 31/1/71 | GET HAPPY | CBS | 64577 |
| re-recorded 1989<br>Jorge Calandrelli | ASTORIA:PORTRAIT OF THE ARTIST | COLUMBIA | 466005 |
| **THERE'LL BE NO TEARDROPS TONIGHT**<br>H.Williams<br>Columbia recorded 4/12/53<br>Percy Faith | THE VOICE OF YOUR CHOICE<br>16 ORIGINAL HITS<br>A STRING OF HITS<br>SINGLE | PHILIPS<br>EVEREST<br>CBS<br>PHILIPS | BBR8051<br>LP16-19<br>66010<br>PB267 |
| **THERE'LL BE SOME CHANGES MADE**<br>W.Overstreet/B.Higgins<br>Improv recorded c1975<br>Torrie Zito | LIFE IS BEAUTIFUL<br>UNFORGETTABLE<br>SINGLE | IMPROV<br>CASTLE<br>IMPROV | 7112<br>UNLP019<br>711 105 |
| ✓ **THERE'S A LULL IN MY LIFE**<br>M.Gordon/H.Revel<br>Columbia recorded 14/10/64<br>George Siravo | WHO CAN I TURN TO<br>TONY! | CBS<br>CBS | 62486<br>32171 |
| ✓ **THERE'S A SMALL HOTEL**<br>R.Rodgers/L.Hart<br>Improv recorded c1973<br>with the Ruby Braff/<br>George Barnes Quartet | MORE RODGERS & HART SONGS<br>RODGERS & HART SONGBOOK<br>UNFORGETTABLE<br>STAGE & SCREEN HITS | IMPROV<br>NELSON<br>CASTLE<br>DBM | 7120<br>CD1129<br>UNLP019<br>1001 |
| **THERE'S ALWAYS TOMORROW**<br>T.Zito/S.Cahn<br>Improv recorded c1976<br>Torrie Zito | SINGLE | IMPROV | 713 106 |
| ✓ **THESE FOOLISH THINGS**<br>J.Strachey/H.Link/H.Marvell<br>Columbia recorded 12/9/56<br>Ray Conniff | TONY<br>TONY BENNETT SHOWCASE | COLUMBIA<br>PHILIPS | CL938<br>BBL7138 |

| | | | |
|---|---|---|---|
| **THEY ALL LAUGHED**<br>I.Gershwin/G.Gershwin<br>Columbia recorded 25/11/68<br>Torrie Zito | I'VE GOTTA BE ME<br>WHEN I FALL IN LOVE | CBS<br>HALLMARK | 63685<br>SHM817 |
| ✓ re-recorded Columbia 1994<br>Tony Bennett & Ralph Sharon | STEPPIN' OUT | COLUMBIA | 474360 |
| **THEY CAN'T TAKE THAT**<br>**AWAY FROM ME**<br>I.Gershwin/G.Gershwin<br>Columbia recorded 16/10/67<br>Torrie Zito<br>featuring Burt Collins | FOR ONCE IN MY LIFE<br>LOVE STORY<br>TONY BENNETT SINGS | CBS<br>CBS<br>R/DIGEST | 63166<br>64368<br>8070 |
| ✓ re-recorded Columbia 1994<br>Tony Bennett & Ralph Sharon | STEPPIN' OUT | COLUMBIA | 474360 |
| Live MTV recorded 4/94<br>with the Ralph Sharon trio<br>duet with Elvis Costello | MTV UNPLUGGED | COLUMBIA | 477170 |
| **THEY SAY IT'S WONDERFUL**<br>I.Berlin<br>Columbia recorded 1987<br>Tony Bennett | BENNETT:BERLIN<br>UNFORGETTABLE ROMANTIC<br>   SONGS (DE KUYPER)<br>GREAT SONGS FROM THE SHOWS | CBS<br><br>COLUMBIA<br>PICKWICK | 460450<br><br>983298<br>4171 |
| **THINK HOW IT'S GONNA BE**<br>**(WHEN WE'RE TOGETHER**<br>**AGAIN)**<br>C.Strouse/L.Adams<br>Columbia recorded 2/4/70<br>Peter Matz | SOMETHING | CBS | 64217 |
| re-recorded Columbia<br>Peter Matz c30/6/70 | SINGLE | COLUMBIA | 4-45157 |
| **THIS CAN'T BE LOVE**<br>R.Rodgers/L.Hart<br>✓ Improv recorded c1973<br>with the Ruby Braff/<br>George Barnes Quartet | 10 RODGERS & HART SONGS<br>RODGERS & HART SONGBOOK<br>HOLLYWOOD & BROADWAY | IMPROV<br>NELSON<br>NELSON | 7113<br>CD1129<br>1145 |
| **THIS COULD BE THE START**<br>**OF SOMETHING** BIG<br>Columbia recorded 14/1/60<br>Ralph Sharon<br>not released<br>   - 9/6/62   CARNEGIE HALL<br>✓ live Columbia recorded 8/4/64<br>Louis Basil with Ralph Sharon Trio<br>not released | | | |

| | | | |
|---|---|---|---|
| **THIS FUNNY WORLD**<br>R.Rodgers/L.Hart<br>Improv recorded c1973<br>Torrie Zito | LIFE IS BEAUTIFUL<br>THE MAGIC OF TONY BENNETT<br>STAGE & SCREEN HITS<br>HOLLYWOOD & BROADWAY | IMPROV<br>NELSON<br>DBM<br>NELSON | 7112<br>CYU106<br>1001<br>1145 |
| re-recorded Improv c1973<br>with the Ruby Braff/<br>George Barnes Quartet | MORE RODGERS & HART SONGS<br>RODGERS & HART SONGBOOK | IMPROV<br>NELSON | 7120<br>CD1129 |
| **THIS IS ALL I ASK**<br>G.Jenkins<br>Columbia recorded 1/3/60<br>Frank de Vol | ALONE TOGETHER<br>MILLION DOLLAR MEMORIES | COLUMBIA<br>R/DIGEST | CL1471<br>8061/9 |
| live Columbia recorded 8/4/64<br>Louis Basil with Ralph Sharon Trio<br>not released | | | |
| re-recorded Columbia<br>Ralph Burns 26/4/63 | THIS IS ALL I ASK<br>FORTY YEARS VOL 2<br>THE GOLDEN TOUCH<br>ALL TIME HALL OF FAME HITS<br>16 MOST REQUESTED SONGS<br>GREATEST HITS<br>ALL-TIME GREATEST HITS<br>SINGLE | CBS<br>COLUMBIA<br>COLUMBIA<br>CBS<br>CBS<br>CBS<br>CBS<br>CBS | 62205<br>46843<br>P12789<br>64200<br>57056<br>62821<br>68200<br>AAG165 |
| **THIS IS THE TIME**<br>Columbia recorded 14/7/50<br>Percy Faith<br>not released | | | |
| **THIS TIME THE DREAM'S ON ME**<br>H.Arlen/J.Mercer<br>Columbia recorded 18/8/60<br>Glenn Osser | A STRING OF HAROLD ARLEN<br>LET'S FALL IN LOVE WITH..<br>FORTY YEARS VOL 2 | COLUMBIA<br>CBS<br>COLUMBIA | CL1559<br>88131<br>46843 |
| **THOU SWELL**<br>R.Rodgers/L.Hart<br>Improv recorded c1973<br>with the Ruby Braff/<br>George Barnes Quartet | MORE RODGERS & HART SONGS<br>RODGERS & HART SONGBOOK<br>UNFORGETTABLE<br>HOLLYWOOD & BROADWAY | IMPROV<br>NELSON<br>CASTLE<br>NELSON | 7120<br>CD1129<br>UNLP019<br>1145 |
| **TILL**<br>C.Danvers/C.Sigman<br>Columbia recorded 11/11/59<br>Frank De Vol | TO MY WONDERFUL ONE<br>SUMMER OF '42<br>MILLION DOLLAR MEMORIES<br>FORTY YEARS VOL 1<br>LOVE SONGS<br>TONY BENNETT SINGS<br>SINGLE | COLUMBIA<br>CBS<br>R/DIGEST<br>COLUMBIA<br>CBS<br>PHILIPS<br>PHILIPS | CL1429<br>64648<br>8061/9<br>46843<br>66297<br>BBE12424<br>PB1079 |

| | | | |
|---|---|---|---|
| ✓ TIME AFTER TIME<br>S.Cahn/J.Styne<br>Columbia recorded 9/4/58<br>Frank De Vol | LONG AGO AND FAR AWAY | COLUMBIA | CL1186 |
| live Columbia recorded 8/4/64<br>Louis Basil with Ralph Sharon Trio<br>not released | | | |
| ✓ re-recorded Columbia 1993<br>with the Ralph Sharon Trio | PERFECTLY FRANK | COLUMBIA | 472222 |
| ✓ TOOT, TOOT, TOOTSIE!<br>(GOODBYE)<br>Kahn/Fioreto/Erdman/Russo<br>Columbia recorded 5/4/61<br>Ralph Burns | MY HEART SINGS<br>FORTY YEARS VOL 2 | COLUMBIA<br>COLUMBIA | CL1658<br>46843 |
| ✓ R. SHARON 9/6/62<br>TOP HAT, WHITE TIE<br>AND TAILS<br>I.Berlin<br>Columbia recorded 1994<br>Tony Bennett & Ralph Sharon | CARNEGIE HALL<br>STEPPIN' OUT | COLUMBIA | 474360 |
| ✓ TOUCH THE EARTH<br>J.Southern/G.Allen<br>Columbia recorded 11/6/66<br>Ralph Burns | A TIME FOR LOVE | CBS | 62800 |
| ✓ TRAPPED (IN THE WEB<br>OF LOVE)<br>J.Burns<br>Columbia recorded 14/6/60<br>Ralph Sharon | A TIME FOR LOVE | CBS | 62800 |
| TRICKS<br>A.Brandt/B.Haymes<br>Columbia recorded 26/4/63<br>Ralph Burns | THIS IS ALL I ASK | CBS | 62205 |
| TRUE BLUE LOU<br>L.Robin/S.Coslow/R.Whiting<br>Columbia recorded 24/4/61<br>Ralph Burns | THIS IS ALL I ASK<br>SINGLE | CBS<br>CBS | 62205<br>AAG165 |
| ✓ TWILIGHT WORLD<br>J.Mercer/M.McPartland<br>Columbia recorded 10/10/71<br>Robert Farnon | WITH LOVE | CBS | 64849 |

| TWO BY TWO | SONGS FOR THE JET SET (US) | COLUMBIA | CL1559 |
| S.Sondheim/R.Rodgers | IF I RULED THE WORLD | EMBASSY | 31058 |
| Columbia recorded 19/2/65 | | | |
| Don Costa | | | |

| UNTIL I MET YOU | I WANNA BE AROUND | CBS | 62149 |
| F.Green/D.Wolf | FORTY YEARS VOL 2 | COLUMBIA | 46843 |
| Columbia recorded 16/3/62 | ON THE GLORY ROAD+ | COLUMBIA | CL1813 |
| Marty Manning | | | |
| +album unreleased | | | |

| UNTIL YESTERDAY | BLUE VELVET | COLUMBIA | CL1292 |
| Engvick/Fanciulli | SINGLE | PHILIPS | PB322 |
| Columbia recorded 4/12/53 | | | |
| Percy Faith | | | |

**VANITY**
Columbia recorded 6/11/63
Dick Hyman
not released

| VIENI QUI | SINGLE | LESLIE | |
| G.Simon | | | |
| Leslie label c1947 | | | |
| as Joe Bari | | | |

This is the first known recording by Tony Bennett using his first stage name,Joe Bari. Both songs were issued on a 78 rpm by Leslie records, a company owned by George Simon. The 1968 Billboard profile "20 years with Tony Bennett" states that the only known copy of this record disintegrated sometime in the 60's.

| WAIT TILL YOU SEE HER | 10 RODGERS & HART SONGS | IMPROV | 7113 |
| R.Rodgers/L.Hart | RODGERS & HART SONGBOOK | NELSON | CD1129 |
| Improv recorded c1973 | HOLLYWOOD & BROADWAY | NELSON | 1145 |
| with the Ruby Braff/ | | | |
| George Barnes Quartet | | | |

| WALK IN THE COUNTRY | ALONE TOGETHER | COLUMBIA | CL1471 |
| B.Howard | | | |
| Columbia recorded 1/3/60 | | | |
| Frank De Vol | | | |

| WALKABOUT | SUMMER OF '42 | CBS | 64648 |
| D.Black/J.Barry | | | |
| Columbia recorded 11/8/71 | | | |
| Robert Farnon | | | |

| WALTZ FOR DEBBIE | WHO CAN I TURN TO | CBS | 62486 |
| B.Evans/G.Lees | FORTY YEARS VOL 3 | COLUMBIA | 46843 |
| Columbia recorded 4/9/64 | | | |
| George Siravo | | | |
| alternative take to above | SINGLE | COLUMBIA | 4-41341 |

| | | | |
|---|---|---|---|
| ✓ re-recorded Fantasy<br>Bill Evans 10-13/6/75 | BENNETT/BILL EVANS ALBUM | FANTASY | FT527 |
| **WASH YOUR BLUES AWAY**<br>**WITH TEARDROPS**<br>Columbia recorded 11/9/63<br>Dick Hyman<br>not released | | | |
| **WATCH WHAT HAPPENS**<br>N.Gimbel/M.LeGrand<br>Columbia recorded 4/1/65<br>Don Costa | SONGS FOR THE JET SET<br>GREATEST HITS VOL 2 | CBS<br>CBS | 62544<br>63612 |
| live Improv recording 13-14/5/77<br>with the MacPartlands | THE MACPARTLANDS & FRIENDS<br>MAKE BEAUTIFUL MUSIC | IMPROV | 7123 |
| **WAVE**<br>A.C.Jobim<br>Columbia recorded 13/8/70<br>Peter Matz | SOMETHING | CBS | 64217 |
| ✓ live Columbia recording<br>Robert Farnon 31/1/71 | GET HAPPY | CBS | 64577 |
| **WE MUSTN'T SAY GOODBYE**<br>Dubin/Monaco<br>Columbia recorded 24 & 30/4/52<br>Percy Faith with the Pastels<br>not released | POSSIBLE RELEASE<br>(COLUMBIA PRICELESS EDITION) | COLUMBIA | PE6 |
| re-recorded Columbia 23/10/59<br>Frank De Vol | TO MY WONDERFUL ONE | COLUMBIA | CL1429 |
| **WEARY BLUES FROM WAITIN'**<br>H.Williams<br>Columbia recorded 19/9/57<br>Ray Ellis | SINGLE | COLUMBIA | 41086 |
| **WE'LL BE TOGETHER AGAIN**<br>Fischer/Laine<br>Columbia recorded 26/2/64<br>not released | | | |
| ✓ re-recorded Fantasy<br>Bill Evans 10-13/6/75 | BENNETT/BILL EVANS ALBUM | FANTASY | FT527 |
| **WHAT A WONDERFUL WORLD**<br>G.Weiss/G.Douglas<br>Columbia recorded 13/8/70<br>Peter Matz | SOMETHING | CBS | 64217 |

| | | | |
|---|---|---|---|
| ✓ **WHAT ARE YOU AFRAID OF?** <br> J.Segal/R.Wells <br> Columbia recorded 9/1/86 <br> Jorge Calandrelli | THE ART OF EXCELLENCE <br> FORTY YEARS VOL 4 | CBS <br> COLUMBIA | 26990 <br> 46843 |
| **WHAT CHILD IS THIS?** <br> Trad <br> Columbia recorded 1/9/67 <br> Marion Evans | GREAT SONGS OF CHRISTMAS | COLUMBIA | CSP888 |
| **WHAT GOOD DOES IT DO?** <br> Y.Harburg/H.Arlen <br> Columbia recorded 18/8/60 <br> Glenn Osser | A STRING OF HAROLD ARLEN | COLUMBIA | CL1559 |
| ✓ live recording Columbia <br> Ralph Sharon 9/6/62 | AT CARNEGIE HALL 2 | CBS | 62117 |
| **WHAT MAKES IT HAPPEN?** <br> S.Cahn/J.Van Heusen <br> Columbia recorded 26/11/66 <br> Marion Evans | TONY MAKES IT HAPPEN | CBS | 63055 |
| **WHAT THE WORLD NEEDS** <br>    **NOW IS LOVE** <br> B.Bacharach/H.David <br> Columbia recorded 27/3/69 <br> Torrie Zito | I'VE GOTTA BE ME <br> THE TROLLEY SONG <br> 20 GREATEST HITS | CBS <br> EMBASSY <br> WARWICK | 63685 <br> 31002 <br> PA5021 |
| ✓ live Columbia recording <br> Robert Farnon 31/1/71 | GET HAPPY | CBS | 64577 |
| **WHAT WILL I TELL MY HEART?** <br> Tinturin/Lawrence <br> Columbia recorded 31/7/53 <br> Gil Evans with The Pastels <br> not released | | | |
| re-recorded Columbia 4/1/55 <br> Percy Faith | THE VOICE OF YOUR CHOICE | PHILIPS | BBR 8051 |
| **WHATEVER LOLA WANTS** <br>    **(LOLA GETS)** <br> Adler/Ross <br> Columbia recorded 9/6/55 <br> Sid Feller | ALL STAR POPS <br> SINGLE | COLUMBIA <br> PHILIPS | CL728 <br> PB672 |
| **WHEN DO THE BELLS** <br> ✓   **RING FOR ME?** <br> C.Deforest <br> Columbia recorded 18/5/89 <br> Jorge Calandrelli | ASTORIA:PORTRAIT OF THE <br>   ARTIST <br> FORTY YEARS VOL 4 | CBS <br> COLUMBIA | 466005 <br> 46843 |

| | | | |
|---|---|---|---|
| **WHEN I FALL IN LOVE**<br>V.Young/E.Heyman<br>Columbia recorded 30/12/58<br>Ralph Sharon & Count Basie | IN PERSON!<br>WHEN I FALL IN LOVE | CBS<br>HALLMARK | 62250<br>SHM817 |
| **WHEN I LOOK IN YOUR EYES**<br>L.Bricusse<br>Columbia recorded 2/4/70<br>Peter Matz | SOMETHING | CBS | 64217 |
| ✓ **WHEN I LOST YOU**<br>I.Berlin<br>Columbia recorded 27/5/87<br>Tony Bennett (Acappella) | BENNETT:BERLIN<br>FORTY YEARS VOL 4 | CBS<br>COLUMBIA | 460450<br>46843 |
| ✓ **WHEN IN ROME**<br>C.Coleman/C.Leigh<br>Fantasy recorded 10-13/6/75<br>Bill Evans | BENNETT/BILL EVANS ALBUM | FANTASY | FT527 |
| **WHEN IT'S SLEEPY TIME DOWN SOUTH**<br>Columbia recorded 15/1/68<br>Torrie Zito with Dominic Germano<br>not released | | | |
| ✓ **WHEN JOANNA LOVED ME**<br>R.Wells/J.Segal<br>Columbia recorded 17/9/63<br>Marty Manning | THE MANY MOODS OF TONY<br>GREATEST HITS<br>LOVE STORY<br>20 GREATEST HITS<br>FORTY YEARS VOL 2<br>SINGLE | CBS<br>CBS<br>CBS<br>WARWICK<br>COLUMBIA<br>CBS | 62245<br>62821<br>64368<br>PA5021<br>46843<br>AAG191 |
| live Columbia recorded 8/4/64<br>Louis Basil with Ralph Sharon Trio<br>not released | | | |
| live MTV recorded 4/94<br>with the Ralph Sharon Trio | MTV UNPLUGGED | COLUMBIA | 477170 |
| ✓ **WHEN LIGHTS ARE LOW**<br>Carter/Williams<br>Columbia recorded 26/3/64<br>Ralph Sharon | WHEN LIGHTS ARE LOW<br>JAZZ | CBS<br>CBS | 62296<br>450465 |
| **WHEN LOVE WAS ALL WE HAD**<br>J.Calandrelli/S.Mihanovic<br>Columbia recorded 1985<br>Jorge Calandrelli | THE ART OF EXCELLENCE | CBS | 26990 |

| | | | |
|---|---|---|---|
| **WHEN THE SUN COMES OUT**<br>T.Koehler/H.Arlen<br>Columbia recorded 17/8/60<br>Glenn Osser | A STRING OF HAROLD ARLEN<br>LET'S FALL IN LOVE WITH .. | COLUMBIA<br>CBS | CL1559<br>88131 |
| **WHERE DID THE MAGIC GO?**<br>P.Erickson/B.Weed<br>Columbia recorded 1989<br>Jorge Calandrelli | ASTORIA: PORTRAIT OF THE<br>ARTIST | CBS | 466005 |
| **WHERE DO YOU GO<br>　FROM LOVE?**<br>C.DeForest<br>Columbia recorded 1989<br>Jorge Calandrelli | ASTORIA: PORTRAIT OF THE<br>ARTIST | CBS | 466005 |
| **WHERE IS LOVE?**<br>L.Bart<br>Columbia recorded 1/10/68<br>Robert Farnon | SNOWFALL, THE CHRISTMAS<br>ALBUM | CBS | 477597 |
| **WHERE OR WHEN**<br>R.Rodgers/L.Hart<br>Columbia recorded 28/10/59<br>Ralph Sharon | TONY SINGS FOR TWO<br>LOVE SONGS<br>GREAT SONGS FROM THE SHOWS | COLUMBIA<br>CBS<br>PICKWICK | CL1446<br>66297<br>4171 |
| **WHILE THE MUSIC PLAYS ON**<br>I.Mills/L.Fien/E.Heim<br>Columbia recorded 11/8/54<br>Chuck Wayne | CLOUD 7<br>JAZZ<br>FORTY YEARS VOL 1 | COLUMBIA<br>COLUMBIA<br>COLUMBIA | CL621<br>450465<br>46843 |
| **WHILE WE'RE YOUNG**<br>Engvick/Wilder/Palitz<br>Columbia recorded 31/5/51<br>Percy Faith | BLUE VELVET<br>BECAUSE OF YOU | COLUMBIA<br>COLUMBIA | CL1292<br>CL6221 |
| live recording Improv 13-14/5/77<br>with the MacPartlands | THE MACPARTLANDS & FRIENDS<br>MAKE BEAUTIFUL MUSIC | IMPROV | 7123 |
| **WHITE CHRISTMAS**<br>I.Berlin<br>Columbia recorded 1967<br>Robert Farnon | SNOWFALL, THE CHRISTMAS<br>ALBUM | CBS | 63782 |
| re-recorded Columbia 1987<br>Tony Bennett | BENNETT:BERLIN | CBS | 460450 |

| | | | |
|---|---|---|---|
| **WHO CAN I TURN TO? (WHEN NOBODY NEEDS ME)** L.Bricusse/A.Newley Columbia recorded 14/8/64 George Siravo | WHO CAN I TURN TO TONY BENNETT SINGS FORTY YEARS VOL 3 THE GOLDEN TOUCH ALL-TIME GREATEST HITS GREATEST HITS 20 GREATEST HITS 16 MOST REQUESTED SONGS THE BEST OF TONY BENNETT TONY! GREAT SONGS FROM THE SHOWS SINGLE SINGLE SINGLE (PROMO) | CBS R/DIGEST COLUMBIA COLUMBIA CBS CBS WARWICK CBS CBS CBS PICKWICK CBS CBS CBS | 62486 8070 46843 P12790 68200 62821 PA5021 57056 6151 32171 4171 201735 AAG225 43141 |
| as above with spoken intro 1970 | ALL TIME HALL OF FAME HITS | CBS | 64200 |
| live recording Columbia H.Roberts (A&R) 11/8/67 not released | | | |
| **WHO CARES (SO LONG AS YOU CARE FOR ME)** G.Gershwin/I.Gershwin Columbia recorded 18/7/67 John Bunch | FORTY YEARS VOL 4 | COLUMBIA | 46843 |
| re-recorded 1994 Tony Bennett & Ralph Sharon | STEPPIN' OUT | COLUMBIA | 474360 |
| **WHOEVER YOU ARE, I LOVE YOU** B.Bacharach/H.David Columbia recorded 25/2/69 Torrie Zito | I'VE GOTTA BE ME | CBS | 63685 |
| **WHY DO PEOPLE FALL IN LOVE?/PEOPLE** Lambert/Potter,Styne/Merrill Columbia recorded 11/1/86 Jorge Calandrelli | THE ART OF EXCELLENCE FORTY YEARS VOL 4 | CBS COLUMBIA | 26990 46843 |
| **WHY DOES IT HAVE TO BE ME?** Columbia recorded 13/10/53 Percy Faith | SINGLE | COLUMBIA | 40121 |
| **WINTER WONDERLAND** R.Smith/F.Bernard Columbia recorded 1/10/68 Robert Farnon | SNOWFALL, THE CHRISTMAS ALBUM | CBS | 63782 |

| | | | |
|---|---|---|---|
| **WITH PLENTY OF MONEY AND YOU**<br>Roulette released 1961<br>Count Basie | STRIKE UP THE BAND | ROULETTE | 25231 |
| **WITHOUT A SONG**<br>B.Rose/E.Eliscu/V.Youmans<br>Columbia recorded 12/9/56<br>Ray Conniff | TONY<br>TONY BENNETT SHOWCASE | COLUMBIA<br>PHILIPS | CL938<br>BBL7138 |
| re-recorded Columbia 22/12/58<br>Ralph Sharon & Count Basie  9/6/6L | IN PERSON!   CARNEGIE HALL | CBS | 62250 |
| **WONDERFUL ONE**<br>Terriss/Whiteman/Grofe<br>Columbia recorded 10/11/59<br>Frank De Vol | TO MY WONDERFUL ONE | COLUMBIA | CL1429 |
| **WRAP YOUR TROUBLES IN DREAMS (AND DREAM YOUR TROUBLES AWAY)**<br>T.Koehler/B.Moll/H.Barris<br>Columbia recorded 29/9/64<br>George Siravo | WHO CAN I TURN TO<br>FORTY YEARS VOL 3 | CBS<br>COLUMBIA | 62486<br>46843 |
| re-recorded Columbia 14/10/64<br>George Siravo<br>not released | | | |
| **YELLOW DAYS**<br>A.Bernstein/A.Carrillo<br>Columbia recorded 1970<br>Peter Matz | SOMETHING<br>TONY! | CBS<br>CBS | 64217<br>32171 |
| **YESTERDAY I HEARD THE RAIN (ESTA TARDE VI LLOVER)**<br>G.Lees/A.Manzanero<br>Columbia recorded 26/2/68<br>Torrie Zito | YESTERDAY I HEARD THE RAIN<br>ALL TIME HALL OF FAME HITS<br>GREATEST HITS VOL 2 | CBS<br>CBS<br>CBS | 63351<br>64200<br>63612 |
| **YESTERDAYS**<br>O.Harbach/J.Kern<br>Columbia recorded 26/2/64<br>Ralph Sharon | A TIME FOR LOVE<br>SUNRISE, SUNSET | CBS<br>CBS | 62800<br>32239 |
| **YOU CAN DEPEND ON ME**<br>Columbia recorded 11/9/56<br>Ray Conniff | TONY<br>TONY BENNETT SHOWCASE | COLUMBIA<br>PHILIPS | CL938<br>BBL7138 |

YOU CAN'T LOVE 'EM ALL
S.Cahn/J.Van Heusen
Columbia recorded 23/3/59
Ralph Sharon
Unreleased track

| re-recorded Columbia 24/6/59 | A STRING OF HITS | CBS | 66010 |
| Ralph Burns | SINGLE | PHILIPS | PB961 |

re-recorded Columbia 26/2/64
not released

live Columbia recorded 8/4/64
Louis Basil with Ralph Sharon Trio
not released

re-recorded Columbia 14/10/64
George Siravo
not released

YOU COULD MAKE ME
   SMILE AGAIN     SINGLE     COLUMBIA     39815
Columbia recorded 30/4/52
Percy Faith

YOU DON'T KNOW WHAT
|    LOVE IS | TOGETHER AGAIN | IMPROV | 7117 |
| Raye/DePaul | TOGETHER AGAIN | NELSON | CD1122 |
| Improv recorded c1977 | UNFORGETTABLE | CASTLE | UNLP019 |
| Bill Evans | STAGE & SCREEN HITS | DBM | 1001 |

✓

YOU GO TO MY HEAD
A.Gillespie/J.Coots
Columbia recorded 14/10/57
Ralph Sharon
not released

✓

*THE BEAT OF*
*MY HEART*

| re-recorded Columbia 1993 | PERFECTLY FRANK | COLUMBIA | 472222 |
| with the Ralph Sharon Trio |

✓

| YOU MUST BELIEVE IN SPRING | TOGETHER AGAIN | IMPROV | 7117 |
| Bergman/M.LeGrand | TOGETHER AGAIN | NELSON | CD1122 |
| Improv recorded c1977 | STAGE & SCREEN HITS | DBM | 1001 |
| Bill Evans |

| YOU SHOWED ME THE WAY | HERE'S TO THE LADIES | COLUMBIA | 481266 |
| Green/Fitzgerald/McCrae/Webb |
| Columbia recorded 1995 |
| Jorge Calandrelli & Bill Holman |

✓

| | | | |
|---|---|---|---|
| YOU TOOK ADVANTAGE OF ME<br>R.Rodgers/L.Hart<br>Columbia recorded 4/4/61<br>Ralph Burns | MY HEART SINGS | COLUMBIA | CL1658 |
| re-recorded Improv c1973<br>with the Ruby Braff/<br>George Barnes Quartet | MORE RODGERS & HART SONGS<br>RODGERS & HART SONGBOOK | IMPROV<br>NELSON | 7120<br>CD1129 |
| YOUNG AND FOOLISH<br>Horwitt/Hague<br>Columbia recorded 22/4/63<br>Ralph Burns | THIS IS ALL I ASK | CBS | 62205 |
| re-recorded Fantasy<br>Bill Evans 10-13/6/75 | BENNETT/BILL EVANS ALBUM | FANTASY | FT527 |
| YOUNG AND WARM AND WONDERFUL<br>Zaret/Singer<br>Columbia recorded 10/4/58 | A STRING OF HITS<br>20 ALL TIME GREATS OF 50'S<br>SINGLE | CBS<br>K-TEL<br>PHILIPS | 66010<br>TU440<br>PB831 |
| YOUNG AT HEART<br>C.Leigh/J.Richards<br>Columbia recorded 1994<br>duet with Shawn Colvin | IT COULD HAPPEN TO YOU | COLUMBIA | 66184 |
| YOU'LL NEVER GET AWAY FROM ME<br>S.Sondheim/J.Styne<br>Columbia recorded 23/3/59 | MR BROADWAY<br>A STRING OF HITS<br>SUNRISE, SUNSET<br>SINGLE | COLUMBIA<br>CBS<br>CBS<br>CBS | CL1763<br>66010<br>32239<br>AAG126 |
| YOU'RE ALL THE WORLD TO ME<br>A.Lerner/B.Lane<br>Columbia recorded 1994<br>Tony Bennett & Ralph Sharon | STEPPIN' OUT | COLUMBIA | 474360 |
| live MTV recorded 4/94<br>with the Ralph Sharon Trio | MTV UNPLUGGED | COLUMBIA | 477170 |
| YOU'RE SO EASY TO DANCE WITH/CHANGE PARTNERS/ CHEEK TO CHEEK<br>I.Berlin<br>Columbia recorded 1994<br>Tony Bennett & Ralph Sharon | STEPPIN' OUT | COLUMBIA | 474360 |

| | | | |
|---|---|---|---|
| **YOU'RE NEARER**<br>R.Rodgers/L.Hart<br>Improv recorded c1977<br>Bill Evans | TOGETHER AGAIN<br>TOGETHER AGAIN<br>STAGE & SCREEN HITS | IMPROV<br>NELSON<br>DBM | 7117<br>CD1122<br>1001 |
| **YOU'RE SO RIGHT FOR ME**<br>Randazzo/Pike<br>Columbia recorded 4/2/58<br>Ralph Sharon | HITS FROM OH CAPTAIN! | COLUMBIA | CL1167 |
| **YOU'VE CHANGED**<br>B.Carey/C.Fischer<br>Columbia recorded 13/3/62<br>Ralph Sharon<br>featuring the Noteworthies<br>+album unreleased | THE MANY MOODS OF TONY<br>ON THE GLORY ROAD+ | CBS<br>COLUMBIA | 62245<br>CL1813 |

## THE ALBUMS OF TONY BENNETT

**BECAUSE OF YOU (10")**
ALBUM 7/52 COL CL 6221
Original EP b314 (4-39824-4-39827)
tracks 2,4,5 & 6 Marty Manning
others Percy Faith

| | |
|---|---|
| BECAUSE OF YOU | 1 |
| BOULEVARD OF BROKEN DREAMS | 2 |
| WHILE WE'RE YOUNG | 3 |
| I WANNA BE LOVED | 4 |
| ONCE THERE LIVED A FOOL | 5 |
| THE VALENTINO TANGO | 6 |
| I WON'T CRY ANYMORE | 7 |
| COLD, COLD HEART | 8 |

**CLOUD 7**
ALBUM 2/55 COL CL 621 PHILIPS BBR.8089
Reissued CBS SONY JAPAN 50PJ99 1954
Featuring CHUCK WAYNE on Guitar
My Reverie is not on Philips 10" album
Chuck Wayne

| | |
|---|---|
| I FALL IN LOVE TOO EASILY | 1 |
| MY BABY JUST CARES FOR ME | 2 |
| MY HEART TELLS ME | 3 |
| OLD DEVIL MOON | 4 |
| LOVE LETTERS | 5 |
| MY REVERIE | 6 |
| GIVE ME THE SIMPLE LIFE | 7 |
| WHILE THE MUSIC PLAYS ON | 8 |
| I CAN'T BELIEVE YOU'RE IN LOVE WITH ME | 9 |
| DARN THAT DREAM | 10 |

**ALONE AT LAST (10")**
ALBUM 10/55 COL CL2507 HOUSE PARTY SERIES

| | |
|---|---|
| SING YOU SINNERS | 1 |
| SOMEWHERE ALONG THE WAY | 2 |
| SINCE MY LOVE HAS GONE | 3 |
| STRANGER IN PARADISE | 4 |
| HERE IN MY HEART | 5 |
| PLEASE DRIVER (ONCE AROUND THE PARK AGAIN) | 6 |

**THE VOICE OF YOUR CHOICE**
ALBUM 10" UK PHILIPS BBR 8051
track 3 Sid Feller, remainder Percy Faith

| | |
|---|---|
| THERE'LL BE NO TEARDROPS TONIGHT | 1 |
| TAKE ME BACK AGAIN | 2 |
| SOMETHING'S GOTTA GIVE | 3 |
| STRANGER IN PARADISE | 4 |
| CLOSE YOUR EYES | 5 |
| WHAT WILL I TELL MY HEART? | 6 |
| TELL ME THAT YOU LOVE ME | 7 |
| HOW CAN I REPLACE YOU? | 8 |

**BECAUSE OF YOU**
ALBUM 26/3/56 COL CL 2550
Percy Faith

| | |
|---|---|
| CLOSE YOUR EYES | 1 |
| I CAN'T GIVE YOU ANYTHING BUT LOVE | 2 |
| BOULEVARD OF BROKEN DREAMS | 3 |
| BECAUSE OF YOU | 4 |
| MAY I NEVER LOVE AGAIN | 5 |
| CINNAMON SINNER | 6 |

**TONY BENNETT SHOWCASE**
ALBUM 4/1/57 COL CL 938 as **"TONY"**
CBS/SONY 20 AP 1495
UK PHILIPS BBL 7138 **"TONY BENNETT SHOWCASE"**

| | |
|---|---|
| IT HAD TO BE YOU | 1 |
| YOU CAN DEPEND ON ME | 2 |
| I'M JUST A LUCKY SO AND SO | 3 |
| TAKING A CHANCE ON LOVE | 4 |
| THESE FOOLISH THINGS | 5 |

track 11 Percy Faith, remainder Ray Coniff

| | |
|---|---|
| I CAN'T GIVE YOU ANYTHING BUT LOVE | 6 |
| BOULEVARD OF BROKEN DREAMS | 7 |
| I'LL BE SEEING YOU | 8 |
| ALWAYS | 9 |
| LOVE WALKED IN | 10 |
| LOST IN THE STARS | 11 |
| WITHOUT A SONG | 12 |

**THE BEAT OF MY HEART**
ALBUM 9/12/57 COL CL1079/GCB20
PHILIPS BBL7219
Ralph Sharon

| | |
|---|---|
| LET'S BEGIN | 1 |
| LULLABY OF BROADWAY | 2 |
| LET THERE BE LOVE | 3 |
| LOVE FOR SALE | 4 |
| ARMY AIR CORPS SONG | 5 |
| CRAZY RHYTHM | 6 |
| THE BEAT OF MY HEART | 7 |
| SO BEATS MY HEART FOR YOU | 8 |
| BLUES IN THE NIGHT | 9 |
| LAZY AFTERNOON | 10 |
| LET'S FACE THE MUSIC AND DANCE | 11 |
| JUST ONE OF THOSE THINGS | 12 |

**JUST ONE OF THOSE THINGS**
HALLMARK SHM646 CBS HS11340 7/69

as above tracks 5 & 8 deleted

**BENNETT & BASIE - STRIKE UP THE BAND**
ALBUM 1961 ROULETTE SR 25231
(**BASIE/BENNETT SINGS** 1958)
with Count Basie

| | |
|---|---|
| STRIKE UP THE BAND | 1 |
| I GUESS I'LL HAVE TO CHANGE MY PLANS | 2 |
| CHICAGO | 3 |
| WITH PLENTY OF MONEY AND YOU | 4 |
| GROWING PAINS | 5 |
| LIFE IS A SONG | 6 |
| I'VE GROWN ACCUSTOMED TO HER FACE | 7 |
| JEEPERS CREEPERS | 8 |
| ANYTHING GOES | 9 |
| POOR LITTLE RICH GIRL | 10 |
| ARE YOU HAVING ANY FUN? | 11 |

**ONE NIGHT STAND**
ALLEGRO 799

as above track 4 deleted

also issued as:-
THE SONG STYLISTS CLASSIC JAZZ CD1076 1993 with Mel Torme
CHICAGO ASTAN LP 20029 12/84
SINGS FOR YOU CD 1995 CHARLY
BIG BAND BASH
JEEPERS CREEPERS B2634
GOLDEN HOUR WITH SARAH VAUGHAN GH869
TONY BENNETT/AL TORNELLO Guest star G1485 - some tracks (3/5/7/11)
ANYTHING GOES Bulldog bdl 1054 track 1 deleted
COUNT BASIE FEATURING TONY BENNETT PICKWICK
BASIE BENNETT EP esg 7790 - some tracks (3/4/8/10/11)

GREAT ARTISTES - GREAT HITS SAGA EROS 8138 various artists (tracks 7&9)
CAPITOL SINGS COAST TO COAST 80180-2 1994 - Chicago only
THE SINGER AND THE SONG PREMIER JAZZ JA9 - Anything goes
TONY BENNETT/COUNT BASIE EROS 8076
BENNETT & BASIE VOGUE 500005 1985
SONG STYLIST HARMONY LABEL
BENNETT/BASIE LASERLIGHT
MEL TORME/TONY BENNETT FAT BOY
and many others . . .

**BASIE/BENNETT**                    AFTER SUPPER            -
as "Strike up the Band" Roulette
Japan CD TOCS 5378 has bonus track
previously unreleased.

| **LONG AGO AND FAR AWAY** | IT COULD HAPPEN TO YOU | 1 |
|---|---|---|
| ALBUM 28/7/58 COL CL 1186 | EVERYTIME WE SAY GOODBYE | 2 |
| PHILIPS BBL7219 | LONG AGO (AND FAR AWAY) | 3 |
| CBS/SONY 22 AP 2523 1984 | IT AMAZES ME | 4 |
| Frank De Vol except tracks 7 & 11 | THE WAY YOU LOOK TONIGHT | 5 |
| Ralph Sharon | BE CAREFUL, IT'S MY HEART | 6 |
| | MY FOOLISH HEART | 7 |
| | TIME AFTER TIME | 8 |
| | FOOLS RUSH IN | 9 |
| | A COTTAGE FOR SALE | 10 |
| | BLUE MOON | 11 |
| | SO FAR | 12 |

| **IN PERSON! WITH COUNT BASIE** | JUST IN TIME | 1 |
|---|---|---|
| ALBUM 9/3/59 CBS 62250 CL 1294/ CS 8104 | WHEN I FALL IN LOVE | 2 |
| (Fake audience) PHILIPS S/BBL 7308/542 | TAKING A CHANCE ON LOVE | 3 |
| LTD ED CBS CAMEO LE 10125 | WITHOUT A SONG | 4 |
| Repackage RCA SL 4010 **ALL YOURS** | FASCINATIN' RHYTHM | 5 |
| CBS DIAMOND MEMORIES 22184 | SOLITUDE | 6 |
| COL LEGACY CK 64276 CD (without audience) | PENNIES FROM HEAVEN | 7 |
| Ralph Sharon with Count Basie Orchestra | LOST IN THE STARS | 8 |
| | FIREFLY | 9 |
| | THERE WILL NEVER BE ANOTHER YOU | 10 |
| | LULLABY OF BROADWAY | 11 |
| | OL' MAN RIVER | 12 |

| **BLUE VELVET** | BLUE VELVET | 1 |
|---|---|---|
| ALBUM 8/6/59 COL CL1292 | I WON'T CRY ANYMORE | 2 |
| Percy Faith | HAVE A GOOD TIME | 3 |
| | CONGRATULATIONS TO SOMEONE | 4 |
| | HERE COMES THAT HEARTACHE AGAIN | 5 |
| | WHILE WE'RE YOUNG | 6 |
| | SOLITAIRE | 7 |
| | MY HEART WON'T SAY GOODBYE | 8 |
| | UNTIL YESTERDAY | 9 |
| | FUNNY THING | 10 |
| | MAY I NEVER LOVE AGAIN | 11 |
| | IT'S SO PEACEFUL IN THE COUNTRY | 12 |

| | | |
|---|---|---|
| **HOMETOWN, MY TOWN** | THE SKYSCRAPER BLUES | 1 |
| ALBUM 13/7/59 COL CL1301 | PENTHOUSE SERENADE (WHEN WE'RE | |
| Ralph Burns | ALONE) | 2 |
| | BY MYSELF | 3 |
| | I COVER THE WATERFRONT | 4 |
| | LOVE IS HERE TO STAY | 5 |
| | THE PARTY'S OVER | 6 |
| | | |
| **TO MY WONDERFUL ONE** | WONDERFUL ONE | 1 |
| ALBUM 15/2/60 CL1429/CS8226 | TILL | 2 |
| PHILIPS BBL7413 | SEPTEMBER SONG | 3 |
| CBS DIAMOND MEMORIES 22184 | SUDDENLY | 4 |
| Frank De Vol | I'M A FOOL TO WANT YOU | 5 |
| | WE MUSTN'T SAY GOODBYE | 6 |
| | AUTUMN LEAVES | 7 |
| | LAURA | 8 |
| | APRIL IN PARIS | 9 |
| | SPEAK LOW | 10 |
| | TENDERLY | 11 |
| | LAST NIGHT WHEN WE WERE YOUNG | 12 |
| | | |
| **ALONE TOGETHER** | ALONE TOGETHER | 1 |
| ALBUM 11/7/60 CL1471/CS8262 | THIS IS ALL I ASK | 2 |
| PHILIPS BBL7452 | OUT OF THIS WORLD | 3 |
| CBS P11489 | WALK IN THE COUNTRY | 4 |
| Frank De Vol | I'M ALWAYS CHASING RAINBOWS | 5 |
| | POOR BUTTERFLY | 6 |
| | AFTER YOU'VE GONE | 7 |
| | GONE WITH THE WIND | 8 |
| | IT'S MAGIC | 9 |
| | HOW LONG HAS THIS BEEN GOING ON? | 10 |
| | SOPHISTICATED LADY | 11 |
| | FOR HEAVEN'S SAKE | 12 |

**A STRING OF HITS**
Compilation double album CBS 66010 1966
UK issue of US albums **TONY'S GREATEST HITS** and **MORE GREATEST HITS** in one package.

| | | |
|---|---|---|
| **A STRING OF HITS (RECORD 1)** | STRANGER IN PARADISE | 1 |
| (**TONY'S GREATEST HITS**) 3/11/58 | COLD HEART | 2 |
| CL1229/CS8652 COL, | BECAUSE OF YOU | 3 |
| Percy Faith tracks 1-5,9,10,12 | RAGS TO RICHES | 4 |
| Neal Hefti track 8 | BOULEVARD OF BROKEN DREAMS | 5 |
| | YOUNG AND WARM AND WONDERFUL | 6 |
| | IN THE MIDDLE OF AN ISLAND | 7 |
| | CA, C'EST L'AMOUR | 8 |
| | JUST IN TIME | 9 |
| | THERE'LL BE NO TEARDROPS TONIGHT | 10 |
| | ANYWHERE I WANDER | 11 |
| | SING YOU SINNERS | 12 |

**A STRING OF HITS (RECORD 2)**
**(MORE OF TONY'S GREATEST HITS)** 17/10/60
COMPILATION CL1535/CS8335/P13301
Ralph Burns tracks 1,7,8
Ralph Sharon track 2
Ray Ellis tracks 3,10,11
Frank De Vol tracks 4,6,12
Glenn Osser track 6

| | |
|---|---|
| SMILE | 1 |
| YOU'LL NEVER GET AWAY FROM ME | 2 |
| I AM | 3 |
| PUT ON A HAPPY FACE | 4 |
| LOVE LOOK AWAY | 5 |
| I'LL BRING YOU A RAINBOW | 6 |
| ASK ANYONE IN LOVE | 7 |
| YOU CAN'T LOVE THEM ALL | 8 |
| BABY TALK TO ME | 9 |
| FIREFLY | 10 |
| THE NIGHT THAT HEAVEN FELL | 11 |
| CLIMB EVERY MOUNTAIN | 12 |

**A STRING OF HAROLD ARLEN**
ALBUM 14/11/60 COL CL1559/CS8359/CQ356
PHILIPS S/BBL 7455/609
**LET'S FALL IN LOVE WITH SONGS BY**
**HAROLD ARLEN & CY COLEMAN** Record 1
Reissue 5/75 CBS 88131 (2 Tracks del 5&9)
Glenn Osser

| | |
|---|---|
| WHEN THE SUN COMES OUT | 1 |
| OVER THE RAINBOW | 2 |
| HOUSE OF FLOWERS | 3 |
| COME RAIN OR COME SHINE | 4 |
| FOR EVERY MAN THERE'S A WOMAN | 5 |
| LETS FALL IN LOVE | 6 |
| RIGHT AS THE RAIN | 7 |
| IT WAS WRITTEN IN THE STARS | 8 |
| WHAT GOOD DOES IT DO? | 9 |
| FUN TO BE FOOLED | 10 |
| THIS TIME THE DREAM'S ON ME | 11 |
| I'VE GOT THE WORLD ON A STRING | 12 |

**TONY SINGS FOR TWO**
ALBUM 6/2/61 CL1446/CS8242
PHILIPS BBL7479
CBS SONY 22 AP 2416 JAPAN BBL 625
Ralph Sharon

| | |
|---|---|
| I DIDN'T KNOW WHAT TIME IT WAS | 1 |
| BEWITCHED | 2 |
| NOBODY'S HEART BELONGS TO ME | 3 |
| I'M THRU' WITH LOVE | 4 |
| MY FUNNY VALENTINE | 5 |
| THE MAN THAT GOT AWAY | 6 |
| WHERE OR WHEN | 7 |
| A SLEEPIN' BEE | 8 |
| HAPPINESS IS A THING CALLED JOE | 9 |
| MAM'SELLE | 10 |
| JUST FRIENDS | 11 |
| STREET OF DREAMS | 12 |
| SKYLARK (out take cd only) | 13 |

**MY HEART SINGS**
ALBUM 7/8/61 CL1658/CS8458
PHILIPS BBL7495
Ralph Burns

| | |
|---|---|
| DON'T WORRY 'BOUT ME | 1 |
| DANCING IN THE DARK | 2 |
| I'M COMING VIRGINIA | 3 |
| MY HEART SINGS | 4 |
| IT NEVER WAS YOU | 5 |
| YOU TOOK ADVANTAGE OF ME | 6 |
| CLOSE YOUR EYES | 7 |
| STELLA BY STARLIGHT | 8 |
| MORE THAN YOU KNOW | 9 |
| MY SHIP | 10 |
| LOVER MAN | 11 |
| TOOT, TOOT, TOOTSIE! (GOODBYE) | 12 |

**MR BROADWAY: TONY'S GREATEST BROADWAY HITS**
COMPILATION 19/3/62 CL 1763/CS 8563
CBS P13574 SP PRO.
Percy Faith tracks 1,11
Frank De Vol track 3
Glenn Osser track 6
Ralph Burns track 8
Ralph Sharon tracks 5,10,12

| | |
|---|---|
| JUST IN TIME | 1 |
| YOU'LL NEVER GET AWAY FROM ME | 2 |
| PUT ON A HAPPY FACE | 3 |
| FOLLOW ME | 4 |
| CLIMB EVERY MOUNTAIN | 5 |
| LOVE LOOK AWAY | 6 |
| COMES ONCE IN A LIFETIME | 7 |
| THE PARTY'S OVER (Edited) | 8 |
| BABY TALK TO ME | 9 |
| BEGIN THE BEGUINE | 10 |
| STRANGER IN PARADISE | 11 |
| LAZY AFTERNOON | 12 |

**I LEFT MY HEART IN SAN FRANCISCO**
ALBUM 16/6/62 CBS 62201
CL1869/CS8669/CQ493
Reissue CBS 22011/CG 33612 1975 CAMEO 1986
CD 902288 2 1990 COL COLLECTORS CHOICE
CD **TWO ON ONE** 477592 2 1994 COLUMBIA
Reissue **SAN FRANCISCO** DTO 10040A
DITTO MC
Marty Manning tracks 1,2,3,7,8
Cy Coleman track 12
Frank de Vol track 11
Ralph Sharon track 5,6
Ralph Burns track 9

| | |
|---|---|
| (I LEFT MY HEART) IN SAN FRANCISCO | 1 |
| ONCE UPON A TIME | 2 |
| TENDER IS THE NIGHT | 3 |
| SMILE | 4 |
| LOVE FOR SALE | 5 |
| TAKING A CHANCE ON LOVE | 6 |
| CANDY KISSES | 7 |
| HAVE I TOLD YOU LATELY? | 8 |
| THE RULES OF THE ROAD | 9 |
| MARRY YOUNG | 10 |
| I'M ALWAYS CHASING RAINBOWS | 11 |
| THE BEST IS YET TO COME | 12 |

**ON THE GLORY ROAD**
ALBUM UNRELEASED
CL 1813/CS 8613 18/6/62
Ralph Sharon
*Tracks are on
The Many Moods of Tony
**I Wanna Be Around

| | |
|---|---|
| SOMETIMES I'M HAPPY | 1 |
| THAT OLD BLACK MAGIC | 2 |
| CARAVAN* | 3 |
| SOON IT'S GONNA RAIN* | 4 |
| I LOVE YOU | 5 |
| SPEAK LOW | 6 |
| YOU'VE CHANGED* | 7 |
| REVOLVIN' JONES | 8 |
| THE LAMP IS LOW | 9 |
| A FOGGY DAY | 10 |
| UNTIL I MET YOU** | 11 |
| THE GLORY ROAD | 12 |

**TONY BENNETT**
  **AT CARNEGIE HALL PART ONE**
LIVE 24/8/62 CBS 62116 CL2L 23/CC5 823
Some tracks compiled to create
**20 GOLDEN GREATS** DEJA VU DVLP 2026
others on **I GRANDI DEL JAZZ** CDJ 91
Ralph Sharon

| | |
|---|---|
| LULLABY OF BROADWAY | 1 |
| JUST IN TIME | 2 |
| ALL THE THINGS YOU ARE | 3 |
| STRANGER IN PARADISE | 4 |
| LOVE IS HERE TO STAY | 5 |
| CLIMB EVERY MOUNTAIN | 6 |
| OL' MAN RIVER | 7 |
| IT AMAZES ME | 8 |
| FIREFLY | 9 |
| (I LEFT MY HEART) IN SAN FRANCISCO | 10 |

|  |  |  |
|---|---|---|
|  | HOW ABOUT YOU/APRIL IN PARIS | 11 |
|  | SOLITUDE | 12 |
|  | I'M JUST A LUCKY SO AND SO | 13 |

**TONY BENNETT**
**AT CARNEGIE HALL PART TWO**
LIVE 24/8/62 CBS 62117 CL2L 23/CC5 823
Ralph Sharon

| | | |
|---|---|---|
| | ALWAYS | 14 |
| | ANYTHING GOES | 15 |
| | BLUE VELVET | 16 |
| | RAGS TO RICHES | 17 |
| | BECAUSE OF YOU | 18 |
| | WHAT GOOD DOES IT DO? | 19 |
| | LOST IN THE STARS | 20 |
| | ONE FOR MY BABY | 21 |
| | LAZY AFTERNOON | 22 |
| | SING YOU SINNERS | 23 |
| | LOVE LOOK AWAY | 24 |
| | SOMETIMES I'M HAPPY | 25 |
| | MY HEART TELLS ME | 26 |
| | DE GLORY ROAD | 27 |

**THE TONY BENNETT COLLECTION**
**20 GOLDEN GREATS**
DEJA VU DVLP 2026

20 tracks from above two albums

**COME NEXT SPRING – SOUNDTRACK**

COME NEXT SPRING

**TONY BENNETT MEETS GENE KRUPA**
SANDY HOOK SH 2067 selected tracks 1963
6 tracks on SUN LABEL P509
Live radio recordings US NATIONAL GUARD
BROADCAST issued 1979 as TONY & GENE

| | | |
|---|---|---|
| | HAVE I TOLD YOU LATELY? | 2 |
| | APRIL IN PARIS | 3 |
| | JUST IN TIME | 5 |
| | (I LEFT MY HEART) IN SAN FRANCISCO | 7 |
| | SOMETIMES I'M HAPPY | 9 |
| | SMALL WORLD IS'NT IT? | 11 |
| | SUNDAY | 14 |
| | FASCINATIN' RHYTHM | 16 |

**TONY BENNETT, STAN GETZ & FRIENDS**
unreleased album CBS 32276 1963

JUST FRIENDS
HAVE YOU MET MISS JONES
OUT OF THIS WORLD

also known as
**SINGIN' TILL THE GIRLS COME HOME**
Columbia FC 38508. Reissue 1983

**I WANNA BE AROUND**
ALBUM 2/63 CBS 62149 CL
1869/CS8800/P13575
CD **TWO ON ONE** 477592 2
Mini LP STEREO SEVEN 6 Tracks CS8800
CQ 557/RCQ 557
Marty Manning

| | | |
|---|---|---|
| | THE GOOD LIFE | 1 |
| | IF I LOVE AGAIN | 2 |
| | I WANNA BE AROUND | 3 |
| | LOVE LOOK AWAY (UK only) | 4 |
| | I'VE GOT YOUR NUMBER (US album) | 4 |
| | UNTIL I MET YOU | 5 |
| | LET'S FACE THE MUSIC AND DANCE | 6 |
| | ONCE UPON A SUMMERTIME | 7 |
| | IF YOU WERE MINE | 8 |
| | I WILL LIVE MY LIFE FOR YOU | 9 |

|  |  |  |
|---|---|---|
|  | SOMEONE TO LOVE | 10 |
|  | IT WAS ME | 11 |
|  | QUIET NIGHTS OF QUIET STARS | 12 |
|  | (CORCOVADO) |  |
| **THIS IS ALL I ASK** | KEEP SMILING AT TROUBLE | 1 |
| ALBUM 22/7/63 CBS 62205 CL2056/CS8856 | AUTUMN IN ROME | 2 |
| Ralph Burns | TRUE BLUE LOU | 3 |
|  | THE WAY THAT I FEEL | 4 |
|  | THIS IS ALL I ASK | 5 |
|  | THE MOMENT OF TRUTH | 6 |
|  | GOT HER OFF MY HANDS (BUT CAN'T GET HER OFF MY MIND) | 7 |
|  | SANDY'S SMILE | 8 |
|  | LONG ABOUT NOW | 9 |
|  | YOUNG AND FOOLISH | 10 |
|  | TRICKS | 11 |
|  | ON THE OTHER SIDE OF THE TRACKS | 12 |
| **THE MANY MOODS OF TONY** | THE LITTLE BOY | 1 |
| ALBUM 13/1/64 CBS 62245 | WHEN JOANNA LOVED ME | 2 |
| CL2141/CS8941/CQ621 | A TASTE OF HONEY | 3 |
| Dick Hyman tracks 1,3,7,10,12 | SOON IT'S GONNA RAIN | 4 |
| Marty Manning tracks 2 | THE KID'S A DREAMER | 5 |
| and arranger track 6 cond by Harold Arlen | SO LONG, BIG TIME | 6 |
| Ralph Sharon tracks 4,5,8,11 | DON'T WAIT TOO LONG | 7 |
| Don Costa track 9 | CARAVAN | 8 |
|  | SPRING IN MANHATTAN | 9 |
|  | I'LL BE AROUND | 10 |
|  | YOU'VE CHANGED | 11 |
|  | LIMEHOUSE BLUES | 12 |
| **WHEN LIGHTS ARE LOW** | NOBODY ELSE BUT ME | 1 |
| ALBUM 11/5/64 62296 CL2175/CS8975/CQ631 | WHEN LIGHTS ARE LOW | 2 |
| Ralph Sharon Trio | ON GREEN DOLPHIN STREET | 3 |
|  | AIN'T MISBEHAVIN' | 4 |
|  | IT'S A SIN TO TELL A LIE | 5 |
|  | I'VE GOT JUST ABOUT EVERYTHING | 6 |
|  | JUDY | 7 |
|  | OH! YOU CRAZY MOON | 8 |
|  | SPEAK LOW | 9 |
|  | IT HAD TO BE YOU | 10 |
|  | IT COULD HAPPEN TO YOU | 11 |
|  | THE RULES OF THE ROAD | 12 |
| **WHO CAN I TURN TO** | WHO CAN I TURN TO | 1 |
| ALBUM 16/11/64 62486 | WRAP YOUR TROUBLES IN DREAMS | 2 |
| CL2285/CS9085/CQ71 SP PRO P13507 | THERE'S A LULL IN MY LIFE | 3 |
| George Siravo | AUTUMN LEAVES | 4 |
|  | I WALK A LITTLE FASTER | 5 |
|  | THE BRIGHTEST SMILE IN TOWN | 6 |
|  | I'VE NEVER SEEN | 7 |

|  |  |
|---|---|
|  | BETWEEN THE DEVIL AND THE |
|  | DEEP BLUE SEA 8 |
|  | LISTEN LITTLE GIRL 9 |
|  | GOT THE GATE ON THE GOLDEN GATE 10 |
|  | WALTZ FOR DEBBIE 11 |
|  | THE BEST THING TO BE IS A PERSON 12 |

**IF I RULED THE WORLD – TONY BENNETT**
**(SONGS FOR THE JET SET)**
Tracks 6 & 12 Substituted on UK version
ALBUM 19/4/65 62544
CL 2343/CS9143/CQ733
reissue **IF I RULED THE WORLD** EMB 31058
1974 on EMBASSY as US original issue
18 KO 0202/ 14 KO 0202
Don Costa all tracks as US version
UK 6 Ralph Burns
12 Ralph Sharon

| | |
|---|---|
| SONG OF THE JET | 1 |
| FLY ME TO THE MOON (IN OTHER WORDS) | 2 |
| HOW INSENSITIVE | 3 |
| IF I RULED THE WORLD | 4 |
| LOVE SCENE | 5 |
| MY SHIP (UK album) | 6 |
| TAKE THE MOMENT (US album) | 6 |
| THEN WAS THEN AND NOW IS NOW | 7 |
| SWEET LORRAINE | 8 |
| THE RIGHT TO LOVE | 9 |
| WATCH WHAT HAPPENS | 10 |
| ALL MY TOMORROWS | 11 |
| LAZY AFTERNOON (UK album) | 12 |
| TWO BY TWO (US album) | 12 |

**TONY BENNETT'S GREATEST HITS**
US VERSION **VOL 3** CL2373/CS9173/CQ748
COMPILATION 19/7/65 CBS 62821 CL 2373
18/14/16 KO 0222
Marty Manning tracks 1,2,3,4,7,10
Ralph Burns tracks 5,9
George Siravo track 6
Dick Hyman track 8
Cy Coleman track 11
Don Costa track 12

| | |
|---|---|
| (I LEFT MY HEART) IN SAN FRANCISCO | 1 |
| I WANNA BE AROUND | 2 |
| QUIET NIGHTS OF QUIET STARS (CORCOVADO) | 3 |
| WHEN JOANNA LOVED ME | 4 |
| THE MOMENT OF TRUTH | 5 |
| WHO CAN I TURN TO? | 6 |
| THE GOOD LIFE | 7 |
| A TASTE OF HONEY | 8 |
| THIS IS ALL I ASK | 9 |
| ONCE UPON A TIME | 10 |
| THE BEST IS YET TO COME | 11 |
| IF I RULED THE WORLD | 12 |

**THE MOVIE SONG ALBUM**
ALBUM 31/1/66 62677 CL2472/CS9272/CQ815
CBS/SONY 22 AP 2415
18/14 10 0048
Johnny Mandel with
Larry Wilcox tracks 1, 10
Neal Hefti track 2
Luiz Bonfa tracks 3, 6
Quincy Jones track 5
Al Cohn tracks 8,9,12
David Rose track 11

| | |
|---|---|
| THE THEME FROM "THE OSCAR" |  |
| MAYBE SEPTEMBER | 1 |
| GIRL TALK | 2 |
| THE GENTLE RAIN | 3 |
| EMILY | 4 |
| THE PAWNBROKER | 5 |
| SAMBA DE ORFEU | 6 |
| THE SHADOW OF YOUR SMILE | 7 |
| SMILE | 8 |
| THE SECOND TIME AROUND | 9 |
| THE DAYS OF WINE AND ROSES | 10 |
| NEVER TOO LATE | 11 |
| THE TROLLEY SONG | 12 |

**THE OSCAR - SOUNDTRACK**
CBS 62684 CS 2950
Tony Bennett sings Maybe September, all other tracks are themes from soundtrack
Percy Faith

THE THEME FROM "THE OSCAR"
MAYBE SEPTEMBER

**MUSIC FOR THE LATE HOURS**
**THE TONY BENNETT SONG BOOK**
THE RALPH SHARON TRIO - instrumental only
CBS ALBUM 62624 1966

Just in time
The good life
Blues for Mr.T
Born to be blue ·
Stranger in town
I wanna be around
Who can I turn to
One for my baby
The kid's a dreamer
Blues for a rainy day
(I left my heart) in San Francisco
You came a long way from St.Louis

This album does not feature Tony Bennett and is included for interest only.

**A TIME FOR LOVE**
ALBUM 29/8/66 62800 CL2560/CS9360/CQ868
18/14 10 0186
Johnny Mandel tracks 1,8,11
Johnny Keating tracks 2,9
Ralph sharon tracks 3,4,5,6
Ralph Burns tracks 7,10
Bobby Hackett on cornet 2,8,9

| | |
|---|---|
| A TIME FOR LOVE | 1 |
| THE VERY THOUGHT OF YOU | 2 |
| TRAPPED IN THE WEB OF LOVE | 3 |
| MY FUNNY VALENTINE | 4 |
| IN THE WEE SMALL HOURS OF THE MORNING | 5 |
| YESTERDAYS | 6 |
| GEORGIA ROSE | 7 |
| THE SHINING SEA | 8 |
| SLEEPY TIME GAL | 9 |
| TOUCH THE EARTH | 10 |
| I'LL ONLY MISS HER WHEN I THINK OF HER | 11 |

**TONY MAKES IT HAPPEN**
ALBUM 6/3/67 CBS 63055 CL2653
Marion Evans

| | |
|---|---|
| ON THE SUNNY SIDE OF THE STREET | 1 |
| A BEAUTIFUL FRIENDSHIP | 2 |
| DON'T GET AROUND MUCH ANYMORE | 3 |
| WHAT MAKES IT HAPPEN? | 4 |
| THE LADY'S IN LOVE WITH YOU | 5 |
| CAN'T GET OUT OF THIS MOOD | 6 |
| I DON'T KNOW WHY (I JUST DO) | 7 |
| I LET A SONG GO OUT OF MY HEART | 8 |
| COUNTRY GIRL | 9 |
| OLD DEVIL MOON | 10 |
| SHE'S FUNNY THAT WAY | 11 |

**FOR ONCE IN MY LIFE**
ALBUM 6/12/67 CBS 63166
CS9573/CL2773/HC996
SP ED LE 10057
18/14 KO 0348
Marion Evans tracks 2,3,6,7
Torrie Zito tracks 1,4,5,9

| | |
|---|---|
| THEY CAN'T TAKE THAT AWAY FROM ME | 1 |
| SOMETHING IN YOUR SMILE | 2 |
| DAYS OF LOVE | 3 |
| BROADWAY/CRAZY RHYTHM/LULLABY OF BROADWAY | 4 |
| FOR ONCE IN MY LIFE | 5 |
| SOMETIMES I'M HAPPY | 6 |

| | | |
|---|---|---|
| David Rose track 8 | OUT OF THIS WORLD | 7 |
| Ralph Burns track 10 | BABY, DREAM YOUR DREAM | 8 |
| | HOW DO YOU SAY AUF WIEDERSEHEN? | 9 |
| | KEEP SMILING AT TROUBLE (TROUBLE'S A BUBBLE) | 10 |

| | | |
|---|---|---|
| **YESTERDAY I HEARD THE RAIN** | YESTERDAY I HEARD THE RAIN | 1 |
| ALBUM 22/7/68 CBS63351 | HI-HO | 2 |
| CL9678/CQ1044/HC1044 | HUSHABYE MOUNTAIN | 3 |
| SP ED LE 1005618/14 KO 0506 | HOME IS THE PLACE | 4 |
| Torrie Zito | LOVE IS HERE TO STAY | 5 |
| | GET HAPPY | 6 |
| | A FOOL OF FOOLS | 7 |
| | I ONLY HAVE EYES FOR YOU | 8 |
| | SWEET GEORGIE FAME | 9 |
| | ONLY THE YOUNG | 10 |
| | THERE WILL NEVER BE ANOTHER YOU | 11 |

| | | |
|---|---|---|
| **SNOWFALL:THE TONY BENNETT CHRISTMAS ALBUM** | SNOWFALL | 1 |
| ALBUM 6/11/68 CBS 63782 CS 9739 | MY FAVOURITE THINGS | 2 |
| reissue CD 477597 2 1994 Bonus track -10 | THE CHRISTMAS SONG | 3 |
| Robert Farnon 1-9 | MEDLEY/CAROLS: | 4 |
| Track 10 live recording from Jon | We wish you a merry Christmas | |
| Stewart TV Show with Ralph Sharon Trio | Silent Night | |
| | O Come, all ye faithful | |
| | Jingle Bells | |
| | Where is love? | |
| | CHRISTMASLAND | 5 |
| | I LOVE THE WINTERWEATHER/I'VE GOT MY LOVE TO KEEP ME WARM | 6 |
| | WHITE CHRISTMAS | 7 |
| | WINTER WONDERLAND | 8 |
| | HAVE YOURSELF A MERRY LITTLE CHRISTMAS | 9 |
| | I'LL BE HOME FOR CHRISTMAS (cd only) | 10 |

| | | |
|---|---|---|
| **GREATEST HITS VOLUME 2** | PEOPLE | 1 |
| (US VERSION **VOL 4**) | FOR ONCE IN MY LIFE | 2 |
| COMPILATION 9/4/69 CBS 63612 | THE SHADOW OF YOUR SMILE | 3 |
| CS9814/HC1144 | YESTERDAY I HEARD THE RAIN | 4 |
| 18/16 IO 0654 | MY FAVOURITE THINGS | 5 |
| Torrie Zito tracks 1,2,4, | WATCH WHAT HAPPENS | 6 |
| Don Costa tracks 6,7,8 | FLY ME TO THE MOON (IN OTHER WORDS) | 7 |
| Ralph Burns track 9 | HOW INSENSITIVE (edited) | 8 |
| Robert Farnon track 5 | GEORGIA ROSE | 9 |
| Al Cohn track track 11 with Luiz Bonfa | A TIME FOR LOVE | 10 |
| Johnny Mandel tracks 3,10 | THE GENTLE RAIN | 11 |

| | | |
|---|---|---|
| **I'VE GOTTA BE ME** | I'VE GOTTA BE ME | 1 |
| ALBUM 21/7/69 CBS 63685 CS9882/HC1180 | OVER THE SUN | 2 |
| 18/16 IO 0714 | PLAY IT AGAIN, SAM | 3 |
| Torrie Zito | ALFIE | 4 |
| | WHAT THE WORLD NEEDS NOW IS LOVE | 5 |

|  |  |
|---|---|
| BABY DON'T YOU QUIT NOW | 6 |
| THAT NIGHT | 7 |
| THEY ALL LAUGHED | 8 |
| A LONELY PLACE | 9 |
| WHOEVER YOU ARE, I LOVE YOU | 10 |
| THEME FROM "VALLEY OF THE DOLLS" | 11 |

**SOMETHING**
ALBUM 14/10/69 64217
C30280/CA30280/CT30280
Peter Matz

|  |  |
|---|---|
| SOMETHING | 1 |
| THE LONG AND WINDING ROAD | 2 |
| EVERYBODY'S TALKIN' | 3 |
| ON A CLEAR DAY | 4 |
| COCO | 5 |
| THINK HOW IT'S GONNA BE | 6 |
| WAVE | 7 |
| MAKE IT EASY ON YOURSELF | 8 |
| COME SATURDAY MORNING | 9 |
| WHEN I LOOK IN YOUR EYES | 10 |
| YELLOW DAYS | 11 |
| WHAT A WONDERFUL WORLD | 12 |

**TONY SINGS THE GREAT HITS OF TODAY**
ALBUM 22/12/69 CBS 63962 CS9980
reissue CBS 22011/CG 33612 75 (with CL1869)
reissue **SAN FRANCISCO** DTO 10040B
DITTO MC
18/16 IO 0876
Peter Matz except track 6 Dee Barton

|  |  |
|---|---|
| MacARTHUR PARK | 1 |
| SOMETHING | 2 |
| THE LOOK OF LOVE | 3 |
| HERE, THERE AND EVERYWHERE | 4 |
| LIVE FOR LIFE | 5 |
| LITTLE GREEN APPLES | 6 |
| ELEANOR RIGBY | 7 |
| MY CHERIE AMOUR | 8 |
| IS THAT ALL THERE IS? | 9 |
| HERE | 10 |
| SUNRISE, SUNSET | 11 |

**ALL TIME HALL OF FAME HITS**
COMPILATION CBS 64200
C/CA/CT/PC30240
with spoken commentary 21/12/70
John Bunch tracks 2,4,8 new versions
Percy Faith tracks 1,3
Marty Manning tracks 5,6
Ralph Burns track 7
Johnny Mandel track 9
George Siravo track 10
Torrie Zito tracks 11,12

|  |  |
|---|---|
| BECAUSE OF YOU | 1 |
| COLD, COLD HEART | 2 |
| RAGS TO RICHES | 3 |
| ONE FOR MY BABY/IT HAD TO BE YOU | 4 |
| (I LEFT MY HEART) IN SAN FRANCISCO | 5 |
| I WANNA BE AROUND | 6 |
| THIS IS ALL I ASK | 7 |
| THE GOOD LIFE | 8 |
| THE SHADOW OF YOUR SMILE | 9 |
| WHO CAN I TURN TO | 10 |
| YESTERDAY I HEARD THE RAIN | 11 |
| FOR ONCE IN MY LIFE | 12 |

**LOVE STORY**
ALBUM 10/2/71 CBS 64368
C/CA/CR/CT30558
Marty Manning tracks 1,7
Ralph Burns tracks 2,3,4
Torrie Zito tracks 5,6,12

|  |  |
|---|---|
| LOVE STORY (WHERE DO I BEGIN) | 1 |
| TEA FOR TWO | 2 |
| I WANT TO BE HAPPY | 3 |
| INDIVIDUAL THING | 4 |
| I DO NOT KNOW A DAY I DID NOT LOVE YOU | 5 |
| THEY CAN'T TAKE THAT AWAY FROM ME | 6 |

Marion Evans track 8
Al Cohn track 9 with Luiz Bonfa
Dick Hyman tracks 10,11

| | |
|---|---|
| WHEN JOANNA LOVED ME | 7 |
| COUNTRY GIRL | 8 |
| THE GENTLE RAIN | 9 |
| SOON IT'S GONNA RAIN | 10 |
| A TASTE OF HONEY | 11 |
| I'LL BEGIN AGAIN | 12 |

**LOVE SONGS**
DOUBLE ALBUM COMPILATION
10/2/71 CBS 66297
(**LOVE STORY** US - GP 14 18 30 0800)
Frank De Vol tracks 1,7,11,13,19
Ralph Sharon tracks 2,6,12,14,16,18,20
Ralph Burns tracks 8,9,10
Johnny Keating track 3
Marty Manning track 4
Torrie Zito track 5
Larry Wilcox track 15
Al Cohn track 17

| | |
|---|---|
| ALONE TOGETHER | 1 |
| BEWITCHED | 2 |
| THE VERY THOUGHT OF YOU | 3 |
| TENDER IS THE NIGHT | 4 |
| I ONLY HAVE EYES FOR YOU | 5 |
| WHERE OR WHEN | 6 |
| LAURA | 7 |
| PENTHOUSE SERENADE | 8 |
| I COVER THE WATERFRONT | 9 |
| STELLA BY STARLIGHT | 10 |
| TENDERLY | 11 |
| I'M THRU' WITH LOVE | 12 |
| SEPTEMBER SONG | 13 |
| MY FUNNY VALENTINE | 14 |
| THE DAYS OF WINE AND ROSES | 15 |
| STREET OF DREAMS | 16 |
| THE SECOND TIME AROUND | 17 |
| IT HAD TO BE YOU | 18 |
| TILL | 19 |
| LOVE FOR SALE | 20 |

**THE VERY THOUGHT OF YOU**
CBS HALLMARK SHM 760 CBS P13402
COMPILATION 18/8/71
HARMONY KH 30758
Percy Faith tracks 1,4
Marion Evans track 2
Johnny Keating track 3
Al Cohn track 5 Ralph Burns track 6
Frank De Vol tracks 7,8
Marty Manning track 0
Dick Hyman track 10

| | |
|---|---|
| JUST IN TIME | 1 |
| DON'T GET AROUND MUCH ANYMORE | 2 |
| THE VERY THOUGHT OF YOU | 3 |
| STRANGER IN PARADISE | 4 |
| THE SECOND TIME AROUND | 5 |
| STELLA BY STARLIGHT | 6 |
| IT'S MAGIC | 7 |
| LAURA | 8 |
| IF I LOVE AGAIN | 9 |
| I'LL BE AROUND | 10 |

**GET HAPPY**
**LIVE with London Philharmonic Orchestra**
CBS 64577 C/CA30953 22/9/71(rec 31/1/71)
Robert Farnon conducting John Bunch Piano arrangers
Marty Manning tracks 1,7,9,18
Ralph Burns tracks 2,5
Don Costa track 3
Torrie Zito tracks 4,12,15,16,17
Dick Cone track 6
Al Cohn track 8
Marion Evans tracks 10,11,14

| | |
|---|---|
| (I LEFT MY HEART) IN SAN FRANCISCO | 1 |
| I WANT TO BE HAPPY | 2 |
| IF I RULED THE WORLD | 3 |
| GET HAPPY | 4 |
| TEA FOR TWO | 5 |
| LET THERE BE LOVE | 6 |
| LOVE STORY (WHERE DO I BEGIN) | 7 |
| THE TROLLEY SONG | 8 |
| I LEFT MY HEART/I WANNA BE AROUND | 9 |
| OLD DEVIL MOON | 10 |
| COUNTRY GIRL | 11 |
| THERE WILL NEVER BE ANOTHER YOU | 12 |

Peter Matz track 13

| | |
|---|---|
| WAVE | 13 |
| ON THE SUNNY SIDE OF THE STREET | 14 |
| FOR ONCE IN MY LIFE | 15 |
| WHAT THE WORLD NEEDS NOW IS LOVE | 16 |
| I'LL BEGIN AGAIN | 17 |
| CLOSING THEME – SAN FRANCISCO | 18 |

**THE LAST PICTURE
SHOW - SOUNDTRACK**
CBS 70115

| | |
|---|---|
| COLD, COLD HEART | 1 |
| BLUE VELVET | 2 |
| SOLITAIRE | 3 |

**SUMMER OF '42**
ALBUM/COMPILATION 12/1/72
CBS64648 C32119
Johnny Mandel track 11
Torrie Zito tracks 1,4,6,7,8
Robert Farnon tracks 2,9
Marty Manning track 3
Marion Evans track 10
Frank De Vol track 5

| | |
|---|---|
| THE SUMMER KNOWS | 1 |
| WALKABOUT | 2 |
| IT WAS ME | 3 |
| I'M LOSING MY MIND | 4 |
| TILL | 5 |
| SOMEWHERE ALONG THE LINE | 6 |
| COFFEE BREAK | 7 |
| MORE AND MORE | 8 |
| IRENA | 9 |
| MY INAMORATA | 10 |
| THE SHINING SEA | 11 |

**WITH LOVE**
ALBUM 24/5/72 CBS 64849 KC 31460 5 64849
Robert Farnon

| | |
|---|---|
| HERE'S THAT RAINY DAY | 1 |
| REMIND ME | 2 |
| HOW BEAUTIFUL IS NIGHT (WITH YOU) | 3 |
| MAYBE THIS TIME (US substitute for 3) | 3 |
| THE RIVIERA | 4 |
| STREET OF DREAMS | 5 |
| LOVE | 6 |
| TWILIGHT WORLD | 7 |
| LAZY DAY | 8 |
| EASY COME, EASY GO | 9 |
| HARLEM BUTTERFLY | 10 |
| DREAM | 11 |

**TONY!**
COMPILATION 3/73 CBS
HARMONY KH 32171
CBS S53 262 - HOLLAND
George Siravo tracks 1,7
Peter Matz tracks 2,5,6,8
Torrie Zito track 4
Johnny Mandel track 9
Al Cohn track 10
Marty Manning track 3

| | |
|---|---|
| WHO CAN I TURN TO | 1 |
| YELLOW DAYS | 2 |
| SMILE | 3 |
| ALFIE | 4 |
| THE LOOK OF LOVE | 5 |
| SOMETHING | 6 |
| THERE'S A LULL IN MY LIFE | 7 |
| MacARTHUR PARK | 8 |
| I'LL ONLY MISS HER WHEN I THINK OF HER | 9 |
| THE SECOND TIME AROUND | 10 |

**SUNRISE, SUNSET**
COMPILATION 22/6/73 CBS C32239
Larry Wilcox track 1
Ralph Sharon tracks 2,3,10

| | |
|---|---|
| THE DAYS OF WINE AND ROSES | 1 |
| CLIMB EVERY MOUNTAIN | 2 |
| YESTERDAYS | 3 |
| SHE'S FUNNY THAT WAY | 4 |

| | | |
|---|---|---|
| Marion Evans tracks 4,11 | YOU'LL NEVER GET AWAY FROM ME | 5 |
| Peter Matz track 6 | SUNRISE, SUNSET | 6 |
| Marty Manning track 7 | LOVE STORY (WHERE DO I BEGIN) | 7 |
| Ralph Burns track 8 | THE PARTY'S OVER | 8 |
| Frank De Vol track 9 ?5 | PUT ON A HAPPY FACE | 9 |
| | BEGIN THE BEGUINE | 10 |
| | DON'T GET AROUND MUCH ANYMORE | 11 |

**LET'S FALL IN LOVE WITH THE SONGS OF HAROLD ARLEN & CY COLEMAN**
Reissue 5/75 DOUBLE/COMPILATION
CBS 88131 KG 33376
Glenn Osser tracks 1-10
Ralph Burns track 11 ?12
Ralph Sharon tracks 13,14
Robert Farnon track 15
Cy Coleman track 16
George Siravo track 17
Frank De Vol track 18
David Rose track 19
Don Costa track 20

| | |
|---|---|
| WHEN THE SUN COMES OUT | 1 |
| HOUSE OF FLOWERS | 2 |
| COME RAIN OR COME SHINE | 3 |
| LETS FALL IN LOVE | 4 |
| OVER THE RAINBOW | 5 |
| RIGHT AS THE RAIN | 6 |
| IT WAS WRITTEN IN THE STARS | 7 |
| FUN TO BE FOOLED | 8 |
| THIS TIME THE DREAM'S ON ME | 9 |
| I'VE GOT THE WORLD ON A STRING | 10 |
| I'VE GOT YOUR NUMBER | 11 |
| ON THE OTHER SIDE OF THE TRACKS | 12 |
| FIREFLY | 13 |
| THE RULES OF THE ROAD | 14 |
| THE RIVIERA | 15 |
| THE BEST IS YET TO COME | 16 |
| I WALK A LITTLE FASTER | 17 |
| IT AMAZES ME | 18 |
| BABY, DREAM YOUR DREAM | 19 |
| THEN WAS THEN AND NOW IS NOW | 20 |

**TONY BENNETT SINGS**
**READERS DIGEST**
**COMPILATION RDS 8070 CBS**
**MILLION DOLLAR MEMORIES**
Don Costa tracks 1,3,5
George Siravo track 2
Al Cohn track 4
Robert Farnon track 6
Marty Manning track 7
Frank De Vol track 8
Marion Evans track 10
Torrie Zito track 11
Ralph Sharon track 12

| | |
|---|---|
| FLY ME TO THE MOON (IN OTHER WORDS) | 1 |
| WHO CAN I TURN TO | 2 |
| IF I RULED THE WORLD | 3 |
| THE TROLLEY SONG | 4 |
| SWEET LORRAINE | 5 |
| MY FAVOURITE THINGS | 6 |
| CANDY KISSES | 7 |
| PUT ON A HAPPY FACE | 8 |
| A TASTE OF HONEY | 9 |
| COUNTRY GIRL | 10 |
| THEY CAN'T TAKE THAT AWAY FROM ME | 11 |
| CLIMB EVERY MOUNTAIN | 12 |

**COCA COLA PRESENTS TONY BENNETT**
**CBS COMPILATION ZTEP 26851**

| | |
|---|---|
| BECAUSE OF YOU | 1 |
| IN THE MIDDLE OF AN ISLAND | 2 |
| COLD, COLD HEART | 3 |
| RAGS TO RICHES | 4 |
| COME NEXT SPRING | 5 |
| CAN YOU FIND IT IN YOUR HEART? | 6 |

**ALL-TIME GREATEST HITS**
CBS 68200 KG 31494
COLUMBIA 468843 23/8/72
Marty Manning tracks 2,6,10,14,19
Percy Faith tracks 4,7,8,9,15,20
Johnny Mandel tracks 11,17
Peter Matz track 1
Torrie Zito track 5
George Siravo track 12
Ralph Burns track 13
Ralph Sharon track 16
Frank de Vol track 18

| | |
|---|---|
| SOMETHING | 1 |
| LOVE STORY (WHERE DO I BEGIN) | 2 |
| MAYBE THIS TIME | 3 |
| JUST IN TIME | 4 |
| FOR ONCE IN MY LIFE | 5 |
| (I LEFT MY HEART) IN SAN FRANCISCO | 6 |
| BECAUSE OF YOU | 7 |
| BOULEVARD OF BROKEN DREAMS | 8 |
| STRANGER IN PARADISE | 9 |
| I WANNA BE AROUND | 10 |
| A TIME FOR LOVE | 11 |
| WHO CAN I TURN TO | 12 |
| THIS IS ALL I ASK | 13 |
| SMILE | 14 |
| SING YOU SINNERS | 15 |
| FIREFLY | 16 |
| THE SHADOW OF YOUR SMILE | 17 |
| PUT ON A HAPPY FACE | 18 |
| LOVE LOOK AWAY | 19 |
| RAGS TO RICHES | 20 |

**THE TROLLEY SONG**
EMBASSY COMPILATION 1974 31002
Torrie Zito tracks 1,3,4,9
Larry Wilcox track 2
Marion Evans tracks 5,6,8
Ralph Sharon track 7 with Count Basie
Neal Hefti track 10
Al Cohn track 11

| | |
|---|---|
| ALFIE | 1 |
| THE DAYS OF WINE AND ROSES | 2 |
| THERE WILL NEVER BE ANOTHER YOU | 3 |
| WHAT THE WORLD NEEDS NOW IS LOVE | 4 |
| A BEAUTIFUL FRIENDSHIP | 5 |
| SHE'S FUNNY THAT WAY | 6 |
| FASCINATIN' RHYTHM | 7 |
| OLD DEVIL MOON | 8 |
| I'VE GOTTA BE ME | 9 |
| GIRL TALK | 10 |
| THE TROLLEY SONG | 11 |

**WHEN I FALL IN LOVE**
COMPILATION 1974 CBS
HALLMARK SHM 817
Reissued part 2 of **TONY BENNETT COLLECTION**
DBL ALBUM HALLMARK PDA 014
Ralph Sharon tracks 1,2,3,4,8,9,11
Torrie Zito tracks 5,6
Johnny Mandel track 7 with Luiz Bonfa
Frank De Vol track 10
Marion Evans track 12

| | |
|---|---|
| WHEN I FALL IN LOVE | 1 |
| TAKING A CHANCE ON LOVE | 2 |
| PENNIES FROM HEAVEN | 3 |
| OL' MAN RIVER | 4 |
| PLAY IT AGAIN, SAM | 5 |
| THEY ALL LAUGHED | 6 |
| THE GENTLE RAIN | 7 |
| FIREFLY | 8 |
| HOW ABOUT YOU? | 9 |
| APRIL IN PARIS | 10 |
| SOLITUDE | 11 |
| COUNTRY GIRL | 12 |

**THE TONY BENNETT COLLECTION**      as SHM646 and SHM817
HALLMARK DBL PDA 014
Reissue of **JUST ONE OF THOSE THINGS** with
**WHEN I FALL IN LOVE**

| | | |
|---|---|---|
| **MILLION DOLLAR MEMORIES**<br>READERS DIGEST SPECIAL<br>PRODUCT RDS8061-8069<br>CBS 1970 VARIOUS ARTISTS<br>COMPILATION 9 RECORD SET | (I LEFT MY HEART) IN SAN FRANCISCO<br>SMILE<br>THIS IS ALL I ASK<br>TILL<br>BECAUSE OF YOU<br>RAGS TO RICHES<br>STRANGER IN PARADISE | 1<br>2<br>3<br>4<br>5<br>6<br>7 |
| **16 ORIGINAL HITS OF TONY BENNETT**<br>COMPILATION TIMELESS TREASURES<br>EVEREST-EUROPA LP 16-19<br>tracks 7 & 11 unique | (I LEFT MY HEART) IN SAN FRANCISCO<br>BECAUSE OF YOU<br>COLD, COLD HEART<br>RAGS TO RICHES<br>STRANGER IN PARADISE<br>IN THE MIDDLE OF AN ISLAND<br>FROM THE CANDY STORE ON THE CORNER<br>(TO THE CHAPEL ON THE HILL)<br>I WANNA BE AROUND<br>CAN YOU FIND IT IN YOUR HEART?<br>THE GOOD LIFE<br>THE AUTUMN WALTZ<br>THERE'LL BE NO TEARDROPS TONIGHT<br>I WON'T CRY ANYMORE<br>FIREFLY<br>CA, C'EST L'AMOUR<br>BLUE VELVET | 1<br>2<br>3<br>4<br>5<br>6<br>7<br><br>8<br>9<br>10<br>11<br>12<br>13<br>14<br>15<br>16 |
| **THE VERY BEST OF TONY BENNETT**<br>20 GREATEST WARWICK<br>COMPILATION 1977<br>CBS WARWICK PA5021<br>Marty Manning tracks 1,2,3,5,11<br>George Siravo track 4<br>Dick Hyman track 6<br>Don Costa track 7<br>Torrie Zito tracks 8,17,18<br>Ralph Sharon tracks 9,10,14<br>Peter Matz track 12<br>Percy Faith tracks 13,16<br>Frank de Vol track 15<br>Johnny Mandel track 19<br>Robert Farnon track 20 | (I LEFT MY HEART) IN SAN FRANCISCO<br>I WANNA BE AROUND<br>WHEN JOANNA LOVED ME<br>WHO CAN I TURN TO<br>THE GOOD LIFE<br>A TASTE OF HONEY<br>IF I RULED THE WORLD<br>WHAT THE WORLD NEEDS NOW IS LOVE<br>FASCINATIN' RHYTHM<br>TAKING A CHANCE ON LOVE<br>CANDY KISSES<br>SOMETHING<br>JUST IN TIME<br>FIREFLY<br>PUT ON A HAPPY FACE<br>STRANGER IN PARADISE<br>PEOPLE<br>FOR ONCE IN MY LIFE<br>THE SHADOW OF YOUR SMILE<br>MY FAVOURITE THINGS | 1<br>2<br>3<br>4<br>5<br>6<br>7<br>8<br>9<br>10<br>11<br>12<br>13<br>14<br>15<br>16<br>17<br>18<br>19<br>20 |
| **THE GOLDEN TOUCH OF TONY BENNETT**<br>COMPILATION DBL P12789/90 COL SP | (I LEFT MY HEART) IN SAN FRANCISCO<br>JUST IN TIME<br>BLUE VELVET<br>A TASTE OF HONEY | 1<br>2<br>3<br>4 |

| | |
|---|---|
| COLD, COLD HEART | 5 |
| FOR ONCE IN MY LIFE | 6 |
| THIS IS ALL I ASK | 7 |
| RAGS TO RICHES | 8 |
| IF I RULED THE WORLD | 9 |
| IN THE MIDDLE OF AN ISLAND | 10 |
| SMILE | 11 |
| DON'T WAIT TOO LONG | 12 |
| CAN YOU FIND IT IN YOUR HEART? | 13 |
| ONE FOR MY BABY | 14 |
| STRANGER IN PARADISE | 15 |
| FLY ME TO THE MOON (IN OTHER WORDS) | 16 |
| MY FUNNY VALENTINE | 17 |
| CLIMB EVERY MOUNTAIN | 18 |
| SPRING IN MANHATTAN | 19 |
| I WANNA BE AROUND | 20 |
| THE GOOD LIFE | 21 |
| SOLITAIRE | 22 |
| THE SHADOW OF YOUR SMILE | 23 |
| HERE IN MY HEART | 24 |
| WHO CAN I TURN TO | 25 |

**16 MOST REQUESTED SONGS**
CD COMPILATION CBS UK 57056
Percy Faith tracks 1-6
Marty Manning tracks 7,8,12,13,15
George Siravo track 9
Ralph Burns track 11
Torrie Zito track 10
Johnny Mandel track 14

| | |
|---|---|
| BECAUSE OF YOU | 1 |
| STRANGER IN PARADISE | 2 |
| RAGS TO RICHES | 3 |
| BOULEVARD OF BROKEN DREAMS | 4 |
| COLD, COLD HEART | 5 |
| JUST IN TIME | 6 |
| (I LEFT MY HEART) IN SAN FRANCISCO | 7 |
| I WANNA BE AROUND | 8 |
| WHO CAN I TURN TO | 9 |
| FOR ONCE IN MY LIFE | 10 |
| THIS IS ALL I ASK | 11 |
| SMILE | 12 |
| TENDER IS THE NIGHT | 13 |
| THE SHADOW OF YOUR SMILE | 14 |
| LOVE STORY (WHERE DO I BEGIN) | 15 |
| THE GOOD LIFE | 16 |

**SAN FRANCISCO**
DITTO DTO 10040 DBL ALBUM PICKWICK
also issued as special Dbl album set CBS 22011

as I LEFT MY HEART IN SAN FRANCISCO
& SINGS THE GREAT HITS OF TODAY

## PHILIPS/FANTASY/IMPROV RECORDINGS

**THE GOOD THINGS IN LIFE**
ALBUM 1972 PHILIPS 6308 134
MGM VERVE 5088
Robert Farnon all tracks except 2
Torrie Zito track 2
John Bunch Trio on tracks 7,11

| THE GOOD THINGS IN LIFE | 1 |
| --- | --- |
| O SOLE MIO | 2 |
| PASSING STRANGERS | 3 |
| END OF A LOVE AFFAIR | 4 |
| OH! LADY BE GOOD | 5 |
| BLUES FOR BREAKFAST | 6 |
| MIMI | 7 |
| INVITATION | 8 |
| SOMEONE TO LIGHT UP MY LIFE | 9 |
| IT WAS YOU | 10 |
| CUTE | 11 |
| THE MIDNIGHT SUN | 12 |
| LONDON BY NIGHT | 13 |
| THE GOOD THINGS IN LIFE (CLOSING) | 14 |

**LISTEN EASY**
ALBUM 1973 PHILIPS 6308 157
MGM VERVE 5094
Don Costa

| LOVE IS THE THING | 1 |
| --- | --- |
| RAIN, RAIN, (DON'T GO AWAY) | 2 |
| THE HANDS OF TIME | 3 |
| I CONCENTRATE ON YOU | 4 |
| AT LONG LAST LOVE | 5 |
| IF I COULD GO BACK | 6 |
| ON THE SUNNY SIDE OF THE STREET | 7 |
| THE GARDEN (ONCE IN A GARDEN) | 8 |
| MY FUNNY VALENTINE | 9 |
| HOW LITTLE WE KNOW | 10 |
| TELL HER THAT IT'S SNOWING | 11 |

**SPOTLIGHT ON ... TONY BENNETT**
COMPILATION PHILIPS
INTERNATIONAL 6641 297
Robert Farnon tracks 1,2,7,8,13,14,15,17,18
20.22,27
Torrie Zito tracks 3,12 with Ruby Braff/
George Barnes Quartet
Don Costa tracks 4,5,6,9,10,19,21,23,24,25
26,28 Torrie Zito tracks 11,16

| END OF A LOVE AFFAIR | 1 |
| --- | --- |
| PASSING STRANGERS | 2 |
| ALL THAT LOVE WENT TO WASTE | 3 |
| LOVE IS THE THING | 4 |
| ON THE SUNNY SIDE OF THE STREET | 5 |
| THE GARDEN (ONCE IN A GARDEN) | 6 |
| INVITATION | 7 |
| SOMEONE TO LIGHT UP MY LIFE | 8 |
| IF I COULD GO BACK | 9 |
| THE HANDS OF TIME | 10 |
| O SOLE MIO | 11 |
| SOME OF THESE DAYS | 12 |
| THE MIDNIGHT SUN | 13 |
| IT WAS YOU | 14 |
| LONDON BY NIGHT | 15 |
| MY LOVE | 16 |
| OH! LADY BE GOOD | 17 |
| CUTE | 18 |
| I CONCENTRATE ON YOU | 19 |
| MIMI | 20 |
| TELL HER THAT IT'S SNOWING | 21 |
| BLUES FOR BREAKFAST | 22 |
| AT LONG LAST LOVE | 23 |

|  |  |  |
|---|---|---|
|  | MY FUNNY VALENTINE | 24 |
|  | HOW LITTLE WE KNOW | 25 |
|  | RAIN, RAIN, (DON'T GO AWAY) | 26 |
|  | THE GOOD THINGS IN LIFE | 27 |
|  | GIVE ME LOVE, GIVE ME PEACE | 28 |

**AT LONG LAST LOVE**
COMPILATION 1976
PHLIPS SONIC 014 BS
Robert Farnon tracks 1,4,5,7,11
Don Costa tracks 2,3,6,9,12
Torrie Zito tracks 8,10

| SOMEONE TO LIGHT UP MY LIFE | 1 |
|---|---|
| AT LONG LAST LOVE | 2 |
| HOW LITTLE WE KNOW | 3 |
| IT WAS YOU | 4 |
| PASSING STRANGERS | 5 |
| IF I COULD GO BACK | 6 |
| END OF A LOVE AFFAIR | 7 |
| MY LOVE | 8 |
| I CONCENTRATE ON YOU | 9 |
| O SOLE MIO | 10 |
| THE MIDNIGHT SUN | 11 |
| LIVING TOGETHER, GROWING TOGETHER | 12 |

**TONY BENNETT'S GREATEST HITS NO 7**
MGM VERVE US ONLY SE 4929
Torrie Zito tracks 1,8,12, +
arranger track 2 Robert Farnon conductor
Robert Farnon tracks 3,4,5,6 with John
Bunch trio tracks 4,5
Don Costa tracks 7,10,11
Bernie Leighton track 9

| MY LOVE | 1 |
|---|---|
| O SOLE MIO | 2 |
| THE GOOD THINGS IN LIFE | 3 |
| CUTE | 4 |
| MIMI | 5 |
| LONDON BY NIGHT | 6 |
| ON THE SUNNY SIDE OF THE STREET | 7 |
| LET'S DO IT | 8 |
| SOPHISTICATED LADY | 9 |
| LIVING TOGETHER, GROWING TOGETHER | 10 |
| TELL HER IT'S SNOWING (Short version) | 11 |
| GIVE ME LOVE | 12 |

**THE TONY BENNETT/BILL EVANS ALBUM**
ALBUM 1975 FANTASY F9489
UK EMI FT527
with Bill Evans

| YOUNG AND FOOLISH | 1 |
|---|---|
| THE TOUCH OF YOUR LIPS | 2 |
| SOME OTHER TIME | 3 |
| WHEN IN ROME | 4 |
| WE'LL BE TOGETHER AGAIN | 5 |
| MY FOOLISH HEART | 6 |
| WALTZ FOR DEBBIE | 7 |
| BUT BEAUTIFUL | 8 |
| THE DAYS OF WINE AND ROSES | 9 |

**TONY BENNETT SINGS**
 **10 RODGERS & HART SONGS**
ALBUM 9/73 IMPROV 7113
Reissued 1986 HORATIO NELSON
YU 108 rec 2
& CDSIV 1129with IMPROV 7120 as
**THE RODGERS & HART COLLECTION/SONGBOOK**
Tracks repeated on **STAGE & SCREEN HITS**

| THIS CAN'T BE LOVE | 1 |
|---|---|
| BLUE MOON | 2 |
| THE LADY IS A TRAMP | 3 |
| LOVER | 4 |
| MANHATTAN | 5 |
| SPRING IS HERE | 6 |
| HAVE YOU MET MISS JONES? | 7 |
| ISN'T IT ROMANTIC? | 8 |

on **HOLLYWOOD & BROADWAY**
CSIV 1145 1994
and on **20 GREATEST** ANTELOPE 52043 1988
with the Ruby Braff/George Barnes Quartet

| | |
|---|---|
| WAIT TILL YOU SEE HER | 9 |
| I COULD WRITE A BOOK | 10 |

**TONY BENNETT SINGS**
**MORE GREAT RODGERS & HART**
ALBUM 9/73 IMPROV 7120
issued 1986 HORATIO NELSON YU 108 rec 1
& CD SIV 1129 with IMPROV 7113 in UK as
**THE RODGERS & HART**
**COLLECTION/SONGBOOK**
repeated on NELSON ALBUM CD SIV 1119
and on **20 GREATEST** ANTELOPE
52043 CD 1988
with the Ruby Braff/George Barnes Quartet

| | |
|---|---|
| THOU SWELL | 11 |
| THE MOST BEAUTIFUL GIRL IN THE WORLD | 12 |
| THERE'S A SMALL HOTEL | 13 |
| I'VE GOT FIVE DOLLARS | 14 |
| YOU TOOK ADVANTAGE OF ME | 15 |
| I WISH I WERE IN LOVE AGAIN | 16 |
| THIS FUNNY WORLD | 17 |
| MY HEART STOOD STILL | 18 |
| MY ROMANCE | 19 |
| MOUNTAIN GREENERY | 20 |

**SINGS THE RODGERS & HART**
**COLLECTION**
HORATIO NELSON YU108

reissue last two albums

**SINGS THE RODGERS & HART SONGBOOK** as above
HORATIO NELSON CDSIV 1129

**LIFE IS BEAUTIFUL**
ALBUM 1975 IMPROV IMP7112
Torrie Zito

| | |
|---|---|
| LIFE IS BEAUTIFUL | 1 |
| ALL MINE | 2 |
| BRIDGES | 3 |
| REFLECTIONS | 4 |
| EXPERIMENT | 5 |
| THIS FUNNY WORLD | 6 |
| AS TIME GOES BY | 7 |
| I USED TO BE COLOUR BLIND | 8 |
| LOST IN THE STARS | 9 |
| THERE'LL BE SOME CHANGES MADE | 10 |

**TONY BENNETT & BILL EVANS**
  **TOGETHER AGAIN**
ALBUM 1977 IMPROV 7117 US ONLY
issued UK HORATIO NELSON CD SIV 1122
reissued by DRG US MRS 901
tracks on **STAGE & SCREEN HITS**
with Bill Evans
*Bill Evans solo on track 1

| | |
|---|---|
| THE BAD AND THE BEAUTIFUL* | 1 |
| LUCKY TO BE ME | 2 |
| MAKE SOMEONE HAPPY | 3 |
| THE TWO LONELY PEOPLE | 4 |
| A CHILD IS BORN | 5 |
| YOU'RE NEARER | 6 |
| YOU DON'T KNOW WHAT LOVE IS | 7 |
| MAYBE SEPTEMBER | 8 |
| LONELY GIRL | 9 |
| YOU MUST BELIEVE IN SPRING | 10 |

**THE MACPARTLANDS AND FRIENDS**
**MAKE MAGNIFICENT MUSIC**
ALBUM US ONLY IMPROV 7123
13&14 May 1977
Tony Bennett on 4 tracks live

| | |
|---|---|
| WATCH WHAT HAPPENS | 1 |
| WHILE WE'RE YOUNG | 4 |
| IN A MELLOW TONE | 5 |
| S' WONDERFUL/I LEFT MY HEART IN SAN FRANCISCO | 8 |

**THE SPECIAL MAGIC OF TONY BENNETT**
ALBUM US DRG CDMRS801 79 issued in UK as
**THE MAGIC OF TONY BENNETT**
NELSON CYU 106
Tracks repeated on **HOLLYWOOD & BROADWAY**
NELSON CSIV 1145 1994
and on NELSON ALBUM CD SIV 1119
and on **20 GREATEST** ANTELOPE 52043 1988
Torrie Zito

| | |
|---|---|
| COLE PORTER SELECTION 10 SONG MEDLEY | 1 |
| EXPERIMENT | 2 |
| ONE | 3 |
| THIS FUNNY WORLD | 4 |
| LOST IN THE STARS | 5 |
| AS TIME GOES BY | 6 |
| I USED TO BE COLOUR BLIND | 7 |
| MR MAGIC | 8 |

**THE MAGIC OF TONY BENNETT**
HORATIO NELSON CYU 106

as above album

**TONY BENNETT SINGS THE GREATEST HITS OF COLE PORTER & RODGERS & HART**
HORATIO NELSON CDSIV 1119

as above album plus More Rodgers & Hart

**STAGE AND SCREEN HITS**
COMPILATION DBL DBM RECORDS 1001
Record one as **THE MAGIC OF TONY BENNETT**
Record two from RODGERS & HART/EVANS ALBUMS
Torrie Zito tracks 1-8
Ruby Braff/George Barnes Quartet tracks 9-16
Bill Evans tracks 17-22

| | |
|---|---|
| COLE PORTER SELECTION 10 SONG MEDLEY | 1 |
| EXPERIMENT | 2 |
| ONE | 3 |
| THIS FUNNY WORLD | 4 |
| LOST IN THE STARS | 5 |
| AS TIME GOES BY | 6 |
| I USED TO BE COLOUR BLIND | 7 |
| MR MAGIC | 8 |
| THE MOST BEAUTIFUL GIRL IN THE WORLD | 9 |
| THERE'S A SMALL HOTEL | 10 |
| I'VE GOT FIVE DOLLARS | 11 |
| I WISH I WERE IN LOVE AGAIN | 12 |
| MANHATTAN | 13 |
| THE LADY IS A TRAMP | 14 |
| MY ROMANCE | 15 |
| MOUNTAIN GREENERY | 16 |
| LUCKY TO BE ME | 17 |
| MAKE SOMEONE HAPPY | 18 |
| YOU'RE NEARER | 19 |
| YOU DON'T KNOW WHAT LOVE IS | 20 |
| LONELY GIRL | 21 |
| YOU MUST BELIEVE IN SPRING | 22 |

| THE UNFORGETTABLE TONY BENNETT | THERE'LL BE SOME CHANGES MADE | 1 |
| COMPILATION 16 GOLDEN CLASSICS | BLUE MOON | 2 |
| CASTLE UNLP 019 | THE LADY IS A TRAMP | 3 |
| Torrie Zito tracks 1,10,16 | LOVER | 4 |
| Ruby Braff/George Barnes tracks 2-7,14,15 | MANHATTAN | 5 |
| Bill Evans tracks 8,9,11,12,13 | I COULD WRITE A BOOK | 6 |
| | SPRING IS HERE | 7 |
| | A CHILD IS BORN | 8 |
| | MAKE SOMEONE HAPPY | 9 |
| | LIFE IS BEAUTIFUL | 10 |
| | MAYBE SEPTEMBER | 11 |
| | LONELY GIRL | 12 |
| | YOU DON'T KNOW WHAT LOVE IS | 13 |
| | THOU SWELL | 14 |
| | THERE'S A SMALL HOTEL | 15 |
| | AS TIME GOES BY | 16 |

| TONY BENNETT 20 GREATEST HITS | SPRING IS HERE | 1 |
| ANTELOPE ANTC 52043 1988 | HAVE YOU MET MISS JONES? | 2 |
| Improv recordings compilation | ISN'T IT ROMANTIC? | 3 |
| issued under several labels i.e. | WAIT TIL YOU SEE HER | 4 |
| TONY BENNET* STARS | I COULD WRITE A BOOK | 5 |
| PILZ CD FM 8342-2 1994 | EXPERIMENT | 6 |
| (*their spelling) this album shows | THIS CAN'T BE LOVE | 7 |
| incorrect track listing | BLUE MOON | 8 |
| | THE LADY IS A TRAMP | 9 |
| | LOVER | 10 |
| | MANHATTAN | 11 |
| | LIFE IS BEAUTIFUL | 12 |
| | BRIDGES | 13 |
| | THIS FUNNY WORLD | 14 |
| | AS TIME GOES BY | 15 |
| | THE MOST BEAUTIFUL GIRL IN THE WORLD | 16 |
| | I'VE GOT FIVE DOLLARS | 17 |
| | THOU SWELL | 18 |
| | MY HEART STOOD STILL | 19 |
| | MY ROMANCE | 20 |

| HOLLYWOOD & BROADWAY | COLE PORTER SELECTION 10 SONG MEDLEY | 1 |
| COMPILATION 1994 NELSON CSIV 1145 | LONELY GIRL | 2 |
| side 1 as STAGE & SCREEN Hits DBM 1001 | MAKE SOMEONE HAPPY | 3 |
| Torrie Zito tracks 1,12,16-18 | THIS CAN'T BE LOVE | 4 |
| Bill Evans tracks 2,3 | THE LADY IS A TRAMP | 5 |
| Ruby Braff/ George Barnes remainder | THE MOST BEAUTIFUL GIRL IN THE WORLD | 6 |
| | I WISH I WERE IN LOVE AGAIN | 7 |
| | MANHATTAN | 8 |
| | WAIT TILL YOU SEE HER | 9 |
| | THOU SWELL | 10 |
| | I'VE GOT FIVE DOLLARS | 11 |
| | EXPERIMENT | 12 |
| | ONE | 13 |
| | THIS FUNNY WORLD | 14 |
| | LOST IN THE STARS | 15 |
| | I USED TO BE COLOUR BLIND | 16 |
| | MR MAGIC | 17 |
| | AS TIME GOES BY | 18 |

## COLUMBIA AND OTHER RECORDINGS ISSUED FROM 1986

| | | |
|---|---|---|
| THE ART OF EXCELLENCE | WHY DO PEOPLE FALL IN LOVE?/PEOPLE | 1 |
| ALBUM 1986 CBS 26990 | MOMENTS LIKE THIS | 2 |
| CD UK Columbia CK 40344 | WHAT ARE YOU AFRAID OF? | 3 |
| Jorge Calandrelli | WHEN LOVE WAS ALL WE HAD | 4 |
| | SO MANY STARS (cd only) | 5 |
| | EVERYBODY HAS THE BLUES (with Ray Charles) | 6 |
| | HOW DO YOU KEEP THE MUSIC PLAYING? | 7 |
| | CITY OF THE ANGELS | 8 |
| | FORGET THE WOMAN | 9 |
| | A RAINY DAY (cd only) | 10 |
| | I GOT LOST IN HER ARMS | 11 |
| | THE DAY YOU LEAVE ME | 12 |

| | | |
|---|---|---|
| THAT'S LIFE (Sound Track) | LIFE IN A LOOKING GLASS | |
| Columbia 1986 | | |

| | | |
|---|---|---|
| TONY BENNETT/JAZZ | I CAN'T BELIEVE YOU'RE IN LOVE WITH ME | 1 |
| COMPILATION 13/3/87 CBS 450465 DOUBLE | DON'T GET AROUND MUCH ANYMORE | 2 |
| Chuck Wayne tracks 1,15,18 | STELLA BY STARLIGHT | 3 |
| Marion Evans tracks 2,10 | ON GREEN DOLPHIN STREET | 4 |
| Ralph Burns tracks 3,9,19 | LET'S FACE THE MUSIC AND DANCE | 5 |
| Ralph Sharon 4-8,11-14,16,24 | I'M THRU' WITH LOVE | 6 |
| Don Costa track 17 | SOLITUDE | 7 |
| Stan Getz tracks 20-23 | LULLABY OF BROADWAY | 8 |
| | DANCING IN THE DARK | 9 |
| | I LET A SONG GO OUT OF MY HEART | 10 |
| | WHEN LIGHTS ARE LOW | 11 |
| | JUST ONE OF THOSE THINGS | 12 |
| | CRAZY RHYTHM | 13 |
| | JUDY | 14 |
| | GIVE ME THE SIMPLE LIFE | 15 |
| | STREET OF DREAMS | 16 |
| | LOVE SCENE | 17 |
| | WHILE THE MUSIC PLAYS ON | 18 |
| | CLOSE YOUR EYES | 19 |
| | OUT OF THIS WORLD | 20 |
| | JUST FRIENDS | 21 |
| | HAVE YOU MET MISS JONES? | 22 |
| | DANNY BOY | 23 |
| | SWEET LORRAINE | 24 |

| | | |
|---|---|---|
| BENNETT:BERLIN | THEY SAY IT'S WONDERFUL | 1 |
| ALBUM 10/87 CBS 460450 | ISN'T THIS A LOVELY DAY? | 2 |
| Tony Bennett arranger | ALL OF MY LIFE | 3 |
| with Ralph Sharon Trio | NOW IT CAN BE TOLD | 4 |
| | THE SONG IS ENDED | 5 |
| | WHEN I LOST YOU | 6 |

| | | |
|---|---|---|
| | CHEEK TO CHEEK | 7 |
| | LET YOURSELF GO | 8 |
| | LET'S FACE THE MUSIC AND DANCE | 9 |
| | SHAKIN' THE BLUES AWAY | 10 |
| | RUSSIAN LULLABY | 11 |
| | WHITE CHRISTMAS | 12 |
| **ASTORIA:PORTRAIT OF THE ARTIST** | WHEN DO THE BELLS RING FOR ME? | 1 |
| ALBUM 12/89 CBS 466005 | I WAS LOST I WAS DRIFTING | 2 |
| Jorge Calandrelli | A LITTLE STREET WHERE OLD FRIENDS MEET | 3 |
| UK Orchestra and Ralph Sharon Trio | THE GIRL I LOVE | 4 |
| | IT'S LIKE REACHING FOR THE MOON | 5 |
| | SPEAK LOW | 6 |
| | THE FOLKS WHO LIVE ON THE HILL | 7 |
| | ANTONIA | 8 |
| | A WEAVER OF DREAMS/ THERE WILL NEVER BE ANOTHER YOU | 9 |
| | BODY AND SOUL | 10 |
| | WHERE DO YOU GO FROM LOVE? | 11 |
| | THE BOULEVARD OF BROKEN DREAMS | 12 |
| | WHERE DID THE MAGIC GO? | 13 |
| | I'VE COME HOME AGAIN | 14 |

**FORTY YEARS – THE ARTISTRY OF TONY BENNETT A 4 CD COMPILATION**

| | | |
|---|---|---|
| **FORTY YEARS: VOL 1** | THE BOULEVARD OF BROKEN DREAMS | 1 |
| COMPILATION 1991 CBS LEGACY 46843 | BECAUSE OF YOU | 2 |
| Marty Manning track 1 | COLD, COLD HEART | 3 |
| Percy Faith tracks 2-6,8-10 | BLUE VELVET | 4 |
| Ralph Sharon tracks 11,13,16-21 | RAGS TO RICHES | 5 |
| Neal Hefti track 12 | STRANGER IN PARADISE | 6 |
| Frank De Vol tracks 14,22,23 | WHILE THE MUSIC PLAYS ON | 7 |
| Ralph Burns track 15 | MAY I NEVER LOVE AGAIN | 8 |
| *previously unreleased | SING YOU SINNERS | 9 |
| **edited – no strings | **JUST IN TIME | 10 |
| ***alternative versions | LAZY AFTERNOON | 11 |
| | CA, CES'T L'AMOUR | 12 |
| | *I GET A KICK OUT OF YOU | 13 |
| | IT AMAZES ME | 14 |
| | PENTHOUSE SERENADE | 15 |
| | LOST IN THE STARS | 16 |
| | LULLABY OF BROADWAY | 17 |
| | FIREFLY | 18 |
| | A SLEEPIN' BEE | 19 |
| | ***THE MAN THAT GOT AWAY | 20 |
| | *SKYLARK | 21 |
| | SEPTEMBER SONG | 22 |
| | TILL | 23 |

**FORTY YEARS: VOL 2**
COMPILATION 1991 CBS LEGACY 46843
Ralph Sharon track 1
Frank De Vol track 2
Cy Coleman track 3
Glenn Osser track 4
Ralph Burns tracks 5-8,18,19
Marty Manning tracks 9-16,21
Don Costa track 17
Dick Hyman tracks 20,22

| | |
|---|---|
| BEGIN THE BEGUINE | 1 |
| PUT ON A HAPPY FACE | 2 |
| THE BEST IS YET TO COME | 3 |
| THIS TIME THE DREAM'S ON ME | 4 |
| CLOSE YOUR EYES | 5 |
| TOOT, TOOT, TOOTSIE! (GOODBYE) | 6 |
| DANCING IN THE DARK | 7 |
| STELLA BY STARLIGHT | 8 |
| TENDER IS THE NIGHT | 9 |
| ONCE UPON A TIME | 10 |
| (I LEFT MY HEART) IN SAN FRANCISCO | 11 |
| UNTIL I MET YOU | 12 |
| IF I LOVE AGAIN | 13 |
| I WANNA BE AROUND | 14 |
| THE GOOD LIFE | 15 |
| IT WAS ME | 16 |
| SPRING IN MANHATTAN | 17 |
| THE MOMENT OF TRUTH | 18 |
| THIS IS ALL I ASK | 19 |
| A TASTE OF HONEY | 20 |
| WHEN JOANNA LOVED ME | 21 |
| I'LL BE AROUND | 22 |

**FORTY YEARS: VOL 3**
COMPILATION 1991 CBS LEGACY 46843
Ralph Sharon tracks 1-3
George Siravo tracks 4-7
Don Costa tracks 8-11
Johnny Mandel tracks 12,13,17,19
David Rose track 14
Al Cohn track 15
Larry Wilcox track 16
Johnny Keating track 18
Marion Evans track 20

| | |
|---|---|
| NOBODY ELSE BUT ME | 1 |
| IT HAD TO BE YOU | 2 |
| I'VE GOT JUST ABOUT EVERYTHING | 3 |
| WHO CAN I TURN TO | 4 |
| WALTZ FOR DEBBIE | 5 |
| I WALK A LITTLE FASTER | 6 |
| WRAP YOUR TROUBLES IN DREAMS | 7 |
| IF I RULED THE WORLD | 8 |
| FLY ME TO THE MOON (IN OTHER WORDS) | 9 |
| LOVE SCENE | 10 |
| SWEET LORRAINE | 11 |
| THE SHADOW OF YOUR SMILE | 12 |
| I'LL ONLY MISS HER WHEN I THINK OF HER | 13 |
| BABY, DREAM YOUR DREAM | 14 |
| SMILE | 15 |
| SONG FROM "THE OSCAR" | |
| MAYBE SEPTEMBER | 16 |
| EMILY | 17 |
| THE VERY THOUGHT OF YOU | 18 |
| A TIME FOR LOVE | 19 |
| COUNTRY GIRL | 20 |

**FORTY YEARS: VOL 4**
COMPILATION 1991 CBS LEGACY 46843
Marion Evans track 1
Ralph Burns track 2
Torrie Zito tracks 3,5,6,8
John Bunch track 4
Peter Matz track 7

| | |
|---|---|
| DAYS OF LOVE | 1 |
| KEEP SMILING AT TROUBLE | 2 |
| FOR ONCE IN MY LIFE | 3 |
| *WHO CARES (SO LONG AS YOU CARE FOR ME) | 4 |
| HI-HO | 5 |
| BABY DON'T YOU QUIT NOW | 6 |
| SOMETHING | 7 |

Bill Evans tracks 9,12-14
Robert Farnon tracks 10,11
Jorge Calandrelli tracks 15-18,21,22
Tony Bennett & Ralph Sharon tracks 19,20
*previously unreleased

| | |
|---|---|
| I DO NOT KNOW A DAY I DID NOT LOVE YOU | 8 |
| OLD DEVIL MOON | 9 |
| REMIND ME | 10 |
| MAYBE THIS TIME | 11 |
| SOME OTHER TIME | 12 |
| MY FOOLISH HEART | 13 |
| BUT BEAUTIFUL | 14 |
| HOW DO YOU KEEP THE MUSIC PLAYING | 15 |
| WHAT ARE YOU AFRAID OF? | 16 |
| WHY DO PEOPLE FALL IN LOVE?/PEOPLE | 17 |
| I GOT LOST IN HER ARMS | 18 |
| WHEN I LOST YOU | 19 |
| SHAKIN' THE BLUES AWAY | 20 |
| ANTONIA | 21 |
| WHEN DO THE BELLS RING FOR ME? | 22 |

**GREAT SONGS FROM THE SHOWS**
COMPILATION 1993 PICKWICK PWKS4171
Robert Farnon track 1
George Siravo track 2
Ralph Sharon tracks 3,4,7,12,14,15,16
Peter Matz track 5
Johnny Mandel track 6
Marion Evans track 8
Percy Faith track 9
Don Costa track 10
Frank De Vol track 11
Stan Getz track 13

| | |
|---|---|
| MAYBE THIS TIME | 1 |
| WHO CAN I TURN TO | 2 |
| OL' MAN RIVER | 3 |
| CLIMB EVERY MOUNTAIN | 4 |
| ON A CLEAR DAY | 5 |
| I'LL ONLY MISS HER WHEN I THINK OF HER | 6 |
| LOVE FOR SALE | 7 |
| OLD DEVIL MOON | 8 |
| STRANGER IN PARADISE | 9 |
| IF I RULED THE WORLD | 10 |
| SEPTEMBER SONG | 11 |
| WHERE OR WHEN | 12 |
| HAVE YOU MET MISS JONES? | 13 |
| THEY SAY IT'S WONDERFUL | 14 |
| MY FUNNY VALENTINE | 15 |
| TAKING A CHANCE ON LOVE | 16 |

**PERFECTLY FRANK**
ALBUM 1993 COLUMBIA 472222 2
Ralph Sharon Trio
*track 19 is correct title

| | |
|---|---|
| TIME AFTER TIME | 1 |
| I FALL IN LOVE TOO EASILY | 2 |
| EAST OF THE SUN (WEST OF THE MOON) | 3 |
| NANCY | 4 |
| I THOUGHT ABOUT YOU | 5 |
| NIGHT AND DAY | 6 |
| I'VE GOT THE WORLD ON A STRING | 7 |
| I'M GLAD THERE IS YOU | 8 |
| A NIGHTINGALE SANG IN BERKELEY SQUARE | 9 |
| I WISHED ON THE MOON | 10 |
| YOU GO TO MY HEAD | 11 |
| THE LADY IS A TRAMP | 12 |
| I SEE YOUR FACE BEFORE ME | 13 |
| DAY IN, DAY OUT | 14 |
| INDIAN SUMMER | 15 |
| CALL ME IRRESPONSIBLE | 16 |
| HERE'S THAT RAINY DAY | 17 |
| LAST NIGHT WHEN WE WERE YOUNG | 18 |
| *I WISH I WERE IN LOVE AGAIN | 19 |

|  |  |
|---|---|
| A FOGGY DAY | 20 |
| DON'T WORRY 'BOUT ME | 21 |
| ONE FOR MY BABY | 22 |
| ANGEL EYES | 23 |
| I'LL BE SEEING YOU | 24 |

**STEPPIN' OUT**
ALBUM 1994 COLUMBIA 474360 2
Tony Bennett & Ralph Sharon

|  |  |
|---|---|
| STEPPIN' OUT WITH MY BABY | 1 |
| WHO CARES? | 2 |
| TOP HAT, WHITE TIE AND TAILS | 3 |
| THEY CAN'T TAKE THAT AWAY FROM ME | 4 |
| DANCING IN THE DARK | 5 |
| SHINE ON YOUR SHOES | 6 |
| HE LOVES AND SHE LOVES | 7 |
| THEY ALL LAUGHED | 8 |
| I CONCENTRATE ON YOU | 9 |
| YOU'RE ALL THE WORLD TO ME | 10 |
| ALL OF YOU | 11 |
| NICE WORK IF YOU CAN GET IT | 12 |
| IT ONLY HAPPENS WHEN I DANCE WITH YOU | 13 |
| SHALL WE DANCE | 14 |
| YOU'RE SO EASY TO DANCE WITH/ CHANGE PARTNERS/CHEEK TO CHEEK | 15 |
| I GUESS I'LL HAVE TO CHANGE MY PLAN | 16 |
| THAT'S ENTERTAINMENT | 17 |
| BY MYSELF | 18 |

**IT COULD HAPPEN TO YOU SOUNDTRACK**
COLUMBIA CK 66184
Johnny Mandel 1 & 3
Ralph Sharon 3

|  |  |
|---|---|
| YOUNG AT HEART with Shawn Colvin | 1 |
| NOW IT CAN BE TOLD | 2 |
| ALWAYS | 3 |

**ELVIS – IT'S NOW OR NEVER**
MERCURY CD 524 072-2 live recording 1994
Ralph Sharon

LOVE ME TENDER

**MTV UNPLUGGED**
LIVE 1994 COLUMBIA 477170 2
with the Ralph Sharon Trio

|  |  |
|---|---|
| OLD DEVIL MOON | 1 |
| SPEAK LOW | 2 |
| IT HAD TO BE YOU | 3 |
| I LOVE A PIANO | 4 |
| IT AMAZES ME | 5 |
| THE GIRL I LOVE | 6 |
| FLY ME TO THE MOON | 7 |
| YOU'RE ALL THE WORLD TO ME | 8 |
| RAGS TO RICHES | 9 |
| WHEN JOANNA LOVED ME | 10 |
| THE GOOD LIFE/I WANNA BE AROUND | 11 |
| (I LEFT MY HEART) IN SAN FRANCISCO | 12 |
| STEPPIN' OUT WITH MY BABY | 13 |
| MOONGLOW with k.d.lang | 14 |

**HERE'S TO THE LADIES**
ALBUM COLUMBIA 1995 481266 2
Jorge Calandrelli & Bill Holman
Ralph Sharon Trio

| | |
|---|---|
| THEY CAN'T TAKE THAT AWAY FROM ME | |
| with Elvis Costello | 15 |
| A FOGGY DAY | 16 |
| ALL OF YOU | 17 |
| BODY AND SOUL | 18 |
| IT DON'T MEAN A THING IF IT AIN'T GOT THAT SWING | 19 |
| AUTUMN LEAVES/INDIAN SUMMER | 20 |
| PEOPLE | 1 |
| I'M IN LOVE AGAIN | 2 |
| SOMEWHERE OVER THE RAINBOW | 3 |
| MY LOVE WENT TO LONDON | 4 |
| POOR BUTTERFLY | 5 |
| SENTIMENTAL JOURNEY | 6 |
| CLOUDY MORNING | 7 |
| TENDERLY | 8 |
| DOWN IN THE DEPTHS | 9 |
| MOONLIGHT IN VERMONT | 10 |
| TANGERINE | 11 |
| GOD BLESS THE CHILD | 12 |
| DAYBREAK | 13 |
| YOU SHOWED ME THE WAY | 14 |
| HONEYSUCKLE ROSE | 15 |
| MAYBE THIS TIME | 16 |
| I GOT RHYTHM | 17 |
| MY IDEAL | 18 |

**DOUBLE ALBUM (vinyl)**
MUTUAL BROADCASTING SYSTEM
for radio promo TN91-51

**THREE CD SET**
for Unistar radio networks as 12 shows
UNISTAR

THE FIRST FORTY YEARS
Interview and album tracks

Interview and tracks from
40 years boxed set, plus
commercials. for broadcasting
July 26-28 1991

## VARIOUS ARTIST ALBUM APPEARANCES

| | |
|---|---|
| **HALL OF FAME**<br>CL 2600 | RAGS TO RICHES |
| **POPULAR FAVORITES**<br>CL6205 | BECAUSE OF YOU<br>COLD, COLD HEART |
| **POPULAR FAVORITES VOL III**<br>CL6284 | STRANGER IN PARADISE<br>RAGS TO RICHES |
| **MUSIC FOR BABYSITTERS**<br>CL688 | RAGS TO RICHES |
| **MUSIC FOR THE ENGAGED**<br>CL687 | CONGRATULATIONS TO SOMEONE |
| **ALL STAR POPS**<br>VARIOUS ARTISTS ALBUM CL728<br>Sid Feller | A BLOSSOM FELL<br>SOMETHINGS GOTTA GIVE<br>HEART<br>WHATEVER LOLA WANTS |
| **TOP 12 VARIOUS ARTISTS**<br>CL937 | HAPPINESS STREET (CORNER SUNSHINE SQ) |
| **TOP 12 VARIOUS ARTISTS VOL 2**<br>CL944 | JUST IN TIME |
| **TOP 12 VARIOUS ARTISTS VOL 4**<br>CL1057 | IN THE MIDDLE OF AN ISLAND |
| **HOUSE PARTY SERIES** (promo)<br>Interviews COL XLP 36210 | TAKIN' A CHANCE ON LOVE (live) |
| **HITS FROM OH CAPTAIN**<br>CL1167 | YOU'RE SO RIGHT FOR ME |
| **POP HIT PARTY VARIOUS ARTISTS**<br>CL1237 | YOUNG AND WARM AND WONDERFUL |
| **POP HIT PARTY VARIOUS ARTISTS (2)**<br>CL1269 | FIREFLY |
| **POP HIT PARTY VARIOUS ARTISTS (3)**<br>CL1306 | LOVE LOOK AWAY |
| **HALL OF FAME HITS VARIOUS ARTISTS**<br>CS 8640 CL 1308 | RAGS TO RICHES |
| **HALL OF FAME SERIES**<br>CL 213 VARIOUS | COLD COLD HEART<br>BECAUSE OF YOU |

HITS FROM THE MOVIES
CL 1421 CS8218 CQ302

SMILE

OUR BEST TO YOU
ABS 2

THE SHADOW OF YOUR SMILE

COLUMBIA BASIC LIBRARY
OF BROADWAY STOPPERS
Col. K3L 235 (KL 5138)
3 LP set

BEST OF '66 VOL 2
AB1 ABS 1

A TASTE OF HONEY

SONGS FOR A SUMMER NIGHT
PM1003 PMS 2003

STELLA BY STARLIGHT

A GOLDEN TRESURY OF THE
GREATEST HITS
C 2X-3 CL 1687

BECAUSE OF YOU

THE GOLDEN DOZEN
CL 1462 VARIOUS

JUST IN TIME

THE HITMAKERS VARIOUS
CL1485 CS8276

I'LL BRING YOU A RAINBOW

MOODS FOR LOVERS ST MICHAEL
M05012115s 1979

FLY ME TO THE MOON
MCARTHUR PARK

WITH A SONG
CSP 142

ONCE UPON A TIME
THE GOOD LIFE
SUDDENLY

CAROLS AND CANDLELIGHT
CSP 12525

I LOVE THE WINTER WEATHER
I'VE GOT MY LOVE TO KEEP ME WARM

THE JOYOUS SONGS OF CHRISTMAS
CSP10400

WINTER WONDERLAND

PARADE OF SHOWSTOPPERS
CSP 237

PUT ON A HAPPY FACE

DIAMOND JUBILEE SHOWCASE
CSP XTV86090

CLIMB EVERY MOUNTAIN

THE SEASON'S BEST VARIOUS
C/CA/CT/30124

HAVE YOURSELF A MERRY LITTLE
CHRISTMAS

2.38 AM RALPH SHARON, QUARTET
& FRIEND
ARGO 635

FRIENDS BLUES (SCAT ONLY)

133

| | |
|---|---|
| **POPULAR FAVOURITES VOL 1**<br>VARIOUS ARTISTS PHILIPS BBR 8030 10" | CINNAMON SINNER |
| **POPULAR FAVOURITES VOL 5**<br>VARIOUS ARTISTS PHILIPS BBR 8084 10" | COME NEXT SPRING |
| **POPULAR FAVOURITES VOL 7**<br>VARIOUS ARTISTS PHILIPS BBR 8108 10" | HEART |
| **POPULAR FAVOURITES NO 14**<br>VARIOUS ARTISTS PHILIPS HOLLAND<br>B13202 R | CA CES'T L'AMOUR |
| **GOLDEN HITS/VARIOUS ARTISTS**<br>S/BBL7331 | STRANGER IN PARADISE |
| **GOLD RECORD HITS**<br>XTV 82067/8 | STRANGER IN PARADISE |
| **THE 50'S GREATEST HITS**<br>G30592 | RAGS TO RICHES |
| **THE BEST OF THE GOLD VOL 50'S**<br>G 32389 | BECAUSE OF YOU |
| **20 YEARS OF NUMBER ONE HITS**<br>KG 32007 | RAGS TO RICHES |
| **GREAT SONGS OF THE 60'S**<br>CSP 129 Safeway Exclusive | THIS IS ALL I ASK |
| **GREAT SONGS OF THE SIXTIES**<br>CSP 138 Safeway Exclusive | PUT ON A HAPPY FACE |
| **THE HEADLINERS**<br>GB7 | BEGIN THE BEGUINE |
| **THE HEADLINERS**<br>CSP D154 | IT COULD HAPPEN TO YOU |
| **REMEMBER HOW GREAT**<br>XTV 69408/9 | BECAUSE OF YOU |
| **SOUNDS COLOURFUL**<br>CSP LSP 13047 | I'M ALWAYS CHASING RAINBOWS |
| **SINGER PRESENTS**<br>CCS 552 | 1 HOUR TV SPECIAL |
| **ZENITH PRESENTS BROADWAY/<br>HOLLYWOOD** | LOVE LOOK AWAY<br>LOVE THEME FROM THE SANDPIPER |

THE LATE, LATE HOURS
CBS BCG 62296

VARIOUS ARTISTS SING 16 NUMBER 1
 HITS
CBS LSP 15203

THE GREAT ONES                          BECAUSE OF YOU
CSP C2 11003 BROOKVILLE

I LOVE N Y                              LULLABY OF BROADWAY
CSP VARIOUS

TED HEATH 21ST ANNIVERSARY ALBUM   tributes with Alan Dell
DECCA SKL 4903s

NARWOOD RECORDS - INTERVIEWS 283/4  with Bill Evans & William B Williams

TONY BENNETT/AL TORNELLO
 GUEST STAR                             see One Night Stand
G1485

COMMAND PERFORMANCE                     GET HAPPY
 VARIOUS ARTISTS                        THE GOOD LIFE
PICKWICK SHM912 CHARITY

GREAT ARTISTES - GREAT HITS             I'VE GROWN ACCUSTOMED TO HER FACE
SAGA EROS 8138 1970 COMPILATION         ANYTHING GOES

DAVE BRUBECK'S SUMMIT SESSIONS
 LIVE                                   THAT OLD BLACK MAGIC
CBS 64311 30522

THE SONGS OF ALEC WILDER –
 VARIOUS                                THE LADY SINGS THE BLUES
JJA19795

MUSIC FROM THE LATE SHOW                THAT OLD BLACK MAGIC
CSP XTV 86356

THE GENE KRUPA COLLECTION               (I LEFT MY HEART) IN SAN FRANCISCO
DVLP 2093 DEJA VU GUARD SESSIONS

RADIO SHOWS ARMY RESERVE
Double Album                            Skitch & Co with 5th Dimension 1975
                                        Skitch & Co with Errol Garner 1974

FABULOUS FIFTIES                        STRANGER IN PARADISE
PICKWICK DITTO DTOL 10252

ALL STAR FAVOURITES                     THE GOOD LIFE
WSR 853

135

| | |
|---|---|
| **TIME FOR TUNES**<br>CBS SP PRO 1967 WSR 854 | WHO CAN I TURN TO |
| **TIME FOR TUNES**<br>WSR 858 | THE SHADOW OF YOUR SMILE |
| **PARTY MOOD**<br>WSR 880 CBS CSQ | LET'S FACE THE MUSIC AND DANCE |
| **STARGAZERS KAZINO TV PROMO**<br>1985 KTV1 | (I LEFT MY HEART) IN SAN FRANCISCO |
| **GREAT SONGS OF CHRISTMAS**<br>WSR 859 VARIOUS | SANTA CLAUS IS COMING TO TOWN |
| **GREAT SONGS OF CHRISTMAS**<br>CSP 888 VARIOUS | WHAT CHILD IS THIS? |
| **THE GREAT SONGS OF CHRISTMAS VOL 7** | SANTA CLAUS IS COMING TO TOWN<br>THE CHRISTMAS SONG |
| **NOEL**<br>VARIOUS ARTISTS TRAX CD701 1988 | HAVE YOURSELF A MERRY LITTLE CHRISTMAS |
| **FOR THOSE WHO BELIEVE IN FATHER CHRISTMAS**<br>CBS 13070 Some tracks by Tony Bennett, others Johnny Matthis | |
| **20 ITALIAN LOVE SONGS**<br>TELSTAR 230S 1983 | AUTUMN IN ROME<br>BEGIN THE BEGUINE |
| **ALWAYS**<br>K-TEL NCD 3377 | STRANGER IN PARADISE |
| **25 YEARS OF ROCK 'N' ROLL**<br>VARIOUS ARTISTS CONNOISSEUR COLLECTION CD63 | THE GOOD LIFE |
| **BACK TO THE FIFTIES**<br>PICKWICK PWKS4151 1993 | CLOSE YOUR EYES |
| **THE 50'S REVISITED**<br>PICKWICK PWKS4152 1993 | STRANGER IN PARADISE |
| **THE SINGER AND THE SONG (PREMIER JAZZ)**<br>MFP CDP 7 98859 2 1993 | ANYTHING GOES |
| **20 ALL TIME GREATS OF THE 50'S**<br>K-TEL NE 490 | YOUNG AND WARM AND WONDERFUL |

**25 YEARS OF ROYAL VARIETY**
   **AT THE PALLADIUM**                (I LEFT MY HEART) IN SAN FRANCISCO
Max Bygraves intro rvp 252S

**20 COMMAND PERFOMANCES**
   **VARIOUS LIVE**                      (I LEFT MY HEART) IN SAN FRANCISCO
Ed Sullivan show
RONCO MSD 2005

**A TOUCH OF CLASS**                  MIMI
PHILIPS 6612 040 DBL 1972       MY FUNNY VALENTINE

**WORDS AND MUSIC – COLE PORTER**   AT LONG LAST LOVE
PHILIPS INT DBL 6641 295          I CONCENTRATE ON YOU

**AH MEN**                                 MY FUNNY VALENTINE
CONTOUR 6870 662

**LOVE SONGS**                     THE LOOK OF LOVE
CBS SPECIAL PRODUCTS 13639 HEINZ

**MAGIC MOMENTS YESTERDAYS HITS**
   **FOR TODAY**                      PENNIES FROM HEAVEN
CBS 54680 1984

**THE FRANK SINATRA DUETS**       MY KIND OF TOWN
PJ INT 001 1984 TV REC 21.4.77

**TONY BENNETT, STAN GETZ & FRIENDS**   JUST FRIENDS
PRESTIGE HB6123                HAVE YOU MET MISS JONES?
not released                          OUT OF THIS WORLD

**SINGIN' TILL THE GIRLS COME HOME**   JUST FRIENDS
COLUMBIA FC38508              HAVE YOU MET MISS JONES?
                                          OUT OF THIS WORLD

**MY CHERRY - UNFORGETTABLE**
   **ROMANTIC SONGS**            THEY SAY IT'S WONDERFUL
DE KUYPER SPECIAL SONY 29-98398-30 1993

**IRVING BERLIN 100 YEARS OF GENIUS**   ALWAYS
CBS 460999 1988                  LET'S FACE THE MUSIC AND DANCE

**DUETS (WITH FRANK SINATRA)**     NEW YORK, NEW YORK
CAPITOL 7243 8 28067 4 5 1994

**TRUE LOVE**                       THE SHADOW OF YOUR SMILE
TELSTAR TCD 2692 1993

**CAPITOL SINGS COAST TO COAST**   CHICAGO
   **ROUTE 66**
CAPITOL 1994 7 80180 2 5 CD

| | |
|---|---|
| **TRIBUTE TO RAY MOORE**<br>BBC RECORDS | THE GOOD THINGS IN LIFE |
| **A TRIBUTE TO DUKE**<br>CONCORD JAZZ CJ 50 VARIOUS | PRELUDE TO A KISS<br>I'M JUST A LUCKY SO AND SO |
| **THAT'S JAZZ**<br>EMI DBL CD 1995 | CHICAGO |
| **50'S THE SONG** STYLIST<br>K-TEL 1995 | 2 Basie/Bennett tracks |
| **50'S THE LOVE SONGS**<br>K-TEL 1995 | 2 Basie/Bennett tracks |
| **ELVIS – IT'S NOW OR NEVER**<br>THE TRIBUTE MERCURY 524072 | LOVE ME TENDER |
| **MANHATTAN TRANSFER XMAS ALBUM**<br>COLUMBIA CL 52968 | THE CHRISTMAS SONG |
| **ONCE MORE WITH FEELING**<br>AMHERST AMH 94405 | I CAN'T GET STARTED |

# EXTENDED PLAY ISSUES

BECAUSE OF YOUAs 10" Album Listing
COL B314

CLOUD 7Tracks 3,8,4,5,6,7 as album
COL B472

CLOUD 7Tracks 1,2,9,10 as album
COL B1960

TONY VOL 1Tracks 1-4 as album
TONY VOL 25-8
TONY VOL 39-12
COL B9381/2/3

THE BEAT OF MY HEARTLET'S BEGIN
COL B10791LET THERE BE LOVE
BLUES IN THE NIGHT

LONG AGO AND FAR AWAYIT COULD HAPPEN TO YOU
COL B11861EV'RYTIME WE SAY GOODBYE
LONG AGO AND FAR AWAY
IT AMAZES ME

IN PERSON!FASCINATIN' RYTHMN
COL B12941WHEN I FALL IN LOVE
PENNIES FROM HEAVEN
THERE WILL NEVER BE ANOTHER YOU

HOMETOWN, MY HOMETOWNPENTHOUSE SERENADE
COL B13011 PHILIPS 12338I COVER THE WATERFRONT
(Skyscraper Blues)

HALL OF FAME SERIESBECAUSE OF YOU
COL B2519COLD, COLD HEART
RAGS TO RICHES
STRANGER IN PARADISE

HALL OF FAME VARIOUSTracks 1,2 as above
COL B1963

BLUE VELVETSING YOU SINNERS
COL B2563BLUE VELVET
BOULEVARD OF BROKEN DREAMS
I WON'T CRY ANYMORE

TONY BENNETT – PHILIPS TV SERIESFIREFLY
UK EP PHILIPS BBE12223I FALL IN LOVE TOO EASILY
IT HAD TO BE YOU
BOULEVARD OF BROKEN DREAMS

**STRANGER IN PARADISE**
UK EP PHILIPS BBE 12009

STRANGER IN PARADISE
TAKE ME BACK AGAIN
MAY I NEVER LOVE AGAIN
PUNCH AND JUDY LOVE

**ONE FOR MY BABY**
COL B2582

ONE FOR MY BABY
I CAN'T GIVE YOU ANYTHING BUT LOVE
SOLITAIRE
ONCE THERE LIVED A FOOL

**JUST SAY I LOVED HER**
COL B2620

JUST SAY I LOVED HER (DICITENCELLO VIVIE)
JUST IN TIME
IN THE MIDDLE OF AN ISLAND
CA, C'EST L'AMOUR

**TONY BENNETT SPOTLITE**
COL B1842

STRANGER IN PARADISE
WHY DOES IT HAVE TO BE ME?
RAGS TO RICHES
CONGRATULATIONS TO SOMEONE

**TONY BENNETT**
COL B2079

A BLOSSOM FELL
SOMETHIN'S GOTTA GIVE
HEART
WHATEVER LOLA WANTS

**TILL**
CBS 6071

TILL
SEPTEMBER SONG
SPEAK LOW
WE MUSN'T SAY GOODBYE

**WHEN JOANNA LOVED ME**
CBS 6066

THIS IS ALL I ASK
A TASTE OF HONEY
FLY ME TO THE MOON
WHEN JOANNA LOVED ME

**THE GOOD LIFE**
UK EP ACG320037 CBS

THE GOOD LIFE
UNTIL I MET YOU
BLUE VELVET
QUIET NIGHTS OF QUIET STARS

**TONY BENNETT SINGS**
UK EP PHILIPS BBE 12424

MARRIAGE-GO-ROUND
SOMEBODY
ASK ANYONE IN LOVE
TILL

**MOMENT OF TRUTH**
UK EP PHILIPS AAG 20052

THE MOMENT OF TRUTH
SO LONG, BIG TIME
YOUNG AND FOOLISH
CARAVAN

**THE BEST OF TONY BENNETT**
UK EP CBS 6151

(I LEFT MY HEART) IN SAN FRANCISCO
THE VERY THOUGHT OF YOU
IF I RULED THE WORLD
WHO CAN I TURN TO

**ALONE TOGETHER**
PHILIPS S/BBE12458/9057

ALONE TOGETHER
THIS IS ALL I ASK
AFTER YOU'VE GONE
HOW LONG HAS THIS BEEN GOING ON

**BASIE - BENNETT**
ESG 7790 ROULETTE

CHICAGO
PLENTY OF MONEY AND YOU
JEEPERS CREEPERS
POOR LITTLE RICH GIRL
ARE YOU HAVING ANY FUN

**TONY BENNETT**
PHILIPS 429 368 BE FRANCE

IN THE MIDDLE OF AN ISLAND
CA C'EST L'AMOUR
WHATEVER LOLA WANTS
ONE KISS FROM HEAVEN

**TONY BENNETT**
PHILIPS 429 088 BE HOLLAND

MY BABY JUST CARES FOR ME
I CAN'T BELIVE YOU'RE IN LOVE WITH ME
LOVE LETTERS
DARN THAT DREAM

## VARIOUS ARTIST EP'S

**POPULAR FAVORITES VOL III**
COL B388

STRANGER IN PARADISE
RAGS TO RICHES

**POPULAR FAVORITES VOL IV**
COL B294

BECAUSE OF YOU
COLD. COLD HEART

**POPULAR HITS VOL 1**
COL B 1648

CONGRATULATIONS TO SOMEONE IN LOVE

**BECAUSE OF YOU VARIOUS**
COL B2055

COLD, COLD HEART

**ALL STAR POPS**
COL B2074

CLOSE YOUR EYES

**HITS FROM KISMET**
COL B1800 PHILIPS BBE 12009

STRANGER IN PARADISE

**HITS FROM THE GIRL IN PINK TIGHTS**
COL B1862

MY HEART WON'T SAY GOODBYE

**HITS FROM BELLS ARE RINGING**
COL B2122 PHILIPS BBE 12148

JUST IN TIME

| | |
|---|---|
| **HITS FROM OH CAPTAIN**<br>COL B2145 | YOU'RE SO RIGHT FOR ME |
| **HITS FROM THE FLOWER DRUM SONG**<br>COL B2151 | LOVE LOOK AWAY |
| **TOP CHOICE '68**<br>WEP 1134 | SOMETHING IN YOUR SMILE |
| **HITS FROM THE SHOWS**<br>EP AMBROSIA | IF I RULED THE WORLD |
| **BIG SHOW ASSORTMENT**<br>EP WEP 1127 QUAKER | STRANGER IN PARADISE |
| **EASY TO GET ON WITH (MARIGOLD GLOVES)**<br>WEP1130 | THEY CAN'T TAKE THAT AWAY FROM ME |
| **TONY AND JULIE SHOWTIME**<br>CSP EP WEP1123<br>BASSETTS JELLY BABIES | CLIMB EVERY MOUNTAIN<br>SMILE |
| **ALL TIME HITS**<br>CSP WEP1133 LYONS | TROLLEY SONG |
| **SHOW FAVOURITES**<br>CSP WEP 1128 | BABY DREAM YOUR DREAM |
| **BIG FOUR NO 7**<br>BBE 12145 | IN THE MIDDLE OF AN ISLAND |
| **BELLS ARE RINGING**<br>PHILIPS EP 12148 | JUST IN TIME |
| **JUST IN TIME**<br>PHILIPS EP 12150 | JUST IN TIME |
| **SOUND OF MUSIC**<br>PHILIPS EP 12437 | CLIMB EVERY MOUNTAIN |

# THE SINGLES

| | | | |
|---|---|---|---|
| FASCINATIN' RHYTHM | A | LESLIE | 1947 |
| VIENI QUI | B | LESLIE | 1947 |
| As Joe Bari | | | |
| | | | |
| THE BOULEVARD OF BROKEN DREAMS | A | DEMO | C1949 |

## THE COLUMBIA SINGLE RELEASES

| | | | |
|---|---|---|---|
| THE BOULEVARD OF BROKEN DREAMS | A | COLUMBIA | 38825 |
| I WANNA BE LOVED | B | COLUMBIA | 38825 |
| | | | |
| LET'S MAKE LOVE | A | COLUMBIA | 38856 |
| I CAN'T GIVE YOU ANYTHING BUT LOVE | B | COLUMBIA | 38856 |
| | | | |
| JUST SAY I LOVE HER | A | COLUMBIA | 38926 |
| OUR LADY OF FATIMA | B | COLUMBIA | 38926 |
| | | | |
| SING YOU SINNERS | A | COLUMBIA | 38989 |
| KISS YOU | B | COLUMBIA | 38989 |
| | | | |
| DON'T CRY BABY | A | COLUMBIA | 39060 |
| ONE LIE LEADS TO ANOTHER | B | COLUMBIA | 39060 |
| | | | |
| ONCE THERE LIVED A FOOL | A | COLUMBIA | 39187 |
| I CAN'T GIVE YOU ANYTHING BUT LOVE | B | COLUMBIA | 39187 |
| | | | |
| BEAUTIFUL MADNESS | A | COLUMBIA | 39209 |
| THE VALENTINO TANGO | B | COLUMBIA | 39209 |
| | | | |
| I WON'T CRY ANYMORE | A | COLUMBIA | 39362 |
| BECAUSE OF YOU | B | COLUMBIA | 39362 |
| | | | |
| COLD, COLD HEART | A | COLUMBIA | 39449 |
| WHILE WE`RE YOUNG | B | COLUMBIA | 39449 |
| | | | |
| BLUE VELVET | A | COLUMBIA | 39555 |
| SOLITAIRE | B | COLUMBIA | 39555 |
| | | | |
| SILLY DREAMER | A | COLUMBIA | 39635 |
| SINCE MY LOVE HAS ONE | B | COLUMBIA | 39635 |
| | | | |
| SLEEPLESS | A | COLUMBIA | 39695 |
| SOMEWHERE ALONG THE WAY | B | COLUMBIA | 39695 |
| | | | |
| HERE IN MY HEART | A | COLUMBIA | 39745 |
| I'M LOST AGAIN | B | COLUMBIA | 39745 |

| | | | |
|---|---|---|---|
| HAVE A GOOD TIME | A | COLUMBIA | 39764 |
| PLEASE, MY LOVE | B | COLUMBIA | 39764 |
| ROSES OF YESTERDAY | A | COLUMBIA | 39815 |
| YOU COULD MAKE ME SMILE AGAIN | B | COLUMBIA | 39815 |
| ANYWHERE I WANDER | A | COLUMBIA | 39866 |
| STAY WHERE YOU ARE | B | COLUMBIA | 39866 |
| CONGRATULATIONS TO SOMEONE | A | COLUMBIA | 39910 |
| TAKE ME | B | COLUMBIA | 39910 |
| I'M THE KING OF BROKEN HEARTS | A | COLUMBIA | 39964 |
| NO ONE WILL EVER KNOW | B | COLUMBIA | 39964 |
| SOMEONE TURNED THE MOON UPSIDE DOWN | A | COLUMBIA | 40004 |
| I'LL GO | B | COLUMBIA | 40004 |
| RAGS TO RICHES | A | COLUMBIA | 40048 |
| HERE COMES THAT HEARTACHE AGAIN | B | COLUMBIA | 40048 |
| STRANGER IN PARADISE | A | COLUMBIA | 40121 |
| WHY DID IT HAVE TO BE ME? | B | COLUMBIA | 40121 |
| MY HEART WON'T SAY GOODBYE | A | COLUMBIA | 40169 |
| THERE'LL BE NO TEARDROPS TONIGHT | B | COLUMBIA | 40169 |
| UNTIL YESTERDAY | A | COLUMBIA | 40213 |
| PLEASE DRIVER | B | COLUMBIA | 40213 |
| CINNAMON SINNER | A | COLUMBIA | 40272 |
| TAKE ME BACK AGAIN | B | COLUMBIA | 40272 |
| MADONNA MADONNA | A | COLUMBIA | 40311 |
| NOT AS A STRANGER | B | COLUMBIA | 40311 |
| FUNNY THING | A | COLUMBIA | 40376 |
| SHOO-GAH (MY PRETTY SUGAR) | B | COLUMBIA | 40376 |
| IT'S TOO SOON TO KNOW | A | COLUMBIA | 40472 |
| CLOSE YOUR EYES | B | COLUMBIA | 40472 |
| WHAT WILL I TELL MY HEART? | A | COLUMBIA | 40491 |
| PUNCH AND JUDY LOVE | B | COLUMBIA | 40491 |
| DON'T TELL ME WHY | A | COLUMBIA | 40523 |
| MAY I NEVER LOVE AGAIN | B | COLUMBIA | 40523 |
| HOW CAN I REPLACE YOU? | A | COLUMBIA | 40567 |
| TELL ME THAT YOU LOVE ME | B | COLUMBIA | 40567 |

| | | | |
|---|---|---|---|
| COME NEXT SPRING | A | COLUMBIA | 40598 |
| AFRAID OF THE DARK | B | COLUMBIA | 40598 |
| | | | |
| SING YOU SINNERS | A | COLUMBIA | 40632 |
| CAPRI IN MAY | B | COLUMBIA | 40632 |
| | | | |
| CAN YOU FIND IT IN YOUR HEART? | A | COLUMBIA | 40667 |
| FORGET HER | B | COLUMBIA | 40667 |
| | | | |
| FROM THE CANDY STORE ON THE CORNER | A | COLUMBIA | 40726 |
| HAPPINESS STREET (CORNER SUNSHINE SQ) | B | COLUMBIA | 40726 |
| | | | |
| JUST IN TIME | A | COLUMBIA | 40770 |
| AUTUMN WALTZ | B | COLUMBIA | 40770 |
| | | | |
| SOLD TO THE MAN WITH THE BROKEN HEART | A | COLUMBIA | 40849 |
| ONE KISS AWAY FROM HEAVEN | B | COLUMBIA | 40849 |
| | | | |
| NO HARD FEELINGS | A | COLUMBIA | 40907 |
| ONE FOR MY BABY | B | COLUMBIA | 40907 |
| | | | |
| I AM | A | COLUMBIA | 40965 |
| IN THE MIDDLE OF AN ISLAND | B | COLUMBIA | 40965 |
| | | | |
| I NEVER FELT MORE LIKE FALLING IN LOVE | A | COLUMBIA | 41032 |
| CA, C'EST L'AMOUR | B | COLUMBIA | 41032 |
| | | | |
| LOVE SONG FROM BEAUTY AND THE BEAST | A | COLUMBIA | 41086 |
| WEARY BLUES FROM WAITIN' | B | COLUMBIA | 41086 |
| | | | |
| YOU'RE SO RIGHT FOR ME | A | COLUMBIA | 41127 |
| ALONE AT LAST | B | COLUMBIA | 41127 |
| | | | |
| THE BEAT OF MY HEART | A | COLUMBIA | 41157 |
| CRAZY RYTHMN | B | COLUMBIA | 41157 |
| | | | |
| YOUNG AND WARM AND WONDERFUL | A | COLUMBIA | 41172 |
| NOW I LAY ME DOWN TO SLEEP | B | COLUMBIA | 41172 |
| | | | |
| FIREFLY | A | COLUMBIA | 41237 |
| THE NIGHT THAT HEAVEN FELL | B | COLUMBIA | 41237 |
| | | | |
| LOVE LOOK AWAY | A | COLUMBIA | 41298 |
| BLUE MOON | B | COLUMBIA | 41298 |
| | | | |
| BEING TRUE TO ONE ANOTHER | A | COLUMBIA | 41341 |
| IT'S SO PEACEFUL IN THE COUNTRY | B | COLUMBIA | 41341 |
| | | | |
| THE COOL SCHOOL | A | COLUMBIA | 41381 |
| YOU'LL NEVER GET AWAY FROM ME | B | COLUMBIA | 41381 |

| | | | |
|---|---|---|---|
| SMILE | A | COLUMBIA | 41434 |
| YOU CAN'T LOVE THEM ALL | B | COLUMBIA | 41434 |
| | | | |
| CLIMB EVERY MOUNTAIN | A | COLUMBIA | 41520 |
| ASK ANYONE IN LOVE | B | COLUMBIA | 41520 |
| | | | |
| ASK ME (I KNOW) | A | COLUMBIA | 41595 |
| I'LL BRING YOU A RAINBOW | B | COLUMBIA | 41595 |
| | | | |
| PUT ON A HAPPY FACE | A | COLUMBIA | 41691 |
| BABY TALK TO ME | B | COLUMBIA | 41691 |
| | | | |
| TILL | A | COLUMBIA | 41770 |
| I AM | B | COLUMBIA | 41770 |
| | | | |
| MARRIAGE-GO-ROUND | A | COLUMBIA | 41874 |
| RAMONA | B | COLUMBIA | 41874 |
| | | | |
| MARRY YOUNG | A | COLUMBIA | 41965 |
| THE BEST IS YET TO COME | B | COLUMBIA | 41965 |
| | | | |
| TOOT, TOOT, TOOTSIE! (GOODBYE) | A | COLUMBIA | 42003 |
| I'M COMING VIRGINIA | B | COLUMBIA | 42003 |
| | | | |
| COMES ONCE IN A LIFETIME | A | COLUMBIA | 42219 |
| TENDER IS THE NIGHT | B | COLUMBIA | 42219 |
| | | | |
| (I LEFT MY HEART) IN SAN FRANCISCO | A | COLUMBIA | 42332 |
| ONCE UPON A TIME | B | COLUMBIA | 42332 |
| | | | |
| CANDY KISSES | A | COLUMBIA | 42395 |
| HAVE I TOLD YOU LATELY? | B | COLUMBIA | 42395 |
| | | | |
| I WILL LIVE MY LIFE FOR YOU | A | COLUMBIA | 42634 |
| I WANNA BE AROUND | B | COLUMBIA | 42634 |
| | | | |
| THE GOOD LIFE | A | COLUMBIA | 42779 |
| SPRING IN MANHATTAN | B | COLUMBIA | 42779 |
| | | | |
| THIS IS ALL I ASK | A | COLUMBIA | 42820 |
| TRUE BLUE LOU | B | COLUMBIA | 42820 |
| | | | |
| LIMEHOUSE BLUES | A | COLUMBIA | 42886 |
| DON'T WAIT TOO LONG | B | COLUMBIA | 42886 |
| | | | |
| THE LITTLE BOY | A | COLUMBIA | 42931 |
| THE MOMENT OF TRUTH | B | COLUMBIA | 42931 |
| | | | |
| WHEN JOANNA LOVED ME | A | COLUMBIA | 42996 |
| THE KID'S A DREAMER | B | COLUMBIA | 42996 |

| | | | |
|---|---|---|---|
| IT'S A SIN TO TELL A LIE | A | COLUMBIA | 43073 |
| A TASTE OF HONEY | B | COLUMBIA | 43073 |
| | | | |
| WHO CAN I TURN TO | A | COLUMBIA | 43141 |
| WALTZ FOR DEBBIE | B | COLUMBIA | 43141 |
| | | | |
| THE BEST THING TO BE IS A PERSON | A | COLUMBIA | 43202 |
| THE BRIGHTEST SMILE IN TOWN | B | COLUMBIA | 43202 |
| | | | |
| IF I RULED THE WORLD | A | COLUMBIA | 43220 |
| TAKE THE MOMENT | B | COLUMBIA | 43220 |
| | | | |
| FLY ME TO THE MOON | A | COLUMBIA | 43331 |
| HOW INSENSITIVE | B | COLUMBIA | 43331 |
| | | | |
| THE SHADOW OF YOUR SMILE | A | COLUMBIA | 43431 |
| I'LL ONLY MISS HER WHEN I THINK OF HER | B | COLUMBIA | 43431 |
| | | | |
| BABY, DREAM YOUR DREAM | A | COLUMBIA | 43508 |
| MAYBE SEPTEMBER | B | COLUMBIA | 43508 |
| | | | |
| GEORGIA ROSE | A | COLUMBIA | 43715 |
| THE VERY THOUGHT OF YOU | B | COLUMBIA | 43715 |
| | | | |
| A TIME FOR LOVE | A | COLUMBIA | 43768 |
| TOUCH THE EARTH | B | COLUMBIA | 43768 |
| | | | |
| WHAT MAKES IT HAPPEN? | A | COLUMBIA | 43954 |
| COUNTRY GIRL | B | COLUMBIA | 43954 |
| | | | |
| DAYS OF LOVE | A | COLUMBIA | 44154 |
| KEEP SMILING AT TROUBLE | B | COLUMBIA | 44154 |
| | | | |
| FOR ONCE IN MY LIFE | A | COLUMBIA | 44258 |
| SOMETHING IN YOUR SMILE | B | COLUMBIA | 44258 |
| | | | |
| A FOOL OF FOOLS | A | COLUMBIA | 44443 |
| THE GLORY OF LOVE | B | COLUMBIA | 44443 |
| | | | |
| YESTERDAY I HEARD THE RAIN | A | COLUMBIA | 44510 |
| SWEET GEORGIE FAME | B | COLUMBIA | 44510 |
| | | | |
| HUSHABYE MOUNTAIN | A | COLUMBIA | 44584 |
| HI-HO | B | COLUMBIA | 44584 |
| | | | |
| MY FAVOURITE THINGS | A | COLUMBIA | 44688 |
| WHERE IS LOVE? | B | COLUMBIA | 44688 |
| | | | |
| PEOPLE | A | COLUMBIA | 44755 |
| THEY ALL LAUGHED | B | COLUMBIA | 44755 |

| | | | |
|---|---|---|---|
| WHOEVER YOU ARE, I LOVE YOU | A | COLUMBIA | 44824 |
| OVER THE SUN | B | COLUMBIA | 44824 |
| | | | |
| PLAY IT AGAIN, SAM | A | COLUMBIA | 44855 |
| WHAT THE WORLD NEEDS NOW IS LOVE | B | COLUMBIA | 44855 |
| | | | |
| I'VE GOTTA BE ME | A | COLUMBIA | 44947 |
| A LONELY PLACE | B | COLUMBIA | 44947 |
| | | | |
| MacARTHUR PARK | A | COLUMBIA | 45032 |
| BEFORE WE SAY GOODBYE | B | COLUMBIA | 45032 |
| | | | |
| COCO | A | COLUMBIA | 45073 |
| LITTLE GREEN APPLES | B | COLUMBIA | 45073 |
| | | | |
| SOMETHING | A | COLUMBIA | 45109 |
| ELEANOR RIGBY | B | COLUMBIA | 45109 |
| | | | |
| THINK HOW IT'S GONNA BE | A | COLUMBIA | 45157 |
| EVERYBODY'S TALKIN' | B | COLUMBIA | 45157 |
| | | | |
| THE VERY THOUGHT OF YOU | A | COLUMBIA | 45247 |
| SLEEPY TIME GAL | B | COLUMBIA | 45247 |
| | | | |
| SOMETHING | A | COLUMBIA | 45205 |
| THINK HOW IT'S GONNA BE | B | COLUMBIA | 45205 |
| | | | |
| I'LL BEGIN AGAIN | A | COLUMBIA | 45256 |
| I DO NOT KNOW A DAY I DID NOT LOVE YOU | B | COLUMBIA | 45256 |
| | | | |
| LOVE STORY (WHERE DO I BEGIN) | A | COLUMBIA | 45316 |
| I'LL BEGIN AGAIN | B | COLUMBIA | 45316 |
| | | | |
| TEA FOR TWO | A | COLUMBIA | 45376 |
| I WANT TO BE HAPPY | B | COLUMBIA | 45376 |
| | | | |
| I'M LOSING MY MIND | A | COLUMBIA | 45411 |
| MORE AND MORE | B | COLUMBIA | 45411 |
| | | | |
| WALKABOUT | A | COLUMBIA | 45449 |
| HOW BEAUTIFUL IS NIGHT (WITH YOU) | B | COLUMBIA | 45449 |
| | | | |
| THE RIVIERA | A | COLUMBIA | 45493 |
| REMIND ME | B | COLUMBIA | 45493 |
| | | | |
| THE SUMMER KNOWS | A | COLUMBIA | 45523 |
| SOMEWHERE ALONG THE LINE | B | COLUMBIA | 45523 |
| | | | |
| TWILIGHT WORLD | A | COLUMBIA | 45573 |
| EASY COME, EASY GO | B | COLUMBIA | 45573 |

| | | | |
|---|---|---|---|
| MAYBE THIS TIME | A | COLUMBIA | 45613 |
| LOVE | B | COLUMBIA | 45613 |
| | | | |
| WHITE CHRISTMAS | A | PROMO | 38.07658 |
| ALL OF MY LIFE | B | RADIO DJ | |

## HALL OF FAME US SINGLES

| | | | |
|---|---|---|---|
| COLD, COLD HEART | A | COLUMBIA | HOF33003 |
| BECAUSE OF YOU | B | COLUMBIA | HOF33003 |
| | | | |
| RAGS TO RICHES | A | COLUMBIA | HOF33035 |
| ONE FOR MY BABY | B | COLUMBIA | HOF33035 |
| | | | |
| (I LEFT MY HEART) IN SAN FRANCISCO | A | COLUMBIA | HOF33062 |
| I WANNA BE AROUND | B | COLUMBIA | HOF33062 |
| | | | |
| THE GOOD LIFE | A | COLUMBIA | HOF33080 |
| THIS IS ALL I ASK | B | COLUMBIA | HOF33080 |
| | | | |
| THE SHADOW OF YOUR SMILE | A | COLUMBIA | HOF33099 |
| WHO CAN I TURN TO? | B | COLUMBIA | HOF33099 |
| | | | |
| YESTERDAY I HEARD THE RAIN | A | COLUMBIA | HOF33144 |
| A FOOL OF FOOLS | B | COLUMBIA | HOF33144 |
| | | | |
| IN THE MIDDLE OF AN ISLAND | A | COLUMBIA | HOF33222 |
| SOMETHING | B | COLUMBIA | HOF33222 |

## COLUMBIA PRICELESS EDITIONS

| | | | |
|---|---|---|---|
| CLOSE YOUR EYES | A | COLUMBIA | PE6 |
| WE MUSTN'T SAY GOODBYE | B | COLUMBIA | PE6 |
| with the Pastels | | | |

## VERVE SINGLES

| | | | |
|---|---|---|---|
| LIVING TOGETHER, GROWING TOGETHER | A | VERVE | MV10690 |
| THE GOOD THINGS IN LIFE | B | | |
| | | | |
| TELL HER THAT IT'S SNOWING | A | VERVE | MV10714 |
| IF I COULD GO BACK | B | | |
| | | | |
| MY LOVE | A | VERVE | K 14607 |
| O' SOLE MIO | B | | |

## PHILIPS RELEASES 1972

| | | | |
|---|---|---|---|
| LIVING TOGETHER, GROWING TOGETHER | A | PHILIPS | 6006 260 |
| GOOD THINGS IN LIFE | B | | |
| | | | |
| GOOD THINGS IN LIFE | A | PHILIPS | 6006 309 |
| LOVE IS THE THING | B | | |
| | | | |
| MY LOVE | A | PHILIPS | 6006 326 |
| GIVE ME LOVE, GIVE ME PEACE | B | | |
| | | | |
| ALL THAT LOVE WENT TO WASTE | A | PHILIPS | 6006 372 |
| SOME OF THESE DAYS | B | | |
| | | | |
| ALL THAT LOVE WENT TO WASTE | A | BRUT | BR813 |
| SOME OF THESE DAYS | B | | |

## IMPROV SINGLES

| | | | |
|---|---|---|---|
| LIFE IS BEAUTIFUL | A | IMPROV | TB711105 |
| THERE'LL BE SOME CHANGES MADE | B | | |
| | | | |
| THERE'S ALWAYS TOMORROW | A | IMPROV | TB713106 |
| I WISH I WERE IN LOVE AGAIN | B | | |
| United Way Charity Single | | | |
| | | | |
| ONE | A | IMPROVE | TB715107 |
| MR MAGIC | B | | |

## PHILIPS BRITISH SINGLE RELEASES 1953-1965 UK

| | | | |
|---|---|---|---|
| MY HEART TELLS ME | A | PHILIPS | B472-1 |
| WHILE THE MUSIC PLAYS ON | B | PHILIPS | B472-1 |
| | | | |
| COLD, COLD HEART | A | PHILIPS | DB2924 |
| BECAUSE OF YOU | B | PHILIPS | DB2924 |
| | | | |
| RAGS TO RICHES | A | PHILIPS | PB216 |
| NO ONE WILL EVER KNOW | B | PHILIPS | PB216 |
| | | | |
| THERE'LL BE NO TEARDROPS TONIGHT | A | PHILIPS | PB267 |
| HERE COMES THAT HEARTACHE AGAIN | B | PHILIPS | PB267 |
| | | | |
| CINNAMON SINNER | A | PHILIPS | PB322 |
| UNTIL YESTERDAY | B | PHILIPS | PB322 |
| | | | |
| MADONNA MADONNA | A | PHILIPS | PB357 |
| NOT AS A STRANGER | B | PHILIPS | PB357 |

| | | | |
|---|---|---|---|
| FUNNY THING | A | PHILIPS | PB390 |
| PLEASE DRIVER (ONCE MORE AROUND THE PARK AGAIN) | B | PHILIPS | PB390 |
| | | | |
| STRANGER IN PARADISE | A | PHILIPS | PB420 |
| TAKE ME BACK AGAIN | B | PHILIPS | PB420 |
| | | | |
| IT'S TOO SOON TO KNOW | A | PHILIPS | PB445 |
| CLOSE YOUR EYES | B | PHILIPS | PB445 |
| | | | |
| KISSES I'LL NEVER FORGET | A | PHILIPS | PB477 |
| PUNCH AND JUDY LOVE | B | PHILIPS | PB477 |
| | | | |
| DON'T TELL ME WHY | A | PHILIPS | PB486 |
| MAY I NEVER LOVE AGAIN | B | PHILIPS | PB486 |
| | | | |
| CAN YOU FIND IT IN YOUR HEART? | A | PHILIPS | PB501 |
| FORGET HER | B | PHILIPS | PB501 |
| | | | |
| HOW CAN I REPLACE YOU? | A | PHILIPS | PB521 |
| TELL ME THAT YOU LOVE ME | B | PHILIPS | PB521 |
| | | | |
| COME NEXT SPRING | A | PHILIPS | PB537 |
| AFRAID OF THE DARK | B | PHILIPS | PB537 |
| | | | |
| SING YOU SINNERS | A | PHILIPS | PB563 |
| CAPRI IN MAY | B | PHILIPS | PB563 |
| | | | |
| FROM THE CANDY STORE ON THE CORNER | A | PHILIPS | PB628 |
| HAPPINESS STREET (CORNER SUNSHINE SQ) | B | PHILIPS | PB628 |
| | | | |
| WHATEVER LOLA WANTS | A | PHILIPS | PB672 |
| HEART | B | PHILIPS | PB672 |
| | | | |
| SOLD TO THE MAN WITH THE BROKEN HEART | A | PHILIPS | PB689 |
| ONE KISS AWAY FROM HEAVEN | B | PHILIPS | PB689 |
| | | | |
| NO HARD FEELING | A | PHILIPS | PB710 |
| ONE FOR MY BABY | B | PHILIPS | PB710 |
| | | | |
| IN THE MIDDLE OF AN ISLAND | A | PHILIPS | PB724 |
| I AM | B | PHILIPS | PB724 |
| | | | |
| JUST IN TIME | A | PHILIPS | PB753 |
| CA, C'EST L'AMOUR | B | PHILIPS | PB753 |
| | | | |
| I NEVER FELT MORE LIKE FALLING IN LOVE | A | PHILIPS | PB786 |
| LOVE ME, LOVE ME, LOVE ME | B | PHILIPS | PB786 |
| | | | |
| YOUNG AND WARM AND WONDERFUL | A | PHILIPS | PB831 |
| NOW I LAY ME DOWN TO SLEEP | B | PHILIPS | PB831 |

| | | | |
|---|---|---|---|
| FIREFLY | A | PHILIPS | PB855 |
| THE NIGHT THAT HEAVEN FELL | B | PHILIPS | PB855 |
| | | | |
| BEING TRUE TO ONE ANOTHER | A | PHILIPS | PB907 |
| IT'S SO PEACEFUL IN THE COUNTRY | B | PHILIPS | PB907 |
| | | | |
| SMILE | A | PHILIPS | PB961 |
| YOU CAN'T LOVE THEM ALL | B | PHILIPS | PB961 |
| | | | |
| THE COOL SCHOOL | A | PHILIPS | PB996 |
| LOVE LOOK AWAY | A | PHILIPS | PB996 |
| | | | |
| ASK ME (I KNOW) | A | PHILIPS | PB1008 |
| I'LL BRING YOU A RAINBOW | B | PHILIPS | PB1008 |
| | | | |
| TILL | A | PHILIPS | PB1079 |
| ASK ANYONE IN LOVE | B | PHILIPS | PB1079 |
| | | | |
| SOMEBODY | A | PHILIPS | PB1089 |
| MARRIAGE-GO-ROUND | B | PHILIPS | PB1089 |
| | | | |
| CLIMB EVERY MOUNTAIN | A | PHILIPS | PB1122 |
| RAMONA | B | PHILIPS | PB1122 |
| | | | |
| PUT ON A HAPPY FACE | A | PHILIPS | PB1149 |
| BABY TALK TO ME | B | PHILIPS | PB1149 |
| | | | |
| THE BEST IS YET TO COME | B | PHILIPS | PB1218 |
| TENDER IS THE NIGHT | B | PHILIPS | PB1218 |

## CBS UK SINGLES RELEASES 1965-1971

| | | | |
|---|---|---|---|
| (I LEFT MY HEART) IN SAN FRANCISCO | A | CBS | AAG121 |
| CANDY KISSES | B | CBS | AAG121 |
| | | | |
| YOU'LL NEVER GET AWAY FROM ME | A | CBS | AAG126 |
| MARRY YOUNG | B | CBS | AAG126 |
| | | | |
| I WANNA BE AROUND | A | CBS | AAG137 |
| I WILL LIVE MY LIFE FOR YOU | B | CBS | AAG137 |
| | | | |
| THE GOOD LIFE | A | CBS | AAG153 |
| SPRING IN MANHATTAN | B | CBS | AAG153 |
| | | | |
| THIS IS ALL I ASK | A | CBS | AAG165 |
| TRUE BLUE LOU | B | CBS | AAG165 |
| | | | |
| DON'T WAIT TOO LONG | A | CBS | AAG176 |
| LIMEHOUSE BLUES | B | CBS | AAG176 |

| | | | |
|---|---|---|---|
| THE LITTLE BOY | A | CBS | AAG184 |
| THE MOMENT OF TRUTH | B | CBS | AAG184 |
| | | | |
| WHEN JOANNA LOVED ME | A | CBS | AAG191 |
| THE KID'S A DREAMER | B | CBS | AAG191 |
| | | | |
| FOLLOW ME | A | CBS | AAG208 |
| SOON IT'S GONNA RAIN | B | CBS | AAG208 |
| | | | |
| WHO CAN I TURN TO | A | CBS | AAG225 |
| QUIET NIGHTS OF QUIET STARS | B | CBS | AAG225 |
| | | | |
| A FOOL OF FOOLS | A | CBS | 3370 |
| THE GLORY OF LOVE | B | CBS | 3370 |
| (with Dominic Germano) | | | |
| | | | |
| MacARTHUR PARK | A | CBS | S5255 |
| ELEANOR RIGBY | B | CBS | S5255 |
| | | | |
| MAYBE THIS TIME | A | CBS | S8095 |
| MORE AND MORE | B | CBS | S8095 |
| | | | |
| (I LEFT MY HEART) IN SAN FRANCISCO | A | CBS | 201730 |
| CANDY KISSES | B | CBS | 201730 |
| | | | |
| IF I RULED THE WORLD | A | CBS | 201735 |
| WHO CAN I TURN TO | B | CBS | 201735 |
| | | | |
| THE VERY THOUGHT OF YOU | A | CBS | 202021 |
| SLEEPY TIME GAL | B | CBS | 202021 |
| | | | |
| WHO CAN I TURN TO | A | CBS | 4-43141 |
| WHO CAN I TURN TO | B | CBS | 4-43141 |
| Red Vinyl Promo | | | |

## TONY BENNETT ON COMPACT DISC
### WORLD WIDE – NOT DEFINITIVE
### (SOME MAY HAVE BEEN DELETED)

### US ISSUES

| | | | |
|---|---|---|---|
| US | COLUMBIA | CK 9272 | THE MOVIE SONG ALBUM |
| US | COLUMBIA | CGK-40215 | 16 MOST REQUESTED SONGS |
| US | COLUMBIA | CK 45348 | ASTORIA – PORTRAIT OF THE ARTIST |
| US | COLUMBIA | CK 8669 | I LEFT MY HEART IN SAN FRANCISCO |
| US | COLUMBIA | CK 9737 | SNOWFALL THE CHRISTMAS ALBUM |
| US | COLUMBIA | CK 57424 | STEPPIN' OUT |
| US | COLUMBIA | CGK-40424 | JAZZ |
| US | COLUMBIA | CK 40344 | THE ART OF EXCELLENCE |
| US | COLUMBIA | CK 52965 | PERFECTLY FRANK |
| US | COLUMBIA | CK 66184 | IT COULD HAPPEN TO YOU - SOUNDTRACK |
| US | COLUMBIA | CK 66214 | MTV UNPLUGGED |
| US | COLUMBIA | LEG6426 | IN PERSON! |
| US | CONCORD | JAZZ | TRIBUTE TO DUKE (TB ON 2 TRACKS) |
| US | CURB | D2-77447 | THE BEST OF TONY BENNETT (EARLY 70'S PHILIPS TRACKS) |
| US | DRG | CDXP-2102 | THE RODGERS & HART SONGBOOK |
| US | DRG | CDMRS-801 | THE SPECIAL MAGIC OF TONY BENNETT |
| US | DRG | CDMR 5901 | TONY BENNETT & BILL EVANS TOGETHER AGAIN |
| US | DUNHILL | DZS-004 | CHICAGO |
| US | FANTASY | CJCCD-439-2 | THE TONY BENNETT/BILL EVANS ALBUM |
| US | MERCURY | 54072-2 | ELVIS – IT'S NOW OR NEVER |
| US | ROULETTE | CDP793899-2 | BASIE/BENNETT |
| US | ROULETTE | RCD-59021 | STRIKE UP THE BAND |
| US | SONY | A 21552 | THE GOOD LIFE |
| US | SONY | CK-53571 | THE ESSENCE OF TONY BENNETT |
| US | SONY | A823 | AT CARNEGIE HALL |
| US | SONY | A8242 | TONY SINGS FOR TWO |
| US | SONY | //// | ... SINGS A STRING OF HAROLD ARLEN |
| US | SONY | A 13302 | THE VERY THOUGHT OF YOU |
| US | COLUMBIA | CK 66503 | WHO CAN I TURN TO |
| US | COLUMBIA | CK 64601 | SOMETHING |
| US | COLUMBIA | CK 66504 | I WANNA BE AROUND |
| US | AMHERST | AMH 94405 | ONCE MORE WITH FEELING |

### UK ISSUES

| | | | |
|---|---|---|---|
| UK | CASTLE | MATCD319 | COUNT BASIE FEATURING TONY BENNETT |
| UK | CBS | 468 843-2 | ALL TIME GREATEST HITS |
| UK | CBS | 468 581-2 | 40 YEARS – THE ARTISTRY OF TONY BENNETT |
| UK | COLUMBIA | 453571 | THE ESSENCE OF TONY BENNETT |
| UK | COLUMBIA | 472222 2 | PERFECTLY FRANK |
| UK | COLUMBIA | 481266 2 | HERE'S TO THE LADIES |
| UK | COLUMBIA | CK 44029 | BENNETT:BERLIN |
| UK | COLUMBIA | 902 288-2 | I LEFT MY HEART IN SAN FRANCISCO |

| | | | |
|---|---|---|---|
| UK | COLUMBIA | CK 45358 | ASTORIA - PORTRAIT OF THE ARTIST |
| UK | COLUMBIA | 477170 2 | MTV UNPLUGGED |
| UK | COLUMBIA | 4775972 2 | SNOWFALL: THE CHRISTMAS ALBUM |
| UK | COLUMBIA | CK 40344 | THE ART OF EXCELLENCE |
| UK | H NELSON | CDSIV 1122 | TONY BENNETT & BILL EVANS TOGETHER AGAIN |
| UK | H NELSON | CDSIV 1106 | THE MAGIC OF TONY BENNETT |
| UK | H NELSON | CDSIV 1129 | SINGS THE RODGERS & HART SONGBOOK |
| UK | H NELSON | CDSIV 1119 | SINGS THE GREATEST HITS OF COLE PORTER AND RODGERS & HART |
| UK | H NELSON | CDSIV 6145 | HOLLYWOOD AND BROADWAY |
| UK | HARMONY | HARCD-105 | PORTRAIT OF A SONG STYLIST |
| UK | PICKWICK | PWK 032 | COUNT BASIE FEATURING TONY BENNETT |
| UK | PICKWICK | PWK 4171 | GREAT SONGS FROM GREAT SHOWS |
| UK | READERS DIGEST | | 40 YEARS – THE ARTISTRY OF TONY BENNETT |
| UK | ROULETTE | ROU 1009 | BASIE/BENNETT |
| UK | SMS | SMS-10 | BENNETT AND BASIE |
| UK | SONY | 477592 2 | I LEFT MY HEART IN SAN FRANCISCO /I WANNA BE AROUND |
| UK | SONY | 473 602-2 | STEPPIN' OUT |
| UK | TRING | JHD053 | THE SPECIAL MAGIC OF TONY BENNETT |

**NETHERLAND ISSUES**

| | | | |
|---|---|---|---|
| NETH | ANTELOPE | ANTC-52043 | 20 GREATEST HITS |
| NETH | CBS | CDCS-57056 | 16 MOST REQUESTED SONGS |
| NETH | CBS | 472 418-2 | 16 MOST REQUESTED SONGS |
| NETH | CBS | 460 450-2 | BENNETT:BERLIN |
| NETH | CBS | 465 445-2 | I LEFT MY HEART IN SAN FRANCISCO (POP MEMORY) |
| NETH | CBS | 472 222-2 | PERFECTLY FRANK |
| NETH | CBS | 462 539-2 | THE ART OF EXCELLENCE |
| NETH | DISKY | VTCD5850 | THE VOCAL TOUCH |

**JAPAN ISSUES**

| | | | |
|---|---|---|---|
| JAPAN | | EJC-747 | GREATEST JAZZ 47 |
| JAPAN | CBS | 32DP-558 | 16 MOST REQUESTED SONGS |
| JAPAN | CBS | CSCS-5244 | ... SINGS A STRING OF HAROLD ARLEN |
| JAPAN | CBS | CSCS-5243 | A TIME FOR LOVE |
| JAPAN | CBS | 32DP-739 | JAZZ |
| JAPAN | CBS | CSCS-5057 | ASTORIA – PORTRAIT OF THE ARTIST |
| JAPAN | CBS | 28DP-5288 | SNOWFALL THE CHRISTMAS ALBUM |
| JAPAN | CBS | 32DP-893 | BENNETT:BERLIN |
| JAPAN | CBS | 32DP-494 | THE ART OF EXCELLENCE |
| JAPAN | CBS | 32DP-568 | ALONE TOGETHER |
| JAPAN | CBS | 32DP-561 | I LEFT MY HEART IN SAN FRANCISCO |
| JAPAN | CBS | CSCS-5241 | I LEFT MY HEART IN SAN FRANCISCO |
| JAPAN | CBS | 25DP-5320 | IF I RULED THE WORLD (SONGS FOR THE JET SET) |
| JAPAN | CBS | 25DP-5507 | STAR BOX |
| JAPAN | CBS | CSCS-5245 | MY HEART SINGS |

| JAPAN | CBS | CSCS-5242 | WHEN LIGHTS ARE LOW |
| --- | --- | --- | --- |
| JAPAN | DRG | KICP-2046 | THE RODGERS & HART SONG BOOK |
| JAPAN | DRG | P28L-20096 | SINGS COLE PORTER AND RODGERS & HART |
| JAPAN | POLYDOR | J33J-20152 | CHICAGO |
| JAPAN | ROULETTE | TOCJ-5378 | BASIE/BENNETT (BONUS AFTER HOURS) |
| JAPAN | SONY | SRCS-6641-4 | 40 YEARS – THE ARTISTRY OF TONY BENNETT |
| JAPAN | SONY | SRCS-6565 | PERFECTLY FRANK |

**OTHERS**

| EEC | ELAP | PK510 | NIGHT AND DAY |
| --- | --- | --- | --- |
| EEC | PILZ | PM8342-2 | GREATEST HITS |
| EEC | ENT | CD273 | THE ENTERTAINERS HIS 28 GREATEST HITS |
| AUS | COLUMBIA | 471 121-2 | GET HAPPY – TONY BENNETT WITH THE LPO |
| AUS | COLUMBIA | 471 135-2 | THE GOOD LIFE |

## TONY BENNETT CD'S BY TITLE

| | | | |
|---|---|---|---|
| 16 MOST REQUESTED SONGS | NETH | CBS | 472 418-2 |
| 16 MOST REQUESTED SONGS | JAPAN | CBS | 32DP-558 |
| 16 MOST REQUESTED SONGS | NETH | CBS | CDCS-57056 |
| 16 MOST REQUESTED SONGS | US | COLUMBIA | CGK-40215 |
| | | | |
| 20 GREATEST HITS | NETH | ANTELOPE | ANTC-52043 |
| | | | |
| 40 YEARS – THE ARTISTRY OF TONY BENNETT | UK | CBS | 468 581-2 |
| 40 YEARS – THE ARTISTRY OF TONY BENNETT | UK | READERS DIGEST | |
| 40 YEARS – THE ARTISTRY OF TONY BENNETT | JAPAN | SONY | SRCS-6641-4 |
| | | | |
| A TIME FOR LOVE | JAPAN | CBS | CSCS-5243 |
| | | | |
| ALL TIME GREATEST HITS | UK | CBS | 468 843-2 |
| | | | |
| ALONE TOGETHER | JAPAN | CBS | 32DP-568 |
| | | | |
| ASTORIA – PORTRAIT OF THE ARTIST | JAPAN | CBS | CSCS-5057 |
| ASTORIA – PORTRAIT OF THE ARTIST | US | COLUMBI | CK 45348 |
| ASTORIA – PORTRAIT OF THE ARTIST | UK | COLUMBIA | CK 45358 |
| | | | |
| AT CARNEGIE HALL | US | SONY | A823 |
| | | | |
| BASIE/BENNETT | US | ROULETTE | CDP793899-2 |
| BASIE/BENNETT | UK | ROULETTE | ROU 1009 |
| BASIE/BENNETT (BONUS AFTER HOURS) | JAPAN | ROULETTE | TOCJ-5378 |
| BENNETT AND BASIE | UK | SMS | SMS-10 |
| | | | |
| BENNETT:BERLIN | NETH | CBS | 460 450-2 |
| BENNETT:BERLIN | JAPAN | CBS | 32DP-893 |
| BENNETT:BERLIN | UK | COLUMBIA | CK 44029 |
| | | | |
| CHICAGO | US | DUNHILL | DZS-004 |
| CHICAGO | JAPAN | POLYDOR | J33J-20152 |
| COUNT BASIE FEATURING TONY BENNETT | UK | CASTLE | MATCD319 |
| COUNT BASIE FEATURING TONY BENNETT | UK | PICKWICK | PWK 032 |
| | | | |
| ELVIS – IT'S NOW OR NEVER | US | MERCURY | 54072-2 |
| | | | |
| GET HAPPY - TONY BENNETT WITH THE LPO | AUS | COLUMBIA | 471 121-2 |
| | | | |
| GREAT SONGS FROM GREAT SHOWS | UK | PICKWICK | PWK 4171 |
| | | | |
| GREATEST JAZZ 47 | JAPAN | | EJC-747 |
| | | | |
| GREATEST HITS | EEC | PILZ | FM 8342 |
| | | | |
| HERE'S TO THE LADIES | UK | COLUMBIA | 481266 2 |

157

| | | | |
|---|---|---|---|
| HOLLYWOOD AND BROADWAY | UK | H NELSON | CDSIV 6145 |
| | | | |
| I LEFT MY HEART IN SAN FRANCISCO | JAPAN | CBS | CSCS-5241 |
| I LEFT MY HEART IN SAN FRANCISCO | JAPAN | CBS | 32DP-561 |
| I LEFT MY HEART IN SAN FRANCISCO | US | COLUMBIA | CK 8669 |
| I LEFT MY HEART IN SAN FRANCISCO | UK | COLUMBIA | 902 288-2 |
| I LEFT MY HEART IN SAN FRANCISCO (POP MEMORY) | NETH | CBS | 465 445-2 |
| | | | |
| I LEFT MY HEART IN SAN FRANCISCO /I WANNA BE AROUND | UK | SONY | 477592 2 |
| | | | |
| IF I RULED THE WORLD (SONGS FOR THE JET SET) | JAPAN | CBS | 25DP-5320 |
| | | | |
| I WANNA BE AROUND | US | COLUMBIA | CK 66504 |
| | | | |
| IN PERSON! | US | COLUMBIA | LEG6426 |
| | | | |
| IT COULD HAPPEN TO YOU – SOUNDTRACK | US | COLUMBIA | CK 66184 |
| | | | |
| JAZZ | JAPAN | CBS | 32DP-739 |
| JAZZ | US | COLUMBIA | CGK-40424 |
| | | | |
| MTV UNPLUGGED | US | COLUMBIA | CK 66214 |
| MTV UNPLUGGED | UK | COLUMBIA | 477170 2 |
| | | | |
| MY HEART SINGS | JAPAN | CBS | CSCS-5245 |
| | | | |
| NIGHT AND DAY | EEC | ELAP | PK 510 |
| | | | |
| PERFECTLY FRANK | NETH | CBS | 472 222-2 |
| PERFECTLY FRANK | US | COLUMBIA | CK 52965 |
| PERFECTLY FRANK | UK | COLUMBIA | 472222 2 |
| PERFECTLY FRANK | JAPAN | SONY | SRCS-6565 |
| | | | |
| PORTRAIT OF A SONG STYLIST | UK | HARMONY | HARCD-105 |
| | | | |
| SINGS A STRING OF HAROLD ARLEN | JAPAN | CBS | CSCS-5244 |
| SINGS A STRING OF HAROLD ARLEN | US | SONY | //// |
| | | | |
| SINGS COLE PORTER AND RODGERS & HART | JAPAN | DRG | P28L-20096 |
| | | | |
| SINGS THE GREATEST HITS OF COLE PORTER AND RODGERS & HART | UK | H NELSON | CDSIV 1119 |
| | | | |
| SINGS THE RODGERS & HART SONGBOOK | UK | H NELSON | CDSIV 1129 |
| | | | |
| SNOWFALL THE CHRISTMAS ALBUM | JAPAN | CBS | 28DP-5288 |
| SNOWFALL THE CHRISTMAS ALBUM | US | COLUMBIA | CK 9737 |
| SNOWFALL THE CHRISTMAS ALBUM | UK | COLUMBIA | 4775972 2 |

| | | | |
|---|---|---|---|
| SOMETHING | US | COLUMBIA | CK 64601 |
| STAR BOX | JAPAN | CBS | 25DP-5507 |
| STEPPIN' OUT | US | COLUMBIA | CK 57424 |
| STEPPIN' OUT | UK | SONY | 473 602-2 |
| STRIKE UP THE BAND | US | ROULETTE | RCD-59021 |
| THE ART OF EXCELLENCE | JAPAN | CBS | 32DP-494 |
| THE ART OF EXCELLENCE | NETH | CBS | 462 539-2 |
| THE ART OF EXCELLENCE | US | COLUMBIA | CK 40344 |
| THE ART OF EXCELLENCE | UK | COLUMBIA | CK 40344 |
| THE BEST OF TONY BENNETT (EARLY 70'S PHILIPS TRACKS) | US | CURB | D2-77447 |
| THE ENTERTAINERS HIS 28 GREATEST HITS | EEC | ENT | CD273 |
| THE ESSENCE OF TONY BENNETT | UK | COLUMBIA | 453571 |
| THE ESSENCE OF TONY BENNETT | US | SONY | CK-53571 |
| THE GOOD LIFE | AUS | COLUMBIA | 471 135-2 |
| THE GOOD LIFE | US | SONY | A 21552 |
| THE MAGIC OF TONY BENNETT | UK | H NELSON | CDSIV 1106 |
| THE MOVIE SONG ALBUM | US | COLUMBIA | CK 9272 |
| THE RODGERS & HART SONG BOOK | JAPAN | DRG | KICP-2046 |
| THE RODGERS & HART SONGBOOK | US | DRG | CDXP-2102 |
| THE SPECIAL MAGIC OF TONY BENNETT | US | DRG | CDMRS-801 |
| THE SPECIAL MAGIC OF TONY BENNETT | UK | TRING | JHD053 |
| THE VERY THOUGHT OF YOU | US | SONY | A 13302 |
| THE VOCAL TOUCH | NETH | DISKY | VTCD5850 |
| THE TONY BENNETT/BILL EVANS ALBUM | US | FANTASY | CJCCD-439-2 |
| TONY BENNETT & BILL EVANS TOGETHER AGAIN | US | DRG | CDMR 5901 |
| TONY BENNETT & BILL EVANS TOGETHER AGAIN | UK | H NELSON | CDSIV 1122 |
| TONY SINGS FOR TWO | US | SONY | A8242 |
| TRIBUTE TO DUKE (TB ON 2 TRACKS) | US | CONCORD | JAZZ |
| WHEN LIGHTS ARE LOW | JAPAN | CBS | CSCS-5242 |
| WHO SHALL I TURN TO | US | COLUMBIA | CK 66503 |

# TONY BENNETT U.S. ALBUMS DISCOGRAPHY

| Label | Record No. | Title | Year |
|---|---|---|---|
| Columbia | CL 6221 | Because of You (10-inch) | 1952 |
| Columbia | CL 613 | Treasure Chest of Song Hits | 1955 |
| Columbia | CL 621 | Cloud 7 | 1955 |
| Columbia | CL 2507 | Alone At Last With Tony Bennett (10-inch) | 1955 |
| Columbia | CL 2550 | Because Of You (10-inch) | 1956 |
| Columbia | CL 938 | Tony | 1957 |
| Columbia | CL 1079 | The Beat Of My Heart | 1957 |
| Columbia | CL 1186 | Long Ago And Far Away | 1958 |
| Columbia | CL 1229 | Tony's Greatest Hits | 1958 |
| Columbia | CL 1292 | Blue Velvet | 1959 |
| Columbia | CL 1294 (M) CS 8104 (S) LE 10125 | In Person! (with Count Basie and his Orchestra) | 1959 |
| Guest Star | GS 1485 | I've Grown Accustomed To Her Face (four tracks by Tony Bennett with the Count Basie Orchestra, the rest by Al Tornello) | ? |
| Columbia | CL 1301 (M) CS 8107 (S) | Hometown, My Town | 1959 |
| Columbia | CL 1429 (M) CS 8226 (S) | To My Wonderful One | 1960 |
| Columbia | CL 1471 (M) CS 8262 (S) | Alone Together | 1960 |
| Columbia | CL 1535 (M) CS 8335 (S) P 13301 | More Tony's Greatest Hits | 1960 |
| Columbia | CL 1553 (M) CS 8359 (S) | Tony Bennett Sings A String Of Harold Arlen | 1960 |
| Columbia | CL 1446 (M) CS 8242 (S) | Tony Bennett Sings For Two | 1961 |
| Columbia | CL 1658 (M) CS 8458 (S) | My Heart Sings | 1961 |
| Roulette | R-25072 (M) SR-25072 (S) | Count Basie Swings/Tony Sings (with Count Basie) | 1961 |
| Roulette | R 25231 (M) SR-25231 (S) | Strike Up The Band (with Count Basie) | 1961 |
| Emus | ES-12026 | | |
| Columbia | CL 1763 (M) CS 8563 (S) P 13574 | "Mr. Broadway": Tony's Greatest Broadway Hits | 1962 |
| Columbia | CL 1852 (M) CS 8652 (S) | Tony's Greatest Hits (reissue of Columbia 1229) | 1962 |
| Columbia | CL 1869 (M) CS 8669 (S) | I Left My Heart In San Francisco | 1962 |
| Columbia | CL 1813 (M) CS 8613 (S) | On The Glory Road (not released) | 1962 |
| Columbia | C2L-23 (M) C2S-863 (S) CC2S 823 | Tony Bennett At Carnegie Hall | 1962 |

| Label | Record No. | Title | Year |
|---|---|---|---|
| Columbia | CL 2000 (M) | I Wanna Be Around . . . | 1963 |
|  | CS 8800 (S) |  |  |
| Columbia | CL 2056 (M) | This Is All I Ask | 1963 |
|  | CS 8856 (S) |  |  |
| Columbia | CL 2141 (M) | The Many Moods Of Tony | 1964 |
|  | CS 8941 (S) |  |  |
| Columbia | CL 2175 (M) | When Lights Are Low | 1964 |
|  | CS 8975 (S) |  |  |
| Columbia | CL 2285 (M) | Who Can I Turn To | 1964 |
|  | CS 9085 (S) |  |  |
|  | P 13507 |  |  |
| Columbia | CL 2343 (M) | If I Ruled The World – For The Jet Set | 1965 |
|  | CS 9143 (S) |  |  |
| Columbia | CL 2373 (M) | Tony's Greatest Hits, Volume III | 1965 |
|  | CS 9173 (S) |  |  |
| Columbia | CL 2472 (M) | The Movie Song Album | 1966 |
|  | CS 9272 (S) |  |  |
| Columbia | CL 2560 (M) | A Time For Love | 1966 |
|  | CS 9360 (S) |  |  |
| Columbia | CL 2653 (M) | Tony Makes It Happen | 1967 |
|  | CS 9453 (S) |  |  |
| Columbia | CL 9458 | My Heart Sings | 1967 |
| Columbia | CL 2773 (M) | For Once In My Life | 1967 |
|  | CS 9573 (S) |  |  |
|  | LE 10057 |  |  |
| Columbia | CS 9678 | Yesterday I Heard The Rain | 1968 |
| Columbia | CS 9739 | Snowfall/The Christmas Album | 1968 |
| Columbia | CS 9814 | Tony Bennett's Greatest Hits, Volume IV | 1969 |
| Columbia | HS 11340 | Just One Of Those Things | 1969 |
| Columbia | CS 9882 | I've Gotta Be Me | 1969 |
|  | LE 10008 |  |  |
| Columbia | CS 9891 | Love Story: 20 All-Time Great Recordings | 1969 |
| Columbia | CS 9980 | Tony Sings The Great Hits Of Today! | 1969 |
| Columbia | C 30280 | Tony Bennett's "Something" | 1970 |
| Columbia | C 30240 | Tony Bennett Sings His All-Time Hall Of Fame Hits | 1970 |
| Columbia | C 30558 | Love Story | 1971 |
| Columbia | KH 30758 | The Very Thought Of You | 1971 |
| Columbia | C 30953 | Get Happy/With The London Philarmonic Orchestra |  |
| Columbia | C 31219 | Summer Of '42 | 1972 |
| Columbia | KC 31460 | With Love | 1972 |
| Columbia | KG 31494 | Tony Bennett's All-Time Greatest Hits | 1972 |
| MGM/Verve | 5088 | The Good Things in Life | 1972 |
| Columbia | KH 32171 | Tony! | 1973 |
| Columbia | C32239 | Sunrise, Sunset | 1973 |
| MGM/Verve | MV-5094 | Listen Easy | 1973 |
| Columbia | KG 33276 | Let's Fall In Love With The Songs Of Harold Arlen And Cy Coleman |  |
| Columbia | CG 33612 | I Left My Heart In San Francisco/Great Hits Of Today | 1975 |
| Improv | 7112 | Tony Bennett Sings 10 Rodgers & Hart Songs | 1975 |
| Fantasy | F-9489 | The Tony Bennett/Bill Evans Album | 1975 |

| Label | Record No. | Title | Year |
|---|---|---|---|
| DRG | CDXP 2102 | The Rodgers And Hart Songbook (reissue of Improv 7113 and Improv 7120) | 1976 |
| DRG | MS 910 | Tony Bennett/The McPartlands and Friends Make Magnificent Music | 1977 |
| Improv | 7117 | Together Again (with Bill Evans) | |
| DRG | MRS 901 | | |
| DRG | CDMRS 901 | | |
| Mobile Fidelity | 1-117 | The Tony Bennett/Bill Evans Albums | |
| Improv | 7120 | Tony Bennett Sings . . . More Great Rodgers & Hart | 1977 |
| DRG | CDMRS 801 | The Special Magic Of Tony Bennett | 1979 |
| Sunbeam | P-509 | Tony & Gene 1963: Fascinatin' Rhythm (with Gene Krupa) | 1979 |
| Pair/CBS | BT 17781 | All-Time Favorites | 1981 |
| Columbia | C 40344 | The Art Of Excellence | 1986 |
| Dunhill | DZS004 | Chicago (with the Count Basie Orchestra) | 1986 |
| CBS | P2S19390 | The Greatest Hits Of Tony Bennett | 1986 |
| Nelson | YU 108 | Tony Bennett Sings The Rodgers And Hart Collection | 1986 |
| Columbia | C2 40424 | Tony Bennett – Jazz | 1987 |
| Columbia | FC 44029 | Bennett/Berlin | 1987 |
| Pair | PCD-2-1237 | Some Pair (with Count Basie and his Orchestra) | |
| Columbia | FC 45348 | Astoria: Portrait Of The Artist | 1990 |
| CBS | A21552 | The Good Life | 1990 |
| Curb | D2-77447 | Best Of Tony Bennett | 1991 |
| Columbia | C4K 46843 | 40 Years: The Artistry Of Tony Bennett | 1991 |
| Columbia | CK 52965 | Perfectly Frank | 1992 |
| Columbia | CK 4743602 | Steppin' Out | 1994 |
| Columbia | CK 66214 | MTV Unplugged | 1994 |
| Columbia | CK 4812662 | Here's To The Ladies | 1995 |

## UNRELEASED CONCERT RECORDINGS

**8 APRIL 1964**

Tony appeared at the Sahara Hotel, Las Vegas, Nevada. Using the Ralph Sharon Trio and Orchestra conducted by Louis Basil.
The show was recorded by Columbia, but only one song has seen a release as a Single.*

THE MOMENT OF TRUTH
SING YOU SINNERS
SPRING IN MANHATTAN
ALWAYS
(I LEFT MY HEART) IN SAN FRANCISCO
I WANNA BE AROUND
*IT'S A SIN TO TELL A LIE
SUNDAY
ONE FOR MY BABY
RULES OF THE ROAD
QUIET NIGHTS (CORCOVADO)
THIS COULD BE THE START OF SOMETHING
MAM'SELLE
FROM THIS MOMENT ON
WHEN JOANNA LOVED ME
RAGS TO RICHES
ONCE UPON A TIME
SMILE WHEN YOU'RE SMILING (MEDLEY)
SPEAK LOW
YOU CAN'T LOVE 'EM ALL
TIME AFTER TIME
KEEP SMILING AT TROUBLE (TROUBLE'S A BUBBLE)
THE SHOW MUST GO ON
LULLABY OF BROADWAY
CHICAGO (THAT TODDLING TOWN)
I'M WAY AHEAD OF THE GAME
AIN'T MISBEHAVIN'
THIS IS ALL I ASK
FIREFLY
PUT ON A HAPPY FACE
IT AMAZES ME

**11 AUGUST 1967**

Columbia recorded a show at The Greek Theatre, Los Angeles, California (A & R H. Roberts).

THE LADY'S IN LOVE WITH YOU
SHE'S FUNNY THAT WAY
GIRL TALK
SHADOW OF YOUR SMILE
BROADWAY
WHO CAN I TURN TO

(I LEFT MY HEART) IN SAN FRANCISCO
FOR ONCE IN MY LIFE
FIREFLY
IF I RULED THE WORLD
KEEP SMILING AT TROUBLE (TROUBLE'S A BUBBLE)
DAYS OF LOVE
OLD DEVIL MOON
ON THE SUNNY SIDE OF THE STREET
(IT'S) NEVER TOO LATE
A TIME FOR LOVE
DON'T GET AROUND MUCH ANYMORE
COUNTRY GIRL
THE MOMENT OF TRUTH
THE TROLLEY SONG